ARCHAEOLOGY AND THE
RELIGION OF ISRAEL

ARCHAEOLOGY AND THE
RELIGION OF ISRAEL

*THE AYER LECTURES OF THE
COLGATE-ROCHESTER DIVINITY SCHOOL*

By

WILLIAM FOXWELL ALBRIGHT

BALTIMORE

THE JOHNS HOPKINS PRESS

Originally published, 1942
Second edition, 1946
Third edition, 1953
Fourth edition, 1956
Fifth edition, 1968

To

JAMES ALAN MONTGOMERY

PH. D., S. T. D., D. H. L., LITT. D.

*President of the American Schools of
Oriental Research*

1921-1933

GENTLEMAN, SCHOLAR, FRIEND

THE AYER LECTURES

OF THE

COLGATE-ROCHESTER DIVINITY SCHOOL

ROCHESTER, NEW YORK

The Ayer Lectureship was founded in May, 1928, in the Rochester Theological Seminary, by the gift of twenty-five thousand dollars from Mr. and Mrs. Wilfred W. Fry, of Camden, New Jersey, to perpetuate the memory of Mrs. Fry's father, the late Mr. Francis Wayland Ayer. At the time of his death, Mr. Ayer was president of the corporation which maintained the Rochester Theological Seminary.

Shortly after the establishment of the Lectureship, the Rochester Theological Seminary and the Colgate Theological Seminary were united under the name of the Colgate-Rochester Divinity School. It is under the auspices of this institution that the Ayer lectures are given.

Under the terms of the Foundation, the lectures are to fall within the broad field of the history of interpretation of the Christian religion and message. It is the desire of those connected with the establishment and the administration of the Lectureship that the lectures shall be religiously constructive, and shall help in the building of Christian faith.

Four lectures are to be given each year at the Colgate-Rochester Divinity School at Rochester, New York, and these lectures are to be published in book form within one year after the time of their delivery. They will be known as the Ayer Lectures.

The lecturer for the year 1940-41 was William Foxwell Albright, W. W. Spence Professor of Semitic Languages, Johns Hopkins University; his subject, "Archaeology and the Religion of Israel."

PREFACE

This book contains the substance of the Ayer Lectures, which I had the honor to deliver at the Colgate-Rochester Divinity School, in April, 1941. I have expanded the four lectures which were actually given then by the addition of Chapter III, as well as by including matter not suitable for oral presentation. The addition of copious notes will, it is hoped, make the volume more useful both to students and to scholars. It is in no sense a reproduction of my larger book, *From the Stone Age to Christianity*, in shorter or more popular form. At least ninety percent of the material in this volume will not be found there at all. Whenever any subject was adequately treated there I refer the reader to it. On the other hand, I have constantly endeavored to complement the treatment of Israelite religion and related matters which was given in that book. In order to make the task of the reader as easy as possible, I have again included a full index of subjects and authors, to which an index of biblical citations has been annexed. Illustrations have been omitted because of their expense, to which may be added the difficulty of obtaining authorization from abroad for reproduction of cuts.

I am greatly indebted to my friends, Dr. H. M. Orlinsky, Professor O. R. Sellers and Mr. John A. Thompson, for their help in reading manuscript and proof, as well as for making many useful suggestions. Manuscript and proofs have also been read, in whole or in part, by my wife, Dr. John Stensvaag and Mr. Cullen I. K. Story, to all of whom I tender my thanks. To Dr. Stensvaag I am also indebted for the preparation of the Index of Biblical Citations and to Mr. Story for his patience and care in compiling the Index of Subjects and Authors. But for my wife's help the book could not have appeared at all.

It is an unusual pleasure to thank the president and the faculty of the Colgate-Rochester Divinity School for affording me the opportunity to give these lectures and to spend an interesting week at the Seminary. President Albert W. Beaven and Mrs. Beaven made my stay unforgettable by their kindly hospitality.

The dedication of this book to my former chief and my friend of many years, Professor James Alan Montgomery of the University of Pennsylvania, is only a slight token of my respect and affection for him. His careful scholarship, catholic spirit and broad culture have long adorned every institution or organization with which he was connected. May he be with us for years to come!

THE AUTHOR

March, 1942

PREFACE TO THE SECOND EDITION

The first edition of this book was exhausted in the spring of 1946, at the same time as the first edition of *From the Stone Age to Christianity*, which was reproduced by photo-offset during the past summer. In preparing this photo-offset second edition of *Archaeology and the Religion of Israel*, over a hundred lines of the text and notes have been revised, besides correction of at least a hundred additional dates, spellings, etc. The paging of the present book has remained unchanged throughout.

For further clarification of my point of view, not always clear to past readers and reviewers of these two complementary volumes, see my remarks in the Preface and the Addenda to the second edition of *From the Stone Age to Christianity*. I am greatly indebted to reviewers and correspondents, notably to the detailed reviews by Professors Millar Burrows of Yale University (*Jour. Am. Or. Soc.*, 1942, pp. 343-346; *Jewish Quar. Rev.*, XXXIII, pp. 471-480), T. J. Meek of the University of

Toronto (*Jour. Near Eastern Stud.*, 1943, pp. 122 f.), W. H. McClellan, S. J., of Woodstock College (*Theological Studies*, II, pp. 112-137), which should be consulted by students who are interested in a perspective view of the problems involved.

The chronology of the second edition of this book has been brought up to date throughout: Mesopotamian dates before 1500 B. C. follow the table in *Bull. Am. Sch. Or. Res.*, No. 88, p. 32 (1942); later Assyrian chronology follows the table of Arno Poebel, *Jour. Near Eastern Stud.*, I, pp. 87 f. (1943); the chronology of the Divided Kingdom follows the system presented in the table in *Bull. Am. Sch. Or. Res.*, No. 100, pp. 20-22.

THE AUTHOR

September, 1946

PREFACE TO THE THIRD EDITION

During the eleven years that have elapsed since the publication of the first edition and the seven years since the appearance of the second, there has been progress all along the line. For technical reasons no changes could be made in the text of this edition, but eight pages of notes have been added to bring it up to date as far as practicable. Many more additions might be made to the bibliography, but we have limited ourselves to citing particularly important items and giving a general idea of the scope of new literature in any field.

Since the first two editions, the writer's *Archaeology of Palestine* (1949) and a long chapter on the history of the Old Testament period in Louis Finkelstein's *The Jews* (also 1949) have provided the archaeological and historical background often needed to clarify the present book. A completely rewritten edition of *From the Stone Age to Christianity* is in preparation.

THE AUTHOR

August, 1953

PREFACE TO THE FOURTH EDITION

During the past three years there has been steady progress in this field of research. Some important discoveries have illuminated whole areas hitherto obscure, and there have been some remarkable advances in the application of Ugaritic and Qumran Scroll data to the interpretation of the Bible. Owing to technical difficulties the pagination has not been changed, but over a hundred lines have been rewritten, especially in pp. 1-106, thus bringing this volume up to date as far as practicable. Two recent books supplement this edition: the new edition of the writer's *Recent Discoveries in Bible Lands* (The Biblical Colloquium, 731 Ridge Ave., Pittsburgh 12, 1956) and the French translation of his *Archaeology of Palestine*, which has been fully revised (*L'archéologie de la Palestine*, Paris, Editions du Cerf, 1955). The revised German translation of the present book, published as *Die Religion Israels im Lichte der archäologischen Ausgrabungen* (München and Basel, Ernst Reinhardt, 1956), will also be found useful. The *Introduction* to the Anchor Series reprint (Doubleday & Co., New York, 1957) of my book, *From the Stone Age to Christianity*, will bring the chief confirmations and modifications of my 1940-1946 points of view.

THE AUTHOR

August, 1956

PREFACE TO THE FIFTH EDITION

Since the appearance of the fourth edition of this book in 1956, publications have multiplied and yet, from my point of view, surprisingly little of its content is antiquated. This somewhat unexpected situation—when one considers the long series of archaeological publications and conclusions drawn from them —is due chiefly to the care taken in writing the original text (in 1941) to avoid controversial areas as much as practicable. Two years earlier (1939) I had written the much more elaborate synthesis contained in my book *From the Stone Age to Christianity*, which covered a great deal of disputed terrain and shocked many scholars by its innovations. In the present work (first published in 1942) I deliberately omitted all specific references to the Patriarchal and Mosaic ages. This book was not intended to be a condensation of *From the Stone Age to Christianity* but was almost entirely supplementary to it both in text and notes. Since I dealt with archaeological and linguistic facts as well as with their historical interpretation—avoiding hypotheses as much as possible—the book has enjoyed moderate but steady distribution, as well as translation into several languages.

The progress of archaeological discovery bearing on the period with which I deal chiefly—the Late Bronze and Iron ages down to the fifth century B. C.—has been very great but not nearly as sensational as the discoveries made during the previous two decades, which included Mari and Ugarit. Thanks to these and many other less important finds, my own thinking has progressed all along the line. For details I refer especially to *The Archaeology of Palestine* (1949-1963, with a new edition proposed); *History, Archaeology and Christian Humanism* (1964), especially Parts I and II (which appear only there, pp. 3-100); and most recently *Yahweh and the Gods of Canaan*

(London and New York, 1968), as well as two briefer books, *Archaeology, Historical Analogy and Early Biblical Tradition* (Baton Rouge, 1966) and *New Horizons in Biblical Research* (London, 1966).

Since I have endeavored to avoid repetition, the present volume, with its elaborate bibliographic notes, remains indispensable for anyone who wishes to master subsequent publications of mine.

CHAPTER I

Archaeology and the Ancient Near-Eastern Mind.—The material given here cannot be found elsewhere and, in my opinion, there has been practically no valid criticism of my approach. My debt to the late Lucien Lévy-Bruhl remains very great, in spite of the fact that I disagreed from the start with some of his basic points of view. For instance, where he used the terms "prelogical" and "logical," I rejected his use of the former term, after first restricting it (1940) to the higher culture of ancient and modern primitives, including religion and magic. All that had to do with the ordinary life of man as well as such unconsciously developed tools as language I designated as *"empiricological."* When I first proposed my new category of thinking, I did not yet know that Lévy-Bruhl himself had already given up his two-stage theory ("prelogical" and "logical") in 1938 (published posthumously in 1947). Lévy-Bruhl's designation as "prelogical" has reference, of course, to the following stage of Greek formal logic. In the third edition of the present book (p. 223) I changed "prelogical" to "protological," since I do not consider this stage as by any means without its own "logic." The category "logical" I limit to rational Hellenic and post-Hellenic thought. For a fuller development of my point of view see my discussion in the first edition of this book, pages 26–30, as well as in *History, Archaeology and Christian Humanism*, pages 66–77.

Meanwhile, the objections which had been raised by many field anthropologists to the categories of Lévy-Bruhl have been taken up and carried much farther by Claude Lévi-Strauss, who began his anthropological work a few years before Lévy-Bruhl's death.

I was first seriously introduced to Lévi-Strauss (see especially the two volumes *Anthropologie structurale* [1958, English translation 1963] and *Mentalité sauvage* [1962, in English as *The Savage Mind*, 1966]) through a French admirer of his in 1960. Unfortunately, the introduction came through his work on the use of mathematical models and mathematical transformations, which are at best a precarious approach to the problem of structure in anthropology. In spite of this excessive tendency to rationalize primitive thinking and to force it into a frame of mathematical type, there can be no doubt that Lévi-Strauss understands the savage mind much better in some ways than Lévy-Bruhl. The reason is simple. Lévy-Bruhl's "primitive mentality" referred, as previously observed, to areas where there is little or no logic, except after magic has been reduced to a pseudo-scientific system. It must be remembered that a great deal of "primitive" thinking in these areas is intimately associated with dream phenomena, which Lévi-Strauss tends to leave out of the picture almost entirely—except when engaged in controversy with the followers of Freud and especially of Jung.

Lévi-Strauss is, however, certainly right in emphasizing the importance of field work in anthropology and in stressing the need of long and repeated contact with "primitives," whom he called "savages" in an obviously deliberate attempt to bypass the whole of anthropological theory based on the assumption that "savages" are survivors of primitive man. I recall vividly how reluctant I was in the 1920's to substitute "primitive" for "savage." There can be no doubt, in my opinion, that there was much diffusion of religious motifs, and especially of magical practices, among the "retarded" peoples of the world. Lévi-Strauss is undoubtedly right when he emphasizes the fact that many "savages" are actually survivors of more advanced populations which were forced out of more favorable environments into the jungle or desert. This is one reason why one can find, especially in South America, fantastically "primitive" Indians still possessing a remarkable range of concepts and categories.

From my point of view, the greatest weaknesses of Lévi-Strauss's work—brilliant as he undoubtedly is—are closely connected with the over-conceptualization of social and cultural anthropology to which I have already referred, as well as to his disregard of history (which often approaches actual contempt) and his apparent lack of interest in the rapidly developing science of animal behavior or ethology. This last science is making such strides at present and is throwing so much light on dark areas of human behavior—primitive, savage and "civilized"—that no future student of the strange vagaries of human ways of thinking can possibly do without it.

CHAPTER II

The Archaeological Background of Old Testament Religion.— There are few significant corrections to what I wrote here except, of course, that one must include subsequent discoveries. The most important of these finds, so far as biblical research and related fields are concerned, are listed in *History, Archaeology and Christian Humanism* (1964), pages 103–56, especially in the numerous supplementary notes. (See also my survey in *The Old Testament and Modern Study* [ed. H. H. Rowley, Oxford, 1951, pp. 1–47].) The most important recent work here is George Ernest Wright's *Biblical Archaeology* (Philadelphia and London, 1957). Owing to the second World War and its train of minor wars during the decade following 1939, advances were chiefly made in studies and museums rather than in the field. In the past few years there has been a tremendous resurgence of actual excavation, most of whose results are not yet published. The publication of the finds at Mari and Ugarit has proceeded at a rather leisurely pace, owing largely to the increasing cost of publication and of the research which must increasingly intervene between excavation and publication.

CHAPTER III

Archaeology and the Religion of the Canaanites.—In this chapter I was able to utilize nearly all the Canaanite mythological epics, and since it was written with the purpose of serving as a general introduction to the subject it still retains most of its value and has not been appreciably antiquated. The elaborate notes to the first three editions still provide the necessary bibliographic and linguistic information. However, it is extensively supplemented by my chapter on Canaanite religion in *Yahweh and the Gods of Canaan* (1968) (pp. 96 ff., 189 ff). It is surprising how few of the once-disputed views presented in *Archaeology and the Religion of Israel* have proved to be wrong. For example, I was correct in insisting that the god Resheph was lord of the underworld and was identified with Nergal. I was right in insisting on the pronunciation *Kôshar* for the craftsman god. In such cases we now have Babylonian bilinguals to prove our points. In the 1968 treatment it has been possible to differentiate between local Canaanite pantheons, but this does not alter our earlier conclusions about the generalized epic pantheon.

CHAPTER IV

Archaeology and the Religion of Early Israel.—This chapter is supplemented and corrected in many cases by Chapters IV and V in *Yahweh and the Gods of Canaan* but still remains the clearest and often fullest account of my point of view with regard to such matters as the status of priests and Levites, as well as the use of images in early Israel and the role of David in organizing the musical guilds.

CHAPTER V

Archaeology and the Religion of Later Israel.—Here we have the only full discussion I have given anywhere of my views on the structure and furnishings of the temple of Solomon, as well as my interpretation of the curious syncretistic religion of the Jewish colony at Elephantine in the sixth and fifth centuries B.C. For the former see also George Ernest Wright's *Biblical Archaeology* (1957) and for the latter see the supplementary notes to the second and third editions, reprinted below.

W. F. ALBRIGHT

Baltimore, August, 1968

TABLE OF CONTENTS

ARCHAEOLOGY AND THE
RELIGION OF ISRAEL

CHAPTER I

ARCHAEOLOGY AND THE ANCIENT NEAR-EASTERN MIND

1. ARCHAEOLOGY, HISTORY AND RELIGION

The rapidly increasing mass of archaeological data from the ancient Near East has hitherto remained singularly sterile, so far as its effect upon our historical thinking is concerned. Specialists have been far too busy accumulating new facts or interpreting facts already collected, to give their time to the task of applying this knowledge to other fields. Where experts in archaeology and philology have strayed into neighboring pastures the results have seldom been happy, owing either to the fact that their ventures were premature or to their own lack of training in the other disciplines into which they strayed. Occasionally the results have been brilliant, as when Sir Flinders Petrie proposed his illuminating theory of historical cycles of civilization, based on his intimate knowledge of Egyptian archaeology,[1] or when Heinrich Schäfer wrote his epoch-making study of the nature of Egyptian line-drawing.[2] However, such instances have been few and far between; most of the attempts to synthesize the archaeology of the Near East have been made by specialists coming from other fields. Examples are numerous: Eduard Meyer, the classical historian; Sir James Frazer, the historian of religions; O. Neugebauer, the mathematician and astronomer; Max Hilzheimer, the vertebrate zoologist— and these are only a few of the many we could name. However, it is not accidental that these incursions from without have hitherto yielded only comparatively restricted insights; specialists in other fields form their views of synthesis and their professional credos on the basis of the doc-

1

trines of their predecessors, supplemented or corrected by new data in their own fields. Such specialists cannot be expected to master the new field so completely that the new data will seriously modify the patterns of thought to which they have become accustomed. Moreover, their strength is here their weakness: thorough indoctrination in the methods and the points of view in their own fields prevents them from grasping the true meaning and configuration of novel patterns. On the other hand, specialists in a new field are likely to accept novel patterns much too hastily, without troubling themselves to acquire the critical approach which only an old, well-organized field can develop.

In our recent volume, *From the Stone Age to Christianity*, we stressed the significance of the new archaeological knowledge for the horizon of the historian.[3] It was easy to show that archaeological history is, in important respects, the most scientific branch of history, since, however fragmentary it may be, its data belong mainly to the epistemological domain of "typical occurrence," that is, they make it possible for the specialist to formulate judgments about recurring facts.[4] In spite of the fact that the historian of social movements and institutions has to deal constantly with such judgments and that the historian of civilization deals with little else, it has become proper in intellectual circles to differentiate sharply between history, as a record of chronologically connected individual facts, and science, as a structure of "laws" governing large bodies of facts. History is often supposed to be subjective and science objective, by the very nature of the subjects. Without repeating our discussion in that volume we must emphasize the fundamental fallacy underlying any such view.[5] There are many branches of history and of historical method which are just as objective and just as logically formulated as corresponding branches of science.[6] There are phases of geology, biology and meteorology which are just as unpredictable as the course of any political history. And the psychologist has at least as much difficulty finding out how the human brain operates as the political historian has in trying to determine the "causes" of popular movements.

At the same time we stressed the organismic character of history.[7] History is not a meaningless record of chance happenings, or even a mere chain of related occurrences; it is a complex web of interacting patterns, each of which has its own structure, however difficult it may be to dissect the structure and to identify its characteristic elements. Moreover, the web is itself constantly changing, and by comparing successive states which it exhibits to the trained eye of the historian we can detect the direction in which it is changing—in other words, its evolution. We also emphasized the fact that the evolution of historical patterns is highly complex and variable; it may move in any direction and it cannot be detected by *a priori* hypotheses nor can it be explained by any deterministic theory. We also pointed out that this organismic nature of history makes uni-linear "historicism" unsuitable as a clue to the complexities of the history of religion.[8] For this reason Wellhausen's Hegelian method was utterly unsuited to become the master-key with which scholars might enter the sanctuary of Israelite religion and acquire a satisfying understanding of it. That it has been a useful tool for historical research we do not, of course, deny.

Hitherto little attention has been paid to one of the richest fields to which archaeology can contribute: the history of the workings of the human mind. There is a rapid and steady increase in the interest taken by scholars in the history of ideas. Historians of science, students of national literature, philologians and philosophers are now converging from all directions upon this fascinating and important new domain of the investigator. At the same time cultural anthropologists, social psychologists, sociologists and philosophers are joining forces to analyze and interpret the workings of the savage mind today. But the gap between savage mentality and the mind of modern man is too great to be easily bridged by direct observation, and the attempt to fill the gap by studying the ideas of half-savage peoples of today is nearly always vitiated by the fact that these peoples have been strongly influenced by more highly developed civilizations, virtually all of which reflect a post-Hellenic stage of progress. In other words, as soon as we begin seriously to study peoples like the Hova, the Nuba, the Kirghiz, we find that their higher culture has been profoundly influenced by civilizations which drew heavily from the Greeks, directly and indirectly. In such cases we can seldom be sure about the aboriginal character of a given cultural element. The only way in which we can bridge this gap satisfactorily is by following the evolution of the human mind in the Near East itself, where we can trace it from the earliest times through successive archaeological ages to the flowering of the Greek spirit. Here is indeed an immensely rich—in fact, almost virgin—field for research. There is only one drawback to intensive cultivation: the would-be investigator must first undergo an arduous training in archaeology and philology; he must learn new languages and master complex scripts; he must work his way painfully through complicated and recondite domains of learning, the "human values" of which are far from being obvious even to the advanced student, unless he possesses a clear vision of his goal.[9]

When we substitute "history of religion" for the closely related "history of ideas," it may be easier to recognize this goal. What we have in mind is nothing less than the ultimate reconstruction, as far as possible, of the route which our cultural ancestors traversed in order to reach Judaeo-Christian heights of spiritual insight and ethical monotheism. In this book we are concerned with the religion of the Old Testament, of which the religion of the New was only the extension and the fulfilment.

We have no illusions about the ease with which this somewhat grandiose task can be accomplished. In this chapter we undertake to make a modest beginning. By systematizing and analyzing the data which Near-Eastern archaeology has accumulated, we can at least provide a foundation on which future scholars can build. The material is so vast and its interpretation so far from being completed that we have had to exercise caution in selecting our data, leaving some of the most striking facts for more adequate future treatment. Moreover, we have only grazed the surface of the available sources, both written and unwritten. Yet we do not believe that our sampling has been one-sided or that we have failed to give a fair picture of what actually exists in this new world of monuments and documents.

After much consideration, we have decided not to seek the collaboration of a professional psychologist. In the first place, our task here is primarily historical, not psychological. In the second place, there is such extraordinary divergence between the views of different contemporary schools of psychology in matters of direct significance to the historian of culture, that a neutral attitude toward the positions of individual schools appears to be indicated. The writer has read extensively in the field of modern psychology during the past twenty years, following an earlier ambition to combine intensive study of psychology with the investigation of the life and thought of the ancient Near East. Omissions are due not to ignorance, but to deliberate intention. The professional psychologist will undoubtedly find classifications and definitions from which he will dissent with good reason. However, it must be remembered that all psychological classification and formulation face

2

a period of revolutionary readjustment, thanks to the unprecedented progress which neurology and experimental psychology are making just now. Accordingly all such points must remain tentative for the present, though their practical utility is seldom affected by their provisional character.

2. ARCHAEOLOGY AND MAN'S AESTHETIC AND IMAGINATIVE FACULTIES

In the three sections which follow we shall for convenience distinguish three categories of mental processes and phenomena. Together these three categories cover most of the activities of the human mind. First we have the aesthetic and imaginative faculties which are mainly involved in art, music and literature. Second come the affective faculties which are primarily responsible for man's emotional and spiritual life. Third we may list the conceptual and reasoning powers which make man a rational animal. It must be emphasized that these categories are not mutually exclusive, but often overlap; and we must stress the fact that two or three of them are generally brought into operation together. Psychologists are now pointing out effectively that mental processes have been analyzed in the past in terms of the results which they achieve, not of their functional relationship as disclosed by factorial and neurological research. As K. S. Lashley states, "even today such terms [in classical psychology] as emotion, perception, imagination, abstraction, or reasoning do not represent functional groupings of processes of like nature, but only classes of such activities as achieve comparable results." [10] The new methods of analysis which have been developed recently by such men as Spearman, Thurstone and Lashley, are discovering functional variables which do not correspond to the functions of classical psychology. We must, for instance, distinguish between capacity to think in terms of the spatial relationship of objects and capacity to understand non-spatial relationships. At the same time, the old psychological categories retain their descriptive and classificatory value. To the historian, who can judge human mentality in the past only by its results, as exhibited in art, literature, religion, etc., these categories are the only ones he can grasp; his interpretations of psychological phenomena may, accordingly, be historically significant, even though they require reinterpretation in the functional language of recent psychology.

In this section, dealing with the aesthetic and imaginative categories of the human mind, we shall draw on literary documents as well as upon artistic remains. Even in the most remote ages which we can control, aesthetic form and imagery played an important role in literature, especially in verse. The urge for artistic expression sometimes appeared simultaneously in art and literature, taking parallel forms in both. Often, however, it was specialized, reaching a high level of achievement in one medium at the same time that it was mute in another. Egypt in the Amarna Age (fourteenth century B. C.) and Attic Greece in the fifth century may be considered as outstanding illustrations of parallel attainment in both graphic art and literature. Early Israel and Homeric Greece afford striking examples of the flowering of literature at a time when graphic art remained on a very low level. To find a time and place in which art flourished but literature languished is more difficult, since apparent instances may be due to the accidental lack of material. It is likely that the Dynasty of Accad in Mesopotamia provides an example of a high level in art and a low one in literature; but this may be a false impression, due to the accidental paucity of poems dating from this dynasty (cir. 2360-2180 B. C.) or attributable to it. It is probable that the Pyramid Age in Egypt (cir. 2600-2300) was wanting in literature which could be correlated with its remarkable artistic development, but here again we may be laboring under a false impression. However, it is remarkable that these two periods, which reached unequalled artistic heights, should have left so little literature which was remembered in later times or which bears intrinsic evidence of belonging to them.

The first phase of art which we can trace, may be called imitative-aesthetic, since it shows little indication of active imagination, but extraordinary development of imitative capacity, combined with an aesthetic feeling which would do credit to a modern European. This phase began between 20,000 and 12,000 B. C., in the Aurignacian Age of southwestern Europe, and continued for many thousands of years until late in the Magdalenian Age. The first examples of this cave art were discovered in 1879, at the site of Altamira near Santander in northern Spain, and they appeared so incredible to prehistorians that it was a full generation before all competent scholars accepted them as genuine. Subsequent finds in southern France, especially in the Dordogne, have added many new caves and countless specimens of palaeolithic art. In the first months of 1941 a cavern near Montignac in Dordogne revealed the finest examples of Aurignacian art yet brought to light.[11] Nearly all of these cave-paintings represent animals: the mammoth, woolly rhinoceros, reindeer, stag, wild horse, wild ox, wild goat, etc. Thanks to a study of stratification in the caves, it is possible to define a number of evolutionary phases in technique and treatment, beginning with the Aurignacian and passing through the Solutrean into the Magdalenian. The separate units of each painting are definitely perceptual rather than conceptual,[12] demonstrating an extraordinary ability to reproduce what the artist actually saw. It is very seldom that we find, e. g., both horns or hoofs of a bison turned toward the observer while the rest of the animal is in profile. However, it must be remembered that a number of objects which belong together in a single scene, are represented conceptually;

i. e., they are drawn separately, without regard to perspective. The most unexpected single feature of these drawings is that in the best period of palaeolithic art we find the paint scraped away from projecting parts of an animal in such a way as to produce true shading. Thanks to this technique the prehistoric artists of southwestern Europe were able to give line drawings the appearance of paintings in perspective—applied only, it is true, to single animals. Accuracy of observation and uncanny ability to portray beasts in unusual postures combine to make these naturalistic paintings of the Palaeolithic superior in some respects, from our modern European point of view, to any other paintings of animals antedating Hellenic times!

It has been demonstrated beyond doubt that the cave-paintings in question were closely associated with hunting, since only animals which were hunted by man appear in them, and since hunters, weapons and traps are of frequent occurrence. It follows with high probability that they served a magical purpose: the animals were portrayed in order to ensure a successful hunt. It is clear that under such circumstances the artist who could draw the most lifelike pictures would be most sought after by hunters; the more realistic the painting the more powerful the sympathetic magic. The sense of beauty which we feel today in looking at these marvelous paintings is in part, of course, a reflection of the ancient artist's accurate rendition of nature; the artist reproduces the simplicity and economy of line with which nature has endowed wild animals. However, there is more than this in these paintings. The artist often gives too little but virtually never too much; with a minimum of line drawing he gives the illusion of completeness, and his lines are often more graceful and more economical than in nature. We are, therefore, fully justified in stressing both the imitative and the aesthetic aspect of the work of palaeolithic artists.

The next great surge of artistic evolution comes in the fourth millennium B. C., in the early Chalcolithic of Southwestern Asia. Several thousand years after man had first learned to sow and reap grain and at least a thousand years after he had manufactured his first clay vessels, we find a flourishing irrigation culture in the alluvial plains and river valleys of the Near East. In Mesopotamia and Syria we call this culture the Halafian; in Palestine a related culture is known as the Ghassulian, which is probably to be dated a little later though still in the same broad archaeological horizon. In the painted pottery of the Halafian and the frescoes of Ghassul we now have astonishing examples of what we may call the imaginative-aesthetic stage of the artistic evolution of Homo sapiens.[13] The geometric repertoire of the Halafian culture seems inexhaustible. Inside shallow bowls we find, in particular, an endless number of different concentric, floral, stellar or radiating patterns in one or more colors. Some of the designs are astonishingly intricate; yet few of them seem tasteless to the modern European. About the same time or a little later we find an even more complex combination of the star motif with concentric bands in a polychrome fresco on the wall of an ordinary house at Teleilât el-Ghassûl in the southern valley of the Jordan. The geometric elaborateness of the design is further heightened by the skillful use of color. It seems at first glance almost unthinkable that the ancient artist should have shown such fertility of invention and such skill in arranging his geometric elements without the use of a kaleidoscope. That the artist's inventiveness was not limited to geometric designs, is shown by the accompanying fragments of heads and bodies of dragons and other, unidentifiable, objects. We have at Ḥalâf and Ghassûl unimpeachable evidence that man's imaginative faculties were already highly developed and that they were already under firm aesthetic control. From about the same general age comes the painted pottery of Susa I, probably from the early fourth millennium, which exhibits astonishing virtuosity in the combination of geometric design with abstract naturalism. In some respects abstract conceptual art reached a height at Susa which it has never equalled since.

As we have pointed out elsewhere,[14] the same general age that witnessed the artistic flowering of the Halafian culture also saw the springtide of mythology. The mythology of early Egypt and Mesopotamia, as well as of Canaan and Asia Minor, presupposes a well developed stage of agriculture and cattle-breeding. Fertility myths were already numerous and varied when we first find allusions to them in written documents, in the Pyramid Texts of Egypt and in the Sumerian religious literature of the third millennium. Nor can there be any reasonable doubt that such elaborate fertility myths as the cycles of Osiris, Horus and Bitis, which we can now trace back in fully developed form to the second millennium, were actually much older. The fertility myths of Canaan and Asia Minor, also found first in texts dating from around 1400 B. C., must certainly go back at least a thousand years, probably much more. In fact, the official mythology of Egypt and Mesopotamia in the second millennium can have been only a small part of the vast mythical world which was still known in the early third millennium, to judge from numerous unintelligible allusions in documents of slightly later date. In this mythical world of the Chalcolithic, fertility myths were superimposed on still older astral myths,[15] producing so complex a mythological syncretism that it is often impossible for us now to analyze the component parts of a given myth or to fix the original nature of a given deity. But for the aesthetic sense which is attested by chalcolithic art, mythology would undoubtedly have become sheer phantasmagoria. The urge toward simplicity of motif and economy of effort saved the day, and the amorphous material was transmuted into individual myths of striking aesthetic balance and even more striking emotional appeal.

After these early pinnacles of human aesthetic achievement, the following ages, from the Warkan of Babylonia in the late fourth millennium to the Late Babylonian and Achaemenian of the sixth century B. C., appear in many ways drab and uninspiring. Man could not easily recapture the *élan* of his youth. For nearly three thousand years men continued to experiment and to acquire discipline. Undisciplined native talent was replaced by disciplined imitation of standards imposed by others. Artistic pinnacles were perhaps not so high, but artistic troughs were fewer and not so deep. Early in the third millennium the Egyptians learned the value of artistic norms, and everything which the artist represented, from the human body to the combination of elements in a group or a scene, was reduced to fixed standards, which were taught to every new generation of artists and which persisted with surprisingly little change for some 2500 years. The quality of Egyptian art might go up and down with the stability of culture as a whole, but it always returned to a high level when the state became strong again and was able to protect and encourage its skilled craftsmen. In Mesopotamia, on the other hand, artistic norms never were standardized for more than a few centuries at a time— usually much less. Seen from our modern European point of view, the artistic level attained in the Warkan period sank slowly through several phases until it reached the low level of the Zur-Nanshe period, when the slim elegance of the human figure in Warkan seals was changed to squat lifelessness, and when symmetrical groups were replaced by bizarre collocations. But in the following Dynasty of Accad (cir. 2360-2180 B. C.) art again surged forward and upward, with astonishingly beautiful results. In the course of successive artistic revolutions and rebirths Mesopotamian art lost many of the primitive conceptual devices which still stifled Egyptian art in the first millennium B. C. Assyrian art seems, accordingly, much more

modern in many respects than Egyptian. The art of Phoenicia
and Syria in the early first millennium drew heavily from both
Egypt and Assyria, selecting motifs and groups which seemed
to possess greatest human appeal or which aroused interest
because of their bizarre character. Phoenician art impresses the
specialist as bastard, since it disregarded all the precise standards which the Egyptian artists had laboriously built up and
preserved. Yet the Phoenicians drew accurately and grace-
fully; and by discarding much of the conventional conceptual-
ism of Egyptian art they paved the way for the Greek miracle
of the fifth century B. C., when accuracy of drawing, combined
with the discovery of shading and perspective, raised art from
the empirical to the logical level. Henceforth Graeco-Roman
art at its best was as remorselessly logical as Aristotle.

Though Israel made no independent artistic contributions
of its own, so far as we know, and though its spiritual leaders
appear rather consistently to have rejected or at least neglected
graphic art, it was part and parcel of the Syro-Phoenician material culture of the day. All through Palestine we find stray
objects of art from Phoenician workshops. The statement that
Israelite art was Phoenician does not, of course, mean that
there were no Israelite artists; it merely indicates that the Israelites imported objects of Phoenician workmanship, that some
Israelites may have worked in Phoenician shops or have
founded ateliers of their own, where they faithfully followed
Phoenician techniques and traditions.[16] It is interesting and
perhaps important to note that Israelite art, from the ninth to
the early sixth century B. C., reflects a stage of Phoenician art
during which the latter was diffused throughout the Mediterranean, transforming Greek art completely. When Judah fell
into Chaldaean hands in the early sixth century, its artistic level
was still higher than that of Greece, as we know from seals,
Astarte figurines, proto-Aeolic pilaster capitals, and decorated

objects of copper or ivory. At the same time it was more modern and more vital than the archaistic art of contemporary Egypt and Babylonia. About a century after the fall of Jerusalem Attic art passed all Asiatic competitors; thenceforth aesthetic culture became increasingly Hellenic.

It is much more difficult to trace the early development of music, since we are restricted almost entirely to musical instruments and to literary texts or monumental scenes which illustrate the importance attached to music in a given time or place.[17] As we shall see in Chapter IV, no ancient people of the Near East devoted more attention to music than the Canaanites. Such figures as the archetype musicians, Koshar and Cinyras, play a leading role in Phoenician and Cypriote mythology. In the second millennium the Egyptians borrowed Canaanite lyres and other instruments, keeping their Semitic names. Canaanite male and especially female musicians were in great demand in the New Empire. The early Israelites were strongly influenced by Canaanite music, and the musical guilds of later Israel traced their origin back to musical families with Canaanite names, which are said to have flourished in the time of David. In the time of Hezekiah (701 B. C.) Jewish musicians were in demand at the court of Assyria. The Greeks also borrowed heavily from Phoenician music, taking over instruments, name and all, as well as myths and musical airs. There can, accordingly, be little doubt that Phoenician music, drawing from all important earlier Near-Eastern sources, distanced all contemporary music and that the Israelites, who adopted it, were thus in the van of the musical world during the Monarchy.

Since poetry and music were so closely related at a time when all poetry was sung or recited to musical accompaniment, we can scarcely be surprised to find essentially the same situation in literature as in music. Canaanite poetic literature of the Bronze Age was not so refined nor so delicate in its nuances as contemporary Egyptian, but it possessed a native force and expressiveness which was lacking in the latter. Artistically it was from our point of view superior to contemporary Accadian verse. In Canaanite poetry we find many rhetorical devices which heightened the effect of rhythm and accompaniment.[18] It is true that some of these and other similar rhetorical devices are found in Old-Accadian poetry in the hymnal-epic dialect, but under the influence of translations from Sumerian they were nearly all abandoned in later times, thus giving Assyro-Babylonian poetry a curiously monotonous effect. The Israelites adopted many of these rhetorical devices from the Canaanites, employing them even more effectively, as we can see from the Song of Miriam, the Song of Deborah, and the Lament of David. Both in early times and later they borrowed very extensively from Canaanite hymnology, trimming away polytheistic expressions and discarding crudities. Meanwhile the later Canaanites and their Phoenician successors had been greatly influenced by Egyptian literary models, some of which have passed into biblical literature through Phoenician channels. Beautiful illustrations of this process and its admirable results may be seen in the Song of Songs and the 104th Psalm, as well as in didactic literature, where, for example, the Proverbs of Amenemope were taken over, very probably through Phoenician channels, into the Book of Proverbs.

As a result of the complex process which we have sketched, Hebrew poetic literature has preserved most of the beauties and few of the crudities of older national literatures. Egyptian, Mesopotamian and Canaanite literatures were replete with idiosyncratic similes, which sounded all right to people who were accustomed to the *besbes* tree and the crocodile, or to the idea that the moon was a celestial tiara, or to far-fetched comparisons in which two gods " gore like bulls, bite like vipers." [19] But such crudities had to be banished from any literature which was to endure and to pass from people to people and from age to age without appreciably losing its universal appeal. This sifting process eliminated innumerable elements which had either come down from an early prelogical stage of thinking or from a barbaric social milieu; it also eliminated virtually all mythological elements, except where they had become acclimated in Israelite cosmogony or had received metaphoric interpretation. Consequently Israelite poetry appears modern in comparison with Egyptian, Babylonian and Canaanite verse. There can be little doubt that the high standards of Phoenician art also had a great deal to do with such matters as the elimination of the strange and weird monsters which people Canaanite mythology.[20] It is true, however, that Phoenician art can scarcely have had much direct influence on Israelite literature, since the latter had evolved to a high level before there is any trace of real Phoenician influence on Israelite art. Moreover, as we have pointed out above, art was at best only tolerated in Israelite religious circles. Music undoubtedly affected Israelite poetry most beneficially. The loss of nearly all vowel endings and the shift of the accent to the end of the word in the last quarter of the second millennium[21] must have revolutionized Hebrew prosody, requiring a wholly new accentual rhythm in place of the old Canaanite metrical system, which seems to have been, at least in part, syllabic. The existence of a highly developed musical system saved the day and gave Israel a new medium, thanks to which Hebrew poetic form became much freer than it had been and better suited to be a spiritual vehicle. Here again we breathe a curiously modern air when we recite the psalms of Israel.

3. ARCHAEOLOGY AND THE AFFECTIVE FACULTIES OF MAN

The feelings and emotions of the human animal are genetically much more fundamental than either his imaginative or his reasoning powers. That we discuss them after his imaginative and aesthetic faculties is solely due to the fact that archaeology cannot throw as direct a light on them. While both imaginative and reasoning powers can be dissociated to a considerable extent from physiology, feelings and emotions are intimately bound up with the physical organism of man. This bond expresses itself in complex neuro-muscular and vascular reactions, controlled by endocrine glands and their hormones in still obscure ways. Emotions have their origin in extremely primitive instincts or drives; some psychologists, like the late W. McDougall, consider feelings and emotions as little more than the by-products of instincts. At all events, it may safely be said that human emotions are the direct result of basic drives, modified in innumerable ways by the influence of imagination, aesthetic impulses (which are themselves faculties of partly affective origin) and reason.[22] It is difficult for experimental psychologists to achieve any agreement with respect to the number of basic drives; it is impossible to agree on the number of different feelings and emotions.[23]

Through the experimental study of animals, especially of white rats and chimpanzees, it is possible to trace the origin of instincts far back in the evolutionary scale. E. C. Tolman distinguishes in the rat some nine different biological drives or appetites, including the maternal drive, the sexual drive, the hunger-satisfying drive, the general activity drive, etc. He also differentiates four corresponding aversions, common to the animals and man: avoidance of cold, heat, danger and obstruction. Following Wolfgang Köhler and R. M. Yerkes, he suggests a tentative list of some eight social drives, all found clearly in the chimpanzee and hence inherited by Homo sapiens from remote sub-human ancestors.[24] This list, which we may give in full, includes gregariousness, loyalty to group when attacked, imitativeness, dominance, submission to a leader, competitive acquisition (piling up material for the future), sharing with others and soliciting from them, tendency to co-operate with others for common gain. Of course, it is hard to make any hard and fast classification of social drives, since loyalty to a group may, for example, result from the imitation of actions performed by a leader, while dominance and sub-mission are merely the opposite faces of a single drive, to dominate if possible and to submit if not.

To take a single example of how a given instinct may be modified by other factors, we may select the sexual urge, from which arises the basic emotion of love between woman and man. To use Tolman's terminology, this drive is affected by other equally basic drives, such as the maternal instinct, the nest-building instinct, the exploratory drive. Social drives, such as group-loyalty, imitativeness, dominance-or-submission, exert great influence on it. Finally, the complex by-play of human imaginative and aesthetic tendencies, of human reason and calculation, introduces an infinite variety of modulations into the picture of sexual love. Many aspects of sexual love may be transferred to another person of the same sex, quite without involving any perversion. In its turn sexual love conditions music, literature, art, until very extensive domains in all three may become closely associated by individuals or groups with love.

The more important emotions characteristic of Homo sapiens may be classified in pairs, such as love and hatred (watered down to liking and dislike, sympathy and antipathy), trustful-ness (confidence, hope) and apprehension (fear), joy and sor-row, but such extreme emotions as anger and jealousy defy this arrangement. That these last two emotions lack true opposites is presumably due to the fact that both anger and jealousy are extremely complex in their origins and hence inherently hard to classify.

We are, in the nature of the case, limited almost exclusively to literary sources in dealing with the affective life of the ancient Near East. It is only with the greatest caution that we can draw on graphic representations for illustrative material. Literary sources are, however, full enough to compensate for the comparative lack of artistic data. In Sumerian religious literature of the third millennium we find rich illustration of such emotions as love and sorrow (especially in the Tammuz cycle, transmitted orally for many centuries before it was reduced to writing in the late third millennium), as sorrow and pain (especially in the numerous lamentations, which span the greater part of the third millennium), as fear and awe, combined with sorrow (in the hymns to the "word" of Ellil),[25] as trust in the gods. The theme of trust in divine solicitude is touchingly developed in the Lamentation over the Destruction of Ur, from the end of the third millennium but employing much older literary materials: [26]

> Like the child(?) of a quarter(?) which has been destroyed Ur
>   seeks a place in thy presence (O Ningal);
> Thy temple, like a man who has lost all, stretches out its hands
>   to thee in supplication; [27]
> The brick wall of thy faithful temple like a man cries, "Where
>   art thou?" [28]

In the Gilgamesh Epic, which seems to have been composed in its Accadian form about 2000 B. C., under the Third Dynasty of Ur,[29] we have vivid descriptions of emotional states. The love of Gilgamesh for Engidu is movingly described; when Engidu died Gilgamesh was not to be comforted. The Old Babylonian version describes it in these words, put into the hero's mouth:

> With me he traversed all hard places—
> Engidu whom I love dearly . . . —
> With me he traversed all hard places.

He went to the destiny of mankind (i. e., he died)—
Day and night I wept over him,
I did not permit him to be buried,
" If a god should see (I said), he might respond to my cry! " [30]
Seven days and seven nights
Like a worm he lay prostrate on his face—
Since his death I have found no life! [31]

Mother love is attributed to the goddess Ishtar in vivid lines, found in a late recension of the Gilgamesh Epic but almost certainly going back to the earliest Accadian text in substantially their present form. Terrified by the great Deluge and distressed by human suffering,

Ishtar cries like a woman in travail,
The Lady of the Gods cries, beautiful of voice,
" The former age has turned to mire
Because I spoke evil in the assembly of the gods.
How could I speak evil in the assembly of the gods?
For the destruction of my people I ordered the onslaught!
Do I cause the birth of my people
That like fishes they may fill the sea? " [32]

The theme of rejoicing in divine worship appears very often in cuneiform psalms. A very early Accadian example, certainly composed before the end of the third millennium, expresses this feeling with naive exuberance:

The song of the Lady of the Gods I will sing—
Friends, attend, warriors hearken!—
It is the song of Mama, sweeter than honey and date-wine,
It is sweeter than honey and date-wine,
It is sweeter than grapes and pomegranates(?)
Than the choicest pure cream . . .[33]

Illustrations of cuneiform literary portrayal of various emotional situations could be multiplied almost indefinitely. For lack of space we shall limit ourselves to one more selection, which shows how well the Babylonians understood the variability of the human temperament toward the end of the second millennium B. C.:

> He who was alive yesterday evening is dead this morning,
> Like a flash he is cast down, in an instant he is broken up;
> One moment he sings a hymn of joy,
> A step (further) he wails like a (professional) mourner.
> Like opening and shutting their mood changes;
> When they are empty they are like a corpse,
> When they are full they compete with their god.
> When all is well they talk of ascending to heaven,
> When they are miserable they speak of descending to Hades.[34]

A more graphic paraphrase of Goethe's "himmelhoch jauchzend, zum Tode betrübt" was never composed!

Turning to Egyptian literature, we abstain from giving additional examples of the same kind. In general Egyptian literature lacks both the sublimity and the poignancy of Sumero-Accadian literature at its best; on the other hand it attains a higher degree of sophistication and shows much greater delicacy in portraying emotions. The love of a young man for a maid is beautifully described in Egyptian love-songs from the New Empire, now greatly extended in volume by the recent publication of the Chester Beatty papyri, which demonstrate the Egyptian origin of the framework of Canticles.[35] The joy of a lover when he sees his mistress approaching and of a girl when she meets her beloved are described with lyric enthusiasm. Love enables the youth to cross the river in defiance of the crocodile; the kiss of his beloved intoxicates him like beer; he longs to be the negress who waits on her, to be the man who washes her garments, to be the ring on her finger. Unrequited love sends the youth to bed, and the efforts of physicians and magicians are vain—only the coming of the dear one herself can heal his illness. The girl longs just as intensely for her beloved: she desires him so intensely that no amount of beating or cruelty can crush her love; she wishes to bathe before him, in order

3

that he may see how beautiful her body is through the wet linen garment which covers her; she offers him her breast, as though he were her child. The maiden sets a snare for her beloved, as though he were a bird; she pours out her love to the swallows. An hour in the garden, while she lies in the arms of her beloved, is sweeter than all the joys of eternity.

Melancholy and *Weltschmerz* are nowhere portrayed in ancient literature more effectively than in the Dialogue of a Man with his Soul, from the end of the third millennium (roughly speaking):

> Death stands before me today
>> as when a sick man becomes well,
>>> as when one goes out after an illness.
> Death stands before me today
>> like the fragrance of myrrh,
>>> like sitting under a sail on a day of breeze.
>
> .   .   .   .
>
> Death stands before me today
>> as when one longs to see his home again
>>> after spending many years in prison.[36]

The literature of Israel seldom rises to emotional heights which cannot be paralleled somewhere in the ancient Near East outside of Palestine. However, biblical literature maintains a much higher average level of feeling. In part this may be due to the fact that the Israelites had developed a previously unknown type of narrative style, simple and direct, equally suited for reciting tales and for recounting historical episodes. Being free from the rhetorical devices which prevented the best Egyptian prose from being spontaneous and natural, as well as from the trammels of verse form, Hebrew prose was able to concentrate on achieving emotional effects. Moreover, Hebrew literature is much younger than the average literary composition which has come down to us from the ancient Near East. Hence it could select the choicest motifs and situations

from its folkloristic and literary inheritance, and could trans-
form them by passing them through the crucible of Israelite
affective and spiritual genius.

Nothing in the ancient Near East can equal the dramatic
portrayal of Joseph's career—Jacob's grief, Joseph's purity and
generosity, the shame and remorse of his brethren. The delicacy
of the story of Ruth remains unsurpassed anywhere; Ruth's
loyalty to her mother-in-law, the scene between her and Boaz
in chapter 3, and the final episode with Naomi (4: 14-17) are
gems of world-literature. The story of David's friendship with
Jonathan is a jewel of the purest water; a comparison between
it and the best ancient oriental parallel, the friendship between Gilgamesh and Engidu, is very instructive. David's grief
over the death of Absalom remains unsurpassed for poignancy.
Nowhere in the entire range of world-literature can we find
an equal to the praise of the love of man for woman in
Canticles 8: 6-7:

> Hang me close to thy heart like a signet,
>   on thy hand, like a ring, do thou wear me!
> For love as Death is strong,
>   and passion as Sheol unyielding.
> Its flames are flames of fire,
>   Its flashes are flashes of lightning.
> Nothing is able to quench it,
>   neither can any streams drown it.
> If one should resign for it all his possessions,
>   could any man therefore contemn him? [37]

We need not remind the reader of the vast treasures of feeling which are contained in the Psalms and the prophetic an-
thologies. Many manuals of biblical literature have listed the
most striking examples, with appropriate classifications and
analyses. The poignancy of the 22nd Psalm, the trusting loyalty
of the 23rd, the majestic theophany of Psalm 29, the deep
yearning for union with God in Psalm 42, the confident trust

in God of Psalm 71—these gems of affective life can be paralleled again and again in the Psalter, while the emotional and spiritual experiences of the prophets have proved normative for two and a half millennia of Judaeo-Christian religious life.

The most exalted emotional experiences known to man, the experiences of religious conversion and mystical union with God, are unknown in the ancient Near East outside of Israel, so far as we can judge from our material. Religious conversion appears first in recorded history in the Hebrew Bible. Nor do we find any examples of it in Greek literature before the Hellenistic period.[38] The idea of turning from doing evil to faith in Yahweh and righteous life is common in the Prophets (e. g., Jer. 31: 18) and the Deuteronomic literature (e. g., Deut. 4: 30). Nearly all of the more important prophets, such as Elisha, Hosea, Amos, Isaiah, Jeremiah, Ezekiel, are said to have received a special vocation from God, through a direct call, through an emotional crisis, or through a tremendous vision. We have elsewhere stressed the fact that the word *nabhî'* does not mean " speaker " but " one who is called (by God)." [39] The central fact of the prophet's consciousness remained thenceforth the memory of that transforming experience, as a result of which he was under special commission from Yahweh to preach to his people.

Another variation on this theme appears in the use of the expression " another heart (*lebh*)," or " a new heart." The former phrase occurs first in I Sam. 10: 9, where we are told that Saul received " another heart" from God after he had been anointed by Samuel. Some recent writers of the pseudo-anthropological school hold that this means that Saul was raised from the profane to the sacred plane by the magical affusion of oil,[40] but there is no basis either in the Bible or in the literature of the ancient Near East for this idea. From innumerable passages in Hebrew and Accadian literature, which have been conveniently collected and classified by Dhorme,[41] we learn that the word for "heart" (*lebh, libbu*) denoted the seat of all affective and reasoning activity of the mind: the emotions of love and hate, desire, joy, sorrow, courage, loyalty, fear, pride were thought to reside in the heart; so also did the faculties of memory, imagination and reasoning. Just what was meant by "another heart" in the case of Saul, we may infer from the use of the same expression in Ezekiel (11: 19) where the prophet describes the coming return from exile and conversion of the people to true religion in the following words: "And I will give them another [42] heart, and I will put a new spirit within them (!); and I will take the heart of stone out of their flesh, and will give them a heart of flesh." In two other passages (18: 31; 36: 26), the prophet speaks of a "new heart and new spirit" in the same sense. It is, of course, true that the idea was prevailingly corporative rather than individual, and that it lacked specifically Christian and—still more—specifically Roman Catholic or Evangelical Protestant nuances; but there can be no doubt that the expression does refer to a powerful emotional experience of religious nature.

4. ARCHAEOLOGY AND THE REASONING FACULTIES OF MAN

From sense-perception, which man shares with the lower animals, the path of psychic evolution leads with relative directness to higher forms of cognition, ending with conceptual and intellectual thinking. The ambiguity and the fluidity of conceptual thinking have been well set forth by Spearman.[48] The archaeologist can control conceptual thought in several ways, through analysis of artistic representations (see above, § 2), through the typological study of artifacts, and through linguistic research. The first method leads to a clear grasp of the way in which the ancient Near-Eastern mind remembered and interpreted perceived objects by selecting dominant external characteristics and grouping them into a simple pattern. The second is at present significant only in so far as it shows that the complex factors which governed man's production of objects for his use, yielded types and sub-types quite comparable to the species and varieties found in nature.[44] There was thus no exception to the undisputed sway of patterns suited to conceptual thought. The third method proves that language then classified and grouped all its material just as systematically as—and even more elaborately than—any comparable modern tongue. Moreover, abstract concepts may be traced back through the instrumentality of comparative linguistics to the fourth and probably to the fifth or sixth millennium B. C.[45] The analogy of modern savage thinking justifies us in tracing the origin of "primitive metaphysics," with such dynamistic concepts as "mana" and "tabu," to a considerably more remote date.[46]

In the writer's book, *From the Stone Age to Christianity* (pp. 84, 123 f.), he briefly discussed three successive stages of reasoning power, basing his treatment on the work of the late Lucien Lévy-Bruhl, with the insertion of another step: prelogical, empirico-logical and logical. The term "prelogical" was coined by a Johns Hopkins psychologist, the late James Mark Baldwin, who first used it in 1906.[47] Lévy-Bruhl's analysis, developed in a long series of studies, remains standard, though further refined or modified by such anthropologists as Preuss,[48] Boas,[49] R. R. Schmidt,[50] and by students of the history of religion, like G. van der Leeuw.[51] A fourth main stage might be added if we adopted the term "hyperlogical," also coined by Baldwin and now being used by opponents of Aristotelian logic to denote the "semantic" phase which they suppose to be now in process of emerging.[52] However, the less said about this speculative bypath the better; that it has a certain theoretical justification we cannot deny, though the designation "para-

logical " is safer. I prefer " proto-logical " to " prelogical,"
since empirical logic was already in use at a lower level.

As illustrated by the thinking processes of modern savages,
proto-logical thought lacks a clear conception of the logical
principles of identity and contradiction. A thing may be what
it is not; it may even be two different things simultaneously.
Proto-logical thought has no idea of causation, for which it is
just as likely to substitute explanation by accidental concomi-
tance or sequence, or by purely superficial resemblance. Characteristic of savage mentality are also collective or corporate
thinking and a dynamistic view of the world. Primitive man
does not regard himself as an individuality, except in concrete
relationships of life; otherwise he is a member of his group,
sharing the feelings and reactions of the group (within the
limits set by his own personality, of course). The boundary
between men and animals or plants, even between men or animals and inanimate objects, is extremely fluid—a mode of
thinking which is very important for the understanding of
ancient Near-Eastern mythology and religion. Corporate thinking leads to dynamism: primitive man feels an impersonal
power or force all around him, a force which is especially
manifest in unusual objects or persons and which may be put
to work through the instrumentality of specific acts and rituals,
to which we apply the term sympathetic magic. Lévy-Bruhl
traces the origin of mysticism to primitive corporativism, which
he calls " the principle of participation " and describes as " collective representation." Most proto-logical thinking is ruled
by affective reactions.

Proto-logical thinking is illustrated in ancient Near-Eastern literature by mythology, especially by the myths relating to
gods of fertility, where sex and personality are fluid, changing
from one to its opposite with the most disconcerting ease. A
deity may be male and female at different times—or simulta-

neously. A goddess may be fruitful mother and virgin at the same time. Heaven may be a cow, a woman, or a sea; the moon may be a young bull, a jeweled tiara, a mother-womb—all in the same hymn. A god may be lord of death and giver of fertility, healer and destroyer. The Canaanite Anath is both the loving mother of her people and the destroying avenger.[53] Cuneiform magic vividly illustrates proto-logical thinking, since all its branches are based upon logically untenable causal relations of dynamistic origin. Thus we may have divination from the movement of drops of oil in a bowl of water, from the appearance of the liver of a sacrificial animal, from the movements of heavenly bodies, etc., etc. However, our oldest Babylonian magical texts already bear the imprint of the empirico-logical stage of thinking, as we shall see presently.

Proto-logical thinking is certainly not restricted to savages or to the ancient world; it also appears constantly in the civilized world of today. Much current superstition is decidedly proto-logical; the intellectual reactions of moronic or uneducated people are often proto-logical. The experimental psychologist of the future will probably find that the mental processes of an educated European are neurologically indistinguishable from those of the savage. This, however, does not alter the fact that the modern mind functions at its best along logical lines which are very different from the best efforts of the ancient Near East. That there is such a difference is due mainly, perhaps entirely, to the fact that the Greeks forged the logical tools which we still use and which enable us to surpass our ancestors without 'having any appreciable change in the capacity or the structure of the brain to thank for our progress.

Empirico-logical thought is as old as Homo sapiens and goes back in simple forms to the animal world. When a dog cuts across a corner he is employing a very rudimentary form of empirical logic. Early man learned by long experience to do a great many things correctly. He was quite able to distinguish between his own person and that of others in all ordinary matters. He learned how to hunt and fish to the greatest advantage, how to sow and reap, how to make tools. He learned how to comport himself to the best advantage in his social relationships. He developed a code of customary law. He learned how to use healing herbs and how to perform simple surgical operations. He learned to invent all kinds of practical devices.[54] He developed elaborate linguistic structures, through which he could communicate rapidly and accurately with others. There are few complex structures in the world of nature which are more logically satisfying than the earliest languages we can trace, such as Indo-European, Hamito-Semitic and Sumerian. Employing very different linguistic devices they still managed to express almost exactly the same concepts of concrete and abstract objects, actions, states and relations, and to express them with maximal efficiency. Nothing can be more erroneous than to say, as is still done by many philosophers who ought to know better, that languages with radically different structures reflect different logical " syntax," and are therefore examples of multi-valued logic.[55]

With primitive man it is, accordingly, empirical logic that governs almost everything he does. It is only when he leaves the world of everyday activity, controlled directly by the senses, that he enters the magical zone of proto-logical thought, a zone where the logical principles of identity and contradiction are flouted constantly, but a world in which man can rise above the petty limitations of his daily routine into a new and wonderful region of direct contact with the superhuman and the divine. Without a proto-logical probation there would have been no poetry, no folk-tales—in short no imaginative literature. There would have been no science, since science arose from primitive magic. Above all, there would have been no religion to distinguish man from the beasts and to carry him into the presence of God.

In the domain of secular literature, of science, and in part of religion, the shift from proto-logical to the empirico-logical stage may be said to have been substantially completed in the third millennium. For two thousand years higher thought was more and more governed by empirico-logical principles. Five great achievements of empirical logic may be singled out for special emphasis: (1) Didactic literature, (2) Systematized and codified law, (3) Morality based on individual rather than on collective responsibility, (4) Early science, (5) Monotheism. The first four were developed in Egypt and Mesopotamia, where the second and fourth reached their culmination [56] before the rise of Hellenic philosophy and science in the sixth century B. C. The first grew to maturity in these centers, but produced its fairest flowers in Israel. The third and fifth were forecast in Egypt and Mesopotamia but are substantially Israel's contribution to the world.

Elsewhere we have sketched the development of didactic literature in Egypt and Mesopotamia.[57] In Egypt we can trace the oldest collections of proverbs and aphorisms back to the Fifth Dynasty, not later than the 24th century B. C. In Babylonia our oldest Sumerian didactic texts go back to about the same age. Most of these texts concern themselves only with advice as to how to get along in the world, but before the end of the third millennium we already find poetic exposition of the basic problems of life and death, sin and suffering. The highest level of pre-philosophical thought which we find documented in Egypt, goes back to the Twelfth Dynasty (cir. 2000-1800 B. C.); in Babylonia our highest level seems to be reached toward the end of the second millennium. During the first half of the last millennium B. C. the Israelites collected and sifted Egyptian, Mesopotamian, Aramaean and especially Phoenician wisdom, producing the incomparable book of Proverbs, which has never been surpassed for practical wisdom. That this wisdom is all empirical does not in the least detract from its accuracy of observation and soundness of conclusion. In the book of Job, from the sixth or fifth century B. C., we have the highest level of pre-philosophical approach to the basic problems of man's relation to God and the world.[58] Thanks to the monotheistic premises of the author, Job remained unequalled by Greek philosophers in its spiritual insight.

Codified law appeared first, as far as we know, in Babylonia toward the end of the third millennium, and our oldest complete document of it is the famous Code of Hammurabi, from about 1690 B. C. In the course of the second millennium we find the Hittite law (extant copies of which date to about the thirteenth century) and extensive fragments of Assyrian laws (cir. 1100 B. C.), as well as the earlier (Z)ur-Nammu, Lipit-Ishtar and Eshnunna codes. Before the end of the second millennium the oldest Hebrew laws make their appearance: fragments of Israelite codes of probably Hebrew origin; fragments of early Israelite apodictic law of Yahwistic origin.[59] Closely related to the development of formal law is the emergence of individual responsibility, which we can best trace in Egypt and which reached its culmination in Israel under the great prophets.[60]

The emergence of science goes back to the third millennium in both Egypt and Mesopotamia, but our oldest extant documents belong in both countries to the period between 2000 and 1600 B. C. Mathematics reached a surprisingly high degree of development at this time: in Egypt such geometrical theorems as the Pythagoraean were empirically discovered, while in Babylonia quadratic equations were solved by the method of false position. Astronomy was particularly cultivated in Babylonia, where the movements of the principal heavenly bodies, including the planet Venus, were carefully observed and recorded.

That astronomical research was motivated by astrological purposes does not alter the fact that it was systematically carried
on. Medicine was systematized and organized by the Egyptians,
who excelled in the use of empirically discovered medicinal
plants and in the practice of surgery along sound anatomical
lines. The Babylonians developed philology to an extraordinary
extent, drawing up elaborate lists of Sumerian signs and words
with their Accadian meanings, preparing lists of grammatical
forms with their Accadian equivalents, compiling exhaustive
lists of names of gods, of animals and plants, of names of
countries, rivers, mountains, etc.[61] All this activity had immediate
practical goals, to simplify the task of learning the sacred language, Sumerian, and to keep accurate knowledge of it alive;
none the less it is obvious that Babylonian scholars were carried
away by the sheer delight of amassing and organizing knowledge. In systematized Babylonian magic we have a very curious
application of empirico-logical methods to prelogical materials.
When the Babylonians compiled elaborate treatises giving all
conceivable varieties of monstrous animal or human births, with
the augury to be derived from each, they were wasting their
time, from our point of view. However, their method was
essentially correct in two important respects: they drew their
first conclusions from what happened after actual cases of
monstrous birth (on the principle *post hoc ergo propter hoc*)
and they codified their lists by the systematic application of
various intuitive principles, such as analogy and polarity. Sometimes these principles were logically correct (though not logically derived) ; e. g., the falcon was unlucky when seen flying
toward the right (since it was an unlucky bird in folk-belief),
but lucky when seen flying toward the unlucky left.[62] This
principle may have been derived by intuitive application of the
principle of polarity, but it yields a logically correct result:
a negative of a negative makes a positive.

We are not primarily concerned here with monotheism, since we have devoted ample space to its emergence elsewhere. Here also the Egyptians and Mesopotamians approached monotheism by intuitive application of the methods of empirical logic, and Israel attained it—humanly speaking—by the same methods. The theologians of the ancient Near East simplified the confusion of deities which they had inherited from their prelogical ancestors by wholesale identification, a process which was bound to lead, sooner or later, to pantheism or monotheism. Similarly, continued empirical observation was likely to attribute the major phenomena of nature to one God, a tendency which may be traced back to very remote antiquity.[63]

Empirical logic achieved a signal triumph in the Old Testament, where survivals from the early proto-logical stage are very few and far between. With it man reached a point where his best judgments about his relation to God, his fellow men and the world, were in most respects not appreciably inferior to ours. In fundamental ethical and spiritual matters we have not progressed at all beyond the empirico-logical world of the Old Testament or the unrivalled fusion of proto-logical intuition,[64] empirico-logical wisdom and logical deduction which we find in the New Testament. In fact a very large section of modern religion, literature and art actually represents a pronounced retrogression when compared with the Old Testament. For example, astrology, spiritism and kindred divagations, which have become religion to tens of millions of Europeans and Americans, are only the outgrowth of proto-logical interpretation of nature, fed by empirico-logical data and covered with a spurious shell of Aristotelian logic and scientific induction. Plastic and graphic art has swung violently away from logical perspective and perceptual accuracy, and has plunged into primordial depths of conceptual drawing and intuitive imagery. While it cannot be denied that this swing from classical art to conceptual and impressionistic art has yielded some valuable results, it is also true that it represents a very extreme retrogression into the proto-logical past. Much of the poetry, drama and fiction which has been written during the past half-century is also a reversion from classical and logical standards of morality and beauty into primitive savagery or pathological abnormality. Some of it has reached such paralogical levels of sophistication that it has lost all power to furnish any standards at all to a generation which has deliberately tried to abandon its entire heritage from the past. All systematic attempts to discredit inherited sexual morality, to substitute dream-states for reflection, and to replace logical writing by jargon, are retreats into the jungle from which man emerged through long and painful millennia of disillusionment. With the same brains and affective reactions as those which our ancestors possessed two thousand years ago, increasing sophistication has not been able to teach us any sounder fundamental principles of life than were known at that time. That the change from empirico-logical to logical thinking is not dependent on any process of biological or psychological evolution, but solely on the discovery of the tools by which empirico-logical principles may be changed into scientific induction and deduction, is clearly proved by the example of Japan, which shifted in a few years from one world to the other. In half a century Japan became a modern nation; in three generations it became strong enough to challenge the supremacy of Europe in the scientific and technological fields which Western civilization had arrogated to itself. That this progress in logical habits, with concomitant material advance, can lead only to disaster when combined with a pagan mentality, largely consisting of proto-logical and empirico-logical components, is now evident. Unless we can continue along the pathway of personal morality and spiritual growth which was marked out for civilized man by the founders of the

Judaeo-Christian tradition, more than two thousand years ago, our superior skill in modifying and even in transforming the material world about us can lead only to repeated disasters, each more terrible than its predecessor. Sound empirical logic is still in general characteristic of the ordinary man in his everyday dealings with his fellows, whatever aberrations may characterize the doctrinaire fusion of prelogical concepts with logical deductions from them which we find in such contemporary movements as National Socialism and Communism. Whatever happens, man will never outgrow the empirical logic of Israel or the Aristotelian logic of Greece. Future progress must conserve all the essential elements of both.

CHAPTER II

THE ARCHAEOLOGICAL BACKGROUND OF OLD
TESTAMENT RELIGION

While the epoch-making archaeological discoveries of the past century have been particularly important because of the new evidence which they bring for cultural history, their significance for the history of religion is much greater than is commonly supposed. The history of Israelite religion, which we find recorded in the Old Testament, can now be much better understood than it was a generation ago. Neither conservative nor liberal interpretation remains unaffected by the flood of archaeological information, though a rational conservative attitude has less to apprehend from the new material than either extreme position.

We use the term "archaeology" in its inclusive sense, covering all written documents and unwritten materials from the ancient Near East. Occasionally, however, we shall restrict "archaeological research" to its narrower meaning, the investigation of unwritten remains, in contrast to "philological investigation."

In this book political and social history will usually be treated only when they are an indispensable prerequisite to our study of the light shed by archaeological discoveries on the religion of the Old Testament. Needless to say, it is often quite futile to deal with religious history until we understand the main lines of political and social development. Where a subject has already been fully or adequately dealt with in *From the Stone Age to Christianity*, we shall not repeat but will refer the reader to the pertinent discussion there.

36

1 THE ARCHAEOLOGICAL SOURCES FOR THE RELIGION
OF THE ANCIENT NEAR EAST

Syria and Palestine.

Though archaeological research goes back over a century in Palestine and Syria, it is only since 1920 that our material has become sufficiently extensive and clearly enough interpreted to be of really decisive value.[1] We shall not attempt to sketch the history of discovery and interpretation here, instructive as this would be, but will describe the principal types of material which are now available to the student. Material of significance for the history of Israelite religion belongs to two main categories, written and unwritten. The former must be studied by the philologist before it can be utilized by the historian; the latter must similarly pass through the hands of field archaeologists and comparative archaeologists before the historian can make use of it. We shall list the written evidence under the following heads, to each of which we shall devote a paragraph: Ugaritica, Accadian and Egyptian texts, Canaanite and Phoenician inscriptions, Aramaic inscriptions from Syria, early Hebrew inscriptions from Palestine. Unwritten data may be summarily classified under the headings: temples and shrines, cult objects, plastic and pictorial representations.

By far the most important epigraphic class is formed by several hundred clay tablets and fragments, excavated by C. F. A. Schaeffer at Ugarit (Ras Shamrah on the coast of northern Syria) between 1929 and today.[2] Published by Ch. Virolleaud and deciphered by H. Bauer and P. Dhorme, these documents in a previously unknown cuneiform alphabet and in a Canaanite dialect closely related to ancestral Hebrew have proved to be epoch-making. Numerous large tablets and fragments belong to several Canaanite epics, relating to Baal and Anath, Dan'el and Aqhat, Keret, etc.; there are also tablets containing other

4

myths and hymns, etc. Many smaller tablets contain liturgies, rituals and documents belonging to the temple administration. A small tablet in this script was found by Elihu Grant at Beth-shemesh in Palestine.[3] The date of these priceless records of Canaanite religion and mythology is about 1400 B. C.,[4] but the original compositions had doubtless been handed down for a long time orally before they were reduced to writing.[5] There are innumerable parallels with the Old Testament in vocabulary and poetic style. Students must beware of using early or inferior translations of the Ugaritic tablets. In particular care must be taken to compare different recent translations and to check them with the aid of C. H. Gordon's *Ugaritic Manual* (Rome, 1955). Where scholars diverge seriously in their views it is usually unsafe to follow any one interpretation.

Second in significance we may place Accadian (Assyro-Babylonian) cuneiform records. The Assyrian royal inscriptions of the period 900-640 B. C. throw a good deal of incidental light on the religions of the West, mostly through the personal names and names of gods, etc., which they contain. Cuneiform lists of divine names also yield numerous names and appella-tions of Syrian deities. The same is true of Assyrian and Neo-Babylonian contract tablets from 900-300 B. C. However, all these sources are strictly secondary and often very indirect. The Amarna Tablets, discovered in Egypt in 1887, were nearly all written in Palestine and Syria, and thus are of first-hand value for the light which they shed on the religions of these countries in the century and a half just before the Israelite conquest.[6] Many Accadian tablets from the period 1500-1200 B. C. have been discovered in the past generation at such sites as Ugarit, Qatna [7] and Alalakh [8] in Syria, Taanach,[9] Shechem,[10] etc., in Palestine; of these we may single out the temple inventories from Qatna (el-Mishrifeh) as particularly signifi-cant for our purposes. In many ways the most important of all these groups is the great mass of tablets excavated in 1936-39 at Mari (Tell el-Ḥarîri) on the Middle Euphrates by André Parrot.[11] These tablets contain a wealth of evidence bearing on the religion of Syria and northwestern Mesopotamia in the eighteenth century B. C. From them we shall learn practically the entire Northwest-Semitic nomenclature in the middle of the Patriarchal Age; we shall also learn the names of many gods, Northwest-Semitic words for religious objects and ideas, together with data bearing on cultic practice in Syria and the Euphrates Valley. Together with the Old-Assyrian documents from Cappadocia (cir. 1800 B. C.) [12] and contemporary documents from Babylonia and Northern Mesopotamia they will enable us to determine the major features of early Hebrew and Amorite religion. We are far from having exhausted the rich material in Accadian cuneiform bearing on our subject—in fact the publication of over twenty thousand tablets from Mari is less than half completed. The student can use the readings and interpretations of recognized specialists with considerable confidence, since Accadian can now be read almost as well as Hebrew. Where specialists go beyond the evidence they are just as dangerous guides as speculative scholars are in any field.

Third come Egyptian sources bearing directly on Syria and Palestine. Of considerable importance for our purpose are Egyptian inscriptions of the New Empire. Besides lists of place-names and personal names, accounts of travel and campaigning in Palestine and Syria, we have many Egyptian texts which throw direct light on Canaanite religion. Among these is even part of an Egyptian translation of a Canaanite mythological poem dealing with Astarte and the Sea-dragon.[13] In temple inscriptions, magical texts, etc., we find many references to Canaanite deities and myths. Recently two groups of imprecatory texts have been published, dating from the Twelfth Dynasty (cir. 2000-1800 B.C.) and containing many Canaanite personal names, which add materially to our knowledge of the divinities then worshipped in Palestine and Syria, especially when taken in conjunction with cuneiform documents of the same period, which they complement beautifully.[14]

Fourth·we may list Canaanite and Phoenician (late Canaar.-ite) inscriptions in the linear alphabet from which Hebrew, Greek and most other alphabets known today are derived. The earliest inscriptions in this alphabet go back to between 1800 and 1500 B. C. and come mostly from Sinai, though a few brief examples have been found at Gezer, Lachish and Shechem in Palestine.[15] Since these early specimens of alphabetic writing have not been deciphered to the satisfaction of all competent scholars, it is much better to disregard them entirely, in spite of various tempting interpretations.[16] Nor is it wise yet to utilize the conflicting translations offered by different scholars for alphabetic inscriptions from the following Late Bronze period (1500-1200 B. C.), though here we are on much safer ground.[17] Not until the twelfth century B. C. do we reach fully intelligible Canaanite inscriptions. At Byblus a number of very important documents have been discovered since 1923, including the sarcophagus of Ahiram, now dated in the tenth century.[18] After 900 B. C. most of our Canaanite inscriptions come from Cyprus, Sardinia, Carthage and other Phoenician colonies in the Western Mediterranean.[19] Carthaginian burial inscriptions yield much interesting matter for estimating Canaanite religion, and two sacrificial tariffs from Carthage (about the fourth century B. C.) are of unique importance for our knowledge of Canaanite sacrificial ritual and practice.[20] Recently two Phoenician magical texts from Arslan Tash have been discovered and one has been published; both date from the seventh century and yield important comparative data.[21]

Fifth may be placed the Aramaic inscriptions and documents from Syria and Egypt. Practically all our Aramaic inscriptions from Syria are on stone, dating from between 900 and 600 B. C. Very important royal documents inscribed on stone have been found at Sham'al (Zendjirli),[22] Sudjîn north of Aleppo,[23] Afis [24] and Nerab [25] in northern Syria. The oaths and curses contained in these documents are of great value for our purposes. Shortly after the drying up of this source of information we begin to have Aramaic papyri from Egypt which throw direct light on the beliefs and practices of the Jewish colonists there. While the Elephantine Papyri have raised new and serious problems for the history of Israelite religion they have proved immensely stimulating and have shed undreamed light on some of the darkest areas of Jewish history.[26]

Last, but not least, are inscriptions in Hebrew from Palestine. The oldest of these is the Gezer Calendar, followed by the Mesha Stone, written by a Moabite king in his own dialect, which was scarcely more remote from the dialect of the Northern Kingdom than the latter was from the dialect of Judah, which we call " Biblical Hebrew." [27] Next in chronological order are the Ostraca of Samaria, formerly dated in the reign of Ahab, but now certainly to be attributed to the reign of Jeroboam II, nearly a century later (cir. 778-770 B. C.).[28] These ostraca are invaluable for the light they shed on personal names and political organization in Israel immediately before the time of Amos. Nearly two hundred years later we have the Lachish Ostraca, over a score of which were excavated in 1935-38. These documents, several of which are completely legible letters, date from the autumn of 589 B. C., less than two years before the destruction of Jerusalem by the Chaldaeans; they furnish useful information about conditions in the time of Jeremiah, in full agreement with the indications in the Bible.[29] In addition to the longer inscriptions we have nearly 150 graffiti on pottery and inscriptions on seals and stamps, all dating between 900 and 500, and most of them between 800 and 587 B. C.[30] From these insignificant looking documents we may collect over two hundred personal names, as well as other evidence of value.

Turning now from written documents to unwritten data from

archaeological undertakings in Syria and Palestine, we may first consider places of worship, temples, smaller shrines and open-air sanctuaries. Until recently the surprising lack of archaeological evidence for the existence of roofed temples in Palestine made many authorities believe that Bronze Age shrines were mostly, if not entirely, of the open-air variety, characterized mainly by standing pillars (*maṣṣeboth*). Since 1925 it has, however, become increasingly clear that this situation was solely due to the limited extent of excavated areas, as well as to chance. Buildings which are certainly to be interpreted as temples have been discovered at Ugarit (temples of Baal and Dagon,[31] identified by inscriptions), Tainât,[32] Qatna[33] and Byblus[34] in Syria, at Beth-shan,[35] Ai,[36] Lachish[37] and Megiddo[38] in Palestine, at Ader[39] in Moab, possibly also at Shechem.[40] Houses discovered at Megiddo, Tell en-Naṣbeh, Beth-shemesh, etc., have been claimed as shrines; see below for a general discussion of the problem and the methods which must be used in solving it. Open-air groups of sacred pillars have unquestionably been found at Gezer, at Ader,[41] at Bâb edh-Dhrâ'[42] in the Dead Sea Valley and at Lejjûn in Moab.[43] A rock-cut outdoor altar of undoubted religious function is known to exist near Zorah in northwestern Judaea, and a very large altar some nine metres in diameter at the base and two metres high has recently been discovered in a stratum dating from cir. 2000 B. C. at Megiddo.[44] A similar Middle Bronze altar was discovered by M. Dothan at Nahariya north of Acre in 1954, and an important Late Bronze shrine was found by Y. Yadin in 1956 at Hazor.

Even more caution is required in dealing with cult-objects than with temples and open-air shrines, as we shall see below. Nearly all cult-objects naturally come from the ruins of temples or just outside sanctuaries. At Tell Beit Mirsim, for example, we discovered a stone lion and libation bowl in a rubbish heap outside the Late Bronze temple, the existence of which we surmise with reason, though it has not yet been cleared.[45] Cult-objects may also be identified by their peculiar form, known from other sources to belong exclusively to some group of cultic equipment. In this way many altars of incense and incense-stands of pottery have been identified.[46] A good many cult-objects can be identified as such by the sculptured or carved representation which they bear. This is true of steles with low relief representing deities or mythological scenes which have been found, e. g., at Ugarit and Tell Beit Mirsim. In some cases objects are considered to be cultic because their practical purpose cannot be divined. A great many mistakes have been made, and stone basins, rock-cut cup-marks, stone pillars, large forks, peculiar types of pottery, etc., have been interpreted without adequate ground as cultic in function.

Plastic and pictorial representations of religious and mythological scenes are rare in Syria and Palestine, comparatively speaking. In this domain the contrast with Egypt and Mesopotamia is very great. Stone sculpture is even rarer. So far we have no large images of divinities which antedate the Iron Age (twelfth century down). Images of the storm-god in stone have been found at Sham'al and Carchemish in northern Syria.[47] Reliefs carved on steles and representing deities have been found at Ugarit,[48] Marathus in Phoenicia,[49] Beth-shan[50] and Tell Beit Mirsim[51] in Palestine, at Shihân[52] and Balû'ah[53] in Moab, etc.[53a] Small bronzes, copper and terra-cotta relief plaques and figurines, mostly representing female divinities, are common and most of our information about pagan Canaanite iconography is derived from them. Mythological scenes are much less abundant, and we can seldom be sure that our interpretations are correct. Many of these scenes, especially on seals and ivories, follow Egyptian, Assyro-Babylonian, or Hittite and Aegean models so closely that we must remain in doubt as to whether they received a Canaanite or Hebrew interpretation at all. This question will be discussed below. A good many miscellaneous bits of information reach us through incised or scrawled designs on stone or pottery.

Mesopotamia and Persia.

In this section we shall deal only with inscriptions and other remains of genuinely Mesopotamian and Iranian character; data bearing directly on Palestine and Syria have already been surveyed in the preceding section. In Mesopotamia inscriptions on stone and clay form by far the most important body of material for the reconstruction of the religion of Babylonia, Assyria and Susiana. In this respect the state of our knowledge contrasts sharply with the situation in Egypt, where pictorial representations and buildings, objects, etc., are scarcely less important for our purpose than written documents. On the other hand, thanks to the enormous number of inscriptions dealing with religion, coming from all periods and from all important parts of the country, it is possible to reconstruct ancient Accadian (Assyro-Babylonian) religion with a historical accuracy and completeness that is impossible in Egypt, in spite of the unequalled significance of the latter for comparative religion in general. Owing to the close ethnic and linguistic ties between the Euphrates Valley and Syria-Palestine, Accadian and Canaanite religion are much more closely related than Canaanite and Egyptian. Many figures of deities and many types of myth were, in fact, common to both lands, and the influence of Mesopotamia on Canaan was practically continuous during the last three thousand years B. C. Moreover, in some respects Israelite religion was more closely akin to Mesopotamian than either was to Canaanite, as we shall see.

In dealing with cuneiform religious sources we must be as summary as practicable, since they are so numerous and so extensive that there would otherwise be no end to our analysis.

All sources for Mesopotamian religion in the strict sense of the term are either in Sumerian or Accadian. Sumerian documents began with the Erech texts, which can only be partially deciphered, and continued down to the final extinction of Sumerian as a spoken tongue, probably before 1800 B. C. However, Sumerian persisted as a ritual and academic language until the first century B. C., and some of the most important Sumerian religious texts are preserved to us only in copies of the Seleucid or Parthian periods.

The most important group of documents for Sumerian religion are the literary tablets found in the temple-library at Nippur, preserved in the archaeological museums of Istanbul and Philadelphia. Only part of these tablets have been published, and the penetrating study of this unilingual material by S. N. Kramer, during recent years, has yielded a wealth of previously unknown epic, didactic and other literary material.[54] Among the thousands of tablets and fragments of literary texts which were excavated at Nippur there are a great many duplicates, which make it possible to restore some of these compositions completely and to recover nearly all of many others. Their interpretation is facilitated enormously by Sumero-Accadian vocabularies, mostly from the library of Assurbanapal at Nineveh, in which the meaning of Sumerian signs and words is given in Semitic Accadian, as well as by many late copies with interlinear translation in Accadian. However, since the number of competent Sumerologists may be counted on one's fingers, and since many of the unilingual tablets (written only in Sumerian) have no bilingual parallels and are written in an obscure dialect ("Eme-sal") and with an ambiguous phonetic orthography, we are far from understanding all their contents.

Besides the literary texts, we have many other Sumerian documents of direct value for the student of ancient religion.

The Fârah tablets, from about 2600 B. C., contain lists of gods, illustrating a type of school activity which continued into much later times and produced the great canonical list of gods from the First Dynasty of Babylon (1730-1530 B. C.). From Lagash come thousands of tablets (24th century) containing documents of the temple administration, which illustrate every aspect of cult except mythology. The royal Sumerian inscriptions, especially those of Gudea (21st century B. C.), are replete with religious matter. Even the business documents from the periods of Accad, Ur III, and Larsa are full of personal names and miscellaneous data of use to the historian of religion.

When we turn to Accadian inscriptions, whether of Sumerian origin or containing matter of strictly Semitic derivation, we find an even greater embarrassment of riches. To survey the vast mass of business and legal documents in Accadian, which cover two and a half millennia, would be largely irrelevant, though we owe a great deal to the personal names and incidental data contained in them for our knowledge of the historical evolution of Mesopotamian religion. The historical inscriptions are of more direct value, since most of them contain prayers and invocations to the gods, as well as curse formulae; many of them, moreover, describe the building of temples and the reorganization of temple ritual.

The oldest group of Accadian religious compositions consists of poems and epics in honor of the gods, written in an archaic dialect known for convenience as the " hymnal-epic dialect." [55] This dialect seems to be the literary form of Babylonian popular speech in the time of the Third Dynasty of Ur (cir. 2070-1960 B. C.), but the dated compositions in it belong to the First Dynasty of Babylon (cir. 1730-1530). The latter dynasty was the classical age of Accadian literature and science (see Chapter I), and the original composition of the majority of extant cuneiform works in these categories may be certainly or probably dated in it. Among these are such important works as the Creation Epic and the Gilgamesh Epic (see above, pp. 19 f.), the Atrakhasis Epic and the Descent of Ishtar. Many rituals and incantations, hymns and didactic texts undoubtedly go back to this period. To it go back also most of the dictionaries, grammars, sign-lists and vocabularies, including the Great List of Gods, nearly all of which received their canonical form at that time. Mathematics and astrology then reached a high point of development, followed closely by all branches of divination, including some (like lecanomancy, the art of predicting events by watching the movements of oil on water) which were much less important in later times.

In subsequent periods we see two trends, the first to revise and modernize the ancient epics, hymns and rituals, the other to compose new works. There was much revision of works of ancient cuneiform literature in the second half of the second millennium B. C., especially in the latter part of the Cossaean Dynasty (cir. 1400-1150 B. C.). Among new compositions which may be dated to this time is the great incantation " Shurpu," which does, however, contain some older matter.[56] After about 1200 B. C. we find great activity in the composition of didactic or gnomic texts, and a whole wisdom literature arose in Assyria as well as in Babylonia. Much of this literature goes back to older sources, in part of Sumerian origin (see above), but there can be no doubt that the extant form of most cuneiform wisdom literature must be dated between 1200 and 800 B. C.[57] After the ninth century B. C. original composition became rare and jejune in Babylonia, though it continued in Assyria until the middle of the seventh century. The elaborate collections of extant literary tablets in the royal library of Assurbanapal (Sardanapalus), between 668 and 626 B. C., and the laborious antiquarian enterprises of Nabonidus, both designed to conserve the past, not to understand it, sounded the death-knell of creative literature, both religious and profane.

Mesopotamia has preserved a wealth of religious constructions and of objects with cultic functions or implications. We have the ground-plan and many architectural details of scores of temples and shrines, extending from the fourth millennium at Erech and Tepe Gawra to the second century B. C. at Erech.[58] Though we must omit the round structures of the Halafian Age (not later than cir. 4000 B. C.), since we cannot be altogether sure of their function, we still find well-built mud-brick temples on stone foundations as far back as Stratum XIII of Tepe Gawra in Assyria, which can scarcely be later than the middle of the fourth millennium B. C. At Erech (Warka) the German excavators have discovered a number of exceedingly archaic shrines from the late fourth and the early third millennium. Religious architecture of the third millennium is best represented by the excavations of the Oriental Institute at Eshnunna (Tell el-Asmar) and neighboring sites in northeastern Babylonia, as well as by Ur and the near-by site of el-'Obeid in southern Babylonia. In Assyria excavations at its early capital, Assur, have yielded a whole series of temples of Ishtar, beginning in the early third millennium and continuing down into the first. In general our knowledge of Mesopotamian religious architecture in the second millennium is relatively slight, though a number of temples in different parts of the country have been dug recently. The first millennium, on the other hand, is very well represented by temples in both Babylonia and Assyria, especially at Babylon, Assur, Nineveh, and Dur-Sharrukin (Khorsabad) The latest Babylonian temple was the " Bit-resh " at Erech, from the early second century B. C., where Babylonian traditions of temple architecture were still followed a century and a half after Alexander's conquest.[59]

While a good many cult-objects have been found in ruined temples or in debris, our knowledge of sacred objects and usages comes largely from pictorial representations, especially from Sumerian reliefs in stone and clay from the period 3200-

2500 B. C., from Assyrian mural reliefs of the period 900-600
B. C., and above all from cylinder seals. These small round
objects, employed for sealing clay covers and documents, enjoyed a vogue of over three thousand years; they have been
published by the thousands and have been studied so intensively
by scholars like H. Frankfort that we are seldom in any doubt
as to the approximate age (within two or three centuries) of a
given piece.[60] The carved scenes or designs on Mesopotamian
seal-cylinders usually have some religious meaning, and it is
scarcely surprising that most of our knowledge of religious
iconography and symbolism in this region is derived from them.

Egypt and Ethiopia.

In Egypt our material, though no less extensive than in
Mesopotamia, is curiously lacking in balance. Buildings are
much more imposing, as a rule, and much better preserved, but
scarcely any cult-objects have ever been excavated in them. The
inscriptions which cover them are excessively formulaic and
repetitious, and papyri of religious character, though numerous,
are far more restricted in time than are cuneifom tablets. A
very large proportion of what we know about the life of ancient
Egypt is derived from the tombs of its dead. Hardly a single
stratified site has been excavated, owing to the fact that almost
all ancient cities are either occupied by modern towns or are
buried under the water-soaked alluvium of the Nile Valley.
Owing to these and other reasons, our knowledge of ancient
Egyptian religion, though very extensive, often lacks precise
form and exhibits gaps. For example, we know very little about
important aspects of Egyptian ritual and liturgy. On the other
hand, we know incomparably more about divine iconography—
how the gods were represented—and about funerary beliefs and
practices than we know about these matters in Mesopotamia.
Moreover, the astonishing conservatism of the Egyptians has
preserved beliefs, practices and representations of incredibly

primitive character, probably going back in many cases to remote predynastic ages, at least to the early fourth millennium B. C. Egyptian religion remains, therefore, classic in its significance for comparative religion.

The oldest body of Egyptian religious literature consists of the magic spells and hymns inscribed on the interior walls of the royal pyramids of the outgoing Old Empire, cir. 2350-2200 B. C.[61] There are over 700 individual spells, most of which are preserved in more than one copy. Nearly all relate to the future life of the king, but a few belonged originally to commoners, and some have nothing at all to do with death, burial, or continued life beyond the grave. A number of the spells are extremely primitive. For example, one hymn praises the dead king as a cannibal who slays and devours the other gods.[62] In some spells the body is said to be buried in earth or sand, in agreement with known predynastic custom.[63] The religious organization presupposed in these texts is often very archaic, antedating the union of Upper and Lower Egypt about 3000 B. C. There can, accordingly, be no doubt that the Pyramid Texts, as these spells are conventionally called, were handed down by oral tradition for many centuries before they were reduced to writing and that some of them must go back over a thousand years in substantially their preserved form.

The corpus of mortuary literature continued to develop in subsequent times. In the Middle Empire (2000-1800 B. C.), the Pyramid Texts were replaced by the so-called Coffin Texts, inscribed on stone coffins of the aristocracy.[64] Numerous spells of the older corpus survived, but their scope was extended to cover all who were rich enough to command proper burial. Certain theological tendencies already manifest in the Pyramid Texts, such as the growing substitution of the god Osiris for the sun-god Rê', are carried still farther in these texts. Several centuries later, in the New Empire (1550-1150 B. C.), a new, democratized, collection of mortuary spells and texts, known as the Book of the Dead, replaced the Coffin Texts.[65] Stray spells from the collection of the Old Empire still persist, but they are usually so buried under a mass of later glosses and explanations that it would be quite impossible to distinguish them without the direct evidence of our written sources. The Book of the Dead remained canonical down to Roman times, though there were abbreviated forms of it in later centuries which replaced the unwieldy bulk of the original. Nearly all papyrus rolls discovered in tombs of the New Empire or later contain copies of this work, in whole or in part, as well as related texts such as the "Amduat" or "Book of what there is in the Underworld."

Outside of the Pyramid Texts no religious literature as such has been preserved to us in originals from the third millennium and very little from the first half of the second. We possess great masses of religious papyri dating from the New Empire and from the first millennium, supplemented by hymns on stone steles and temple walls, etc., as well as by documents of liturgical type inscribed on temple walls. Many of these texts undoubtedly go back to the Old Empire and several may be attributed with confidence to the beginning of the third millennium. However, we are always hampered in such cases by our ignorance of the character of earlier transmission, whether it was oral or written, or both.

Hymns and litanies of the gods are exceedingly abundant in the texts of the last fifteen hundred years B. C. Among the most important may be mentioned the hymns to the sun-god, to Osiris, to the Nile, to Ptah of Memphis, the antiphonal Lamentation of Isis and Nephthys, together with the Song of Isis and Nephthys, also antiphonal.[66] The Hymn to the Aten, from Amarna, is of unique importance because of the light it throws on the development of monotheism. The inscriptions which describe the dramatic "mysteries" of Osiris at Abydos are of outstanding significance for the history of religion.[67] While the mortuary ritual is disproportionally stressed in our sources, and most early information about cultic organization applies solely to cults of dead kings, we have a great deal of miscellaneous material for ritual and temple administration. Among the most important are the festal calendar from Medînet Habu (early twelfth century B. C.) and the contemporary list of gifts to the temples made by Ramesses III in the Papyrus Harris.[68] However, much scholarly research is required before we can have an adequate idea of the historical development or the comparative significance of Egyptian liturgy and temple cult.

In the Middle Empire there was a rich unfolding of didactic literature, nearly all of which is of value to us here for the light it sheds on the operations of the ancient Egyptian mind and its spiritual yearnings and ideals. The Teachings of Ptahhotpe (which may go back to the 23rd century B. C.), of Kagemni, of Merikere', and of Amenemmes rank first in significance; they were copied again and again in later times.[69] At the end of the second millennium there was a revival of didactic literature, best known from the Proverbs of Amenemope and of Ani.[70] Uniquely characteristic of Egypt at the beginning of the second millennium are the prophecies, which tend to merge into records of disillusionment, such as the Dialogue of a Man with his Soul.[71]

Unwritten data bearing on Egyptian religion are singularly rich and significant. Temples and tombs abound in all historical ages. Our knowledge of the development of tombs is extraordinarily extensive and detailed. Beginning with the earliest cemeteries of the Badarian period, probably antedating the year 4000 B. C., we can follow Egyptian tomb construction and burial practices with scarcely any interruption until Roman times. Of particular importance for the religious aspect of Old-Empire mortuary belief and practice are the tombs of the First Dynasty at Abydos, Naqâdah and Saqqârah, and the pyramids and pyramid-temples of the Memphite kings which culminate in the mortuary temple of Zoser, the Great Pyramid of Cheops, the sun-temples of the early Fifth Dynasty and the later pyramids with inscriptions, whose contents (the Pyramid Texts) have been described above.[72] From the end of the Eleventh Dynasty (late 21st century) comes the mortuary temple of Mentu-hotpe III at Deir el-Bahri. The tombs of rich commoners of the Old and Middle Empires, especially at Saqqârah, contain a wealth of mural painting to illustrate mortuary belief and practice. In the New Empire tombs become still richer and more elaborately decorated, as is particularly true of the royal tombs of Dynasties XVIII-XIX. The fabulous luxury of the tomb of Tut-ankh-amûn is familiar to all. In later times we find fewer and fewer comparable examples; but even at the end of the fourth century we have an unusually good illustration in the tomb of Petosiris, which is full of mural paintings in the strangest mixture of Egyptian and Greek technique.[73]

Surprisingly little is known about the temples and shrines of the gods in the Old and Middle Empires, since almost all surviving buildings of this class were built to honor the defunct god-king. Even the temples of the Sun-god at Abusir (Fifth Dynasty) honor the god as his incarnate representative, the king. In the New Empire this is changed. The temples now belong to the gods and his tomb to pharaoh, though the walls of the temples still furnish ample testimony to the belief that the reigning king was the incarnate Amun-Rêʿ. Such tremendous edifices as the Temple of Amûn at Deir-el-Baḥri (fifteenth century B. C.), the great temple of Amûn at Karnak (mainly fourteenth and thirteenth centuries), the temple of Amûn at Medînet Habu (twelfth century), capture our imagination, and their carved walls supply us with data repeated *ad nauseam*; but they are only gigantic examples of a class which is found from Soleb and Abu Simbel in Nubia to Tanis in the northeastern Delta. Scarcely any of the furnishings and equipment of these temples have been found; what we

5

know about images, altars, cult-objects of all kinds, comes almost entirely from scenes carved and painted on the walls of temples and tombs. Though there are gaps in our direct evidence, we can obtain a very fair general idea of their nature from paintings and texts.

Asia Minor: the Hittites.

The recovery of the long-lost Hittite culture and religion is much more recent than the achievements of Assyriology and Egyptology. No attention was paid to the scattered Hittite hieroglyphic inscriptions of Asia Minor until after the discovery of monuments in this script at Hamath in Syria (1871), and the few known tablets in Hittite cuneiform passed practically unnoticed until the excavations of Winckler at the Hittite capital, Boghazköy, in 1907, when many more tablets were found. Since the Hittite hieroglyphs have been only partially deciphered even after Bossert's publication of the Karatepe bilinguals in Hittite and Phoenician, great caution is still needed.[74] A number of hieroglyphs for special deities have been made out, and they are useful as means for the identification of divine figures carved at Yazilikaya and elsewhere in eastern Asia Minor. No long inscriptions in this character seem to appear until after the fall of the Hittite Empire about 1200 and most of these must be dated between cir. 1100 and cir. 700 B. C. Hittite cuneiform was deciphered by Hrozny in 1915 and can now be read almost as well as Accadian and Egyptian, though there are still a good many doubtful words in the religious texts; Hittite cuneiform was in use from about 1900 B. C. to 1100, but especially about 1400-1200.

Since Hittite religious texts bring together elements from six different ethnic horizons, Sumero-Accadian, Hurrian, Nasian or Nesian, Luvian, Balaic, as well as Hattic (Proto-Hittite), it is at present difficult to make a clear separation between them.[75] In view of the fact that these elements all coexist in the Hittite texts, it is better to think of the Hittite culture as highly syncretistic and not as a homogeneous civilization. The gods worshipped in the Hittite Empire reflect all the horizons just mentioned, together with Northwest-Semitic and presumably additional elements, not yet identified with certainty. Mythological texts have three principal identified sources: Hattic, Hurrian and Sumero-Accadian, of which Hurrian is the most important single source, especially when we remember that Accadian myths often reached the Hittites through Hurrian intermediation. Rituals and liturgies, which form the great majority of extant Hittite religious texts, drew on all of these different sources, but were prevailingly of Anatolian origin. These texts undoubtedly provide the most reliable evidence for Hittite religion, especially since the men and women whose practice they reproduce, are nearly always mentioned by name and provenience. Prayers and hymns are rare, and only one hymn worthy of the name has been published. Incantations and divinatory texts are abundant, but show very considerable dependence on Mesopotamian models.

Our knowledge of Hurrian (biblical Horite) religion still remains a mosaic of fragmentary materials drawn from different sources. The Hittite tablets have preserved many fragments of ritual in Hurrian and a considerable number of mythological and other texts translated or adapted from Hurrian originals. Lists of deities and incantations in Hurrian have also been excavated at Ugarit, where they were written in the Canaanite alphabet. A Canaanite hymn to an Accadian goddess seems to have been translated from Hurrian.[76] Mari has yielded several archaic Hurrian incantations from about 1800 B. C. Accadian cuneiform documents and vocabularies also provide a great many items which help materially to understand Hurrian religion. It is already certain that Hurrian exerted decisive influence on many aspects of Western-Asiatic syncretism in the age between its emergence in our available documents, about 2500 B. C., and its extinction toward the end of the second millennium B. C.[77]

Since no Hittite temples have yet been excavated in Asia Minor proper, our knowledge of cult comes almost exclusively from the Hittite cuneiform texts, from the rock-carvings of the fourteenth-thirteenth century at Yazilikaya near Boghazköy, and from rock-carvings and slabs of later date found in Cappadocia and Cilicia. It is perfectly clear that this latter material possesses no little comparative value, but its interpretation has only begun.[78]

Arabia.

It is now just a century since the first decipherment of the South-Arabian inscriptions by Rödiger and Gesenius (1841). Thanks to the explorations of such scholars as Halévy and Glaser, supplemented by an increasing flow of inscriptions through dealers, several thousand inscriptions are now known, most of them very short and stereotyped in content. The language of these inscriptions is related to Arabic and Ethiopic, but is much more archaic than either; in grammar the Sabaean and Minaean dialects closely resembled Canaanite as we know it from the Ugaritic inscriptions.[79] The latest South-Arabian (Himyarite) inscriptions belong to the late sixth or the early seventh century A. D. and the earliest seem to go back to the ninth or tenth century B. C. Formerly scholars like Glaser and Hommel insisted on dating the oldest Minaean documents back to the middle of the second millennium (Hommel's latest date was cir. 1300 B. C.), but the researches of recent scholars, especially of F. V. Winnett, have proved that they were many centuries too high in their chronology.[80] It would appear that the oldest Minaean inscriptions go back to about the fifth (possibly the fourth) century B. C. and that the somewhat more archaic Sabaean inscriptions of the " mukar-

ribs" ascend to the eighth or ninth. The North-Arabian inscriptions from Dedan, Liḥyân and Thamûd, which are in a
similar script, date from the seventh century B. C. (possibly
the sixth) to the fourth or fifth century A. D.[81]

The value of these inscriptions for our purpose consists
principally in their great wealth of personal and divine names,
which enable us to reconstruct the Arabian pantheon in the
first millennium B. C.[82] The Minaean inscriptions from the
last five centuries B. C. are especially interesting for the side-
lights which they shed on religious usages and terms. In the
South-Arabian documents we have numerous references to
temples, temple personnel, construction of buildings and objects
for religious purposes, ceremonial purification, votive offerings,
etc. A number of very interesting altar models and other documents list the names of various kinds of incense used in the cult.
The uncertainties of interpretation are, however, often considerable and it is still too early to draw far-reaching conclusions
as to details of biblical cult from obscure passages in these
documents. Very great progress is now being made by G.
Ryckmans, Maria Höfner, A. Jamme and other scholars.

Cyprus and the Aegean.

Since the treasure-hunts of Cesnola in the seventies of the
past century Cyprus has yielded enormous quantities of objects,
mainly from tombs, but there was little systematic excavation
until after the First World War, when a Swedish expedition
undertook to make good the deficiency and was followed by
others. Aside from Phoenician inscriptions, which have already
been mentioned above, and aside from numerous short inscriptions in Aegean syllabic characters (and mostly in the Greek
language after the seventh century B. C.), only a few early
tablets have been discovered.[83] Among the objects discovered
are many which throw direct light on Israelite cult-objects,
such as the portable lavers of Solomon's temple. Since rela-

tions between Cyprus and the adjacent Syrian coast were always close, most of these objects and representations may safely be considered as of Phoenician origin.

The lands of the Aegean have been so intensively explored by archaeologists in the past seventy years that few important gaps remain in their cultural history. The chronology of pre-Hellenic remains is approximately fixed by cultural synchronisms with Egypt and Western Asia and by observations based on the succession of layers in stratified sites. Once the broad lines of cultural evolution are fixed it is easy to fill in the gaps by typological observations, i. e., by noting changes in form and style which indicate changes in time. The Aegean civilization of the second millennium B. C. was quite as high in material things as the contemporary cultures of the Nile and the Euphrates, though higher culture seems to have been on a much lower plane. Their interesting religion forms a bridge, so to speak, between the world of the Homeric epics and the world of the ancient Near East.[84] Unfortunately, what we know of it is derived mainly from fragmentary frescoes and from carved designs on various objects, especially on gems. The inscriptions, over 2000 of which are now known from Crete and Greece, were deciphered by A. Ventris in 1953, and found to be in archaic Greek.[85] While interpretation is in progress, hypotheses regarding the relation which exists between Homeric and Mycenaean or Minoan religion must remain more or less speculative. Once we understand the texts of Cnossus and Pylus, as well as the dedications on libation-bowls, etc., it will be possible to use the Homeric epics with a great deal more confidence as direct sources for our knowledge of Aegean religion toward the end of the second millennium. Until then we cannot effectually disprove the views of radical critics who insist that the Iliad was not composed until about the eighth century B. C. It should, however, be observed that the evidence already at hand makes it probable that the contents of the Iliad and Odyssey go back in substantially their present form to the period between 1000 and 850; in 1950 I proposed a date in the tenth century B. C.

2. ON THE USE OF ARCHAEOLOGICAL DATA FOR THE HISTORY OF ANCIENT NEAR-EASTERN RELIGION

The Use of Written Documents.

In the preceding survey of the more important sources for our knowledge of ancient Near-Eastern religion and its bearing on the Bible, we have avoided discussions of method, except where they required only a sentence or two. There are a great many significant problems where method is of prime importance, but where a discussion would involve many side-issues. We select a number of problems from Ugaritic, Egyptian and Accadian documents, in order to illustrate the necessity of a critical approach—an *informed* critical approach, since caution or negation without knowledge seldom merits the name "criticism." We shall restrict ourselves to two problems from Ugaritic, one from Egyptian and a complex group of examples from Accadian cuneiform sources.

In 1933 Ch. Virolleaud, the distinguished editor of the Ugaritic documents, published a mythological poem in which he claimed to find allusions to figures of Hebrew prehistory, such as Terah, as well as to places in southern Palestine, such as Beer-sheba, Ashdod and the desert of Kadesh(-barnea). In 1936 he followed this publication by issuing a translation of a tablet belonging to the Keret Epic, in which he saw new references to Terah and his wives, accompanied by mention of the Israelite tribes of Asher and Zebulun, of Edom, the biblical Cherethites (through their alleged eponym, Chereth), etc. In other papers Virolleaud added references to the Red Sea, the town of Jamnia north of Ashdod, etc. Ably seconded by

René Dussaud, the eminent curator of the Louvre, Virolleaud erected an elaborate structure of joint Hebrew-Canaanite prehistory. The two peoples were supposed to have a common original home in the Negeb, that is, in the region south of Palestine, around Midian on the shores of the Red Sea. Terah, Abraham's father, was then a legendary national hero of the two peoples, either originally or secondarily a moon-god, as indicated by the alleged fact that he had two wives, Sin (name of the Accadian moon-god) and *N-k-r* (supposed to be the Sumero-Accadian moon-goddess Nikkal). The Ugaritic epics would then describe legendary events in the common national prehistory of the Hebrews and Phoenicians (Canaanites) such as war between the Terachites and the Edomites and the founda tion of Beer-sheba and Ashdod. In this way Israelite history, secular and religious, might be prolonged back into the early second millennium and an entirely novel reconstruction of early biblical history might become necessary. These indications are sufficient; there is no need to mention the exaggerated embellishments which these two scholars and others added to the picture, which is lurid enough as we have drawn it.[86]

The writer opposed the entire " Negebite " hypothesis from the beginning and one concession which he made at first to Virolleaud and Dussaud was abandoned in 1938.[87] Other scholars have followed suit, with additional arguments and evidence,[88] until the hypothesis is now virtually extinct in serious scholarly circles. Meanwhile it was naturally enough adopted by many scholars of second rank and was widely popularized, finding its way into handbooks and books on archaeology. It has turned out that nearly every one of these " Negebite " figures sprang from misreading or mistranslation of the difficult original text. " Terah " is a verb meaning " to espouse " and the noun *t-r-kh-t* is identical in meaning as well as in form with Accadian *terkhatu,* " marriage-gift." " Ashdod " must be read 'a-sh-l-d, pronounced 'ashôlidu, and means simply " (my two sons whom) I have begotten "(!). The putative tribes of Asher and Zebulun are, respectively, a verb, "they marched," and a common noun related to Hebrew zebûl, " exalted place, etc." The supposed eponymous hero of Beer-sheba, " Shibani," is part of a characteristic verbal form, meaning " be ye sated (with food)." And so on. It is a pity that the authors of the Negebite hypothesis did not seriously ask themselves whether it was historically and archaeologically reasonable before launching their frail craft into such treacherous waters. Needless to say, neither biblical tradition nor archaeology offers the slightest warrant for any aspect of this amazing theory, so it was only to be expected that sound philology would disprove it completely.

Another Ugaritic field in which premature combinations have sadly distorted the true picture is the domain of cultic practice, especially with regard to sacrifice.[89] The Hebrew sacrificial terms shelem, " offering," and asham, " trespass-offering," occur with exactly the right consonants to represent the two sibilants (one standing for s in Arabic, the other for th) and in suitable context in the Ugaritic sacrificial rituals which were first discovered and deciphered. There can, accordingly, be no reasonable doubt that they have been correctly identified. On the other hand, terms like kalîl, " whole burnt offering," and ishsheh, " offering," have been prematurely identified with similar words in Ugaritic literature; the second word, for instance, has turned out to be the ordinary word for " fire," mentioned in connection with the burning of Baal's old temple. Similarly, an Ugaritic " Feast of Tabernacles " has been reconstructed from a passage where the gods are merely said to have been fed by Baal for eight days(?) in celebration of the building of new temples.

In using Egyptian tales the student of comparative religion and culture is seriously handicapped unless he knows exactly the type of literature with which he is dealing. The Story of Sinuhe, which claims to be the record of the adventures of an Egyptian prince of the royal family who was suspected of complicity in the death of Amenemmes I of Egypt about 1980 B. C. and fled to Syria, where he lived for many years until he was exculpated and reinstated in royal favor, is the most striking example. Is the story fiction or does it possess a historical nucleus—or is it even straight biography? There can be no doubt that the story was put into writing within a century after the events which it describes, since we possess manuscripts of it from the latter part of the Middle Empire. The recent discovery of two groups of execration texts, one from the late twentieth, the other from the following century, tells us enough about conditions in Syria and Palestine to make the local color extremely plausible, to say the least. We now know, for instance, that the district to which Sinuhe fled, east (using the Canaanite-Hebrew word *qedem*) of Byblus, was in the following generations just outside of the sphere of direct Egyptian domination, which extended northward as far as the Eleutherus Valley on the coast and as far as the Damascene in the interior.   The primitive, semi-nomadic state of social organization in eastern Syria in the early twentieth century B. C. agrees exactly with our present archaeological and documentary evidence for that period, before the Amorites had settled down, two centuries and a half before the date of the Mari tablets.[90] The Amorite personal names contained in the story are satisfactory for that period and region.   Finally, there is nothing unreasonable in the story itself and the hero's most remarkable achievement, the defeat of a Syrian in hand-to-hand combat, is perfectly credible, especially since Egyptians of high birth were then carefully trained in martial activities. Without taking every statement of the Sinuhe story too literally we are, accordingly, justified in regarding it as a substantially true account of life in its *milieu*.

Employing the same method of approach we are again justified in treating the Report of Wen-amûn as an authentic narrative of events which actually transpired in the odyssey of an Egyptian envoy to Byblus in the early eleventh century B. C. The judgment does not mean that we can uncritically accept every statement in the story as we have it, but rather that its political history and geography are true and that it correctly reflects the cultural horizon and the religious ideas and practices of its time. On the other hand, such romantic tales as the Story of the Shipwrecked Sailor, the Story of the Two Brothers, the Story of the Prince's Fate, all betray their character as fiction by total lack of specific historical or geographical background, as well as by their *mise-en-scène*, which is either mythical or extravagantly improbable. That the Story of the Two Brothers is throughout a myth retold as a folk-tale is now certain, after comparative mythological and literary analysis.[91] It reflects the same literary type as the newly discovered Strife of Horus and Seth, found in the Chester Beatty papyri; the latter is a well-known myth retold in every-day narrative form. In short, while Sinuhe and Wen-amûn belong to the domain of history and may be used with requisite prudence by the historian, the other tales which we have mentioned, belong to the field of the student of comparative literature and mythology, who can use them without apprehending the existence of any historical nucleus. Other stories are both historical and folkloristic at once.[92]

As our Accadian example we shall consider the complex problem invoved in alleged occurrences of the name *Yahweh*, "the Lord," in cuneiform sources. We shall not deal with the meaning of this name, but simply with a number of cuneiform writings which have been asserted to contain this name, sometimes in remote pre-Israelite ages and sometimes in strange or unexpected places. In Old Babylonian tablets, from the early second millennium, we have the names *Iaum-ilum* and *Yawi-ilum* or *Yakhwi-ilum*, which have been explained as

"Yahweh is god," with suitable inferences. A little more knowledge has taught us that this explanation is false. The former is a good Babylonian (Accadian) name, meaning "Mine is God." [93] The latter belongs to an exceedingly common class of Amorite personal names, beginning with a verbal form in imperfect jussive, third person, and ending with a divine name; *Ya(kh)wi-ilum* means "May (the) God . . ." and is strictly parallel to such a name as *Yawi-Dagan*, "May Dagon. . . ." Since cuneiform was a very defective way of transcribing a number of Northwest-Semitic laryngeal consonants such as *'aleph, 'ayin, he,* soft *heth, ghayin,* none of which existed in Accadian any longer and might be omitted entirely or represented by *kh*, we cannot be sure what the first consonant of the verb was, and translation of the verbal form is precarious, to say the least. One of the cuneiform letters from Taanach near Megiddo in Palestine, probably dating from the late fifteenth century B. C., mentions a certain Akhiyami. His name has often been identified with biblical "Ahijah" (*Ahiyahu*, "My Brother is Yahweh") on the ground that Babylonian *m* was pronounced as *w*. Unfortunately, Canaanite *w* is always written with a special sign for *w* in this period and it is only in Late Babylonian that we find *m* used to transcribe Canaanite *w* or transliterated into Hebrew and Aramaic as *waw* (in intervocalic position). So this name (whose meaning is still obscure) cannot be identified with "Ahijah." These are by no means the only cuneiform names which have been supposed to contain the name of the God of Israel, but they are the most commonly quoted, as well as the most plausible in themselves.

The Use of Unwritten Materials.

In the first decades after excavation began in Palestine, there was a strong tendency, undoubtedly of the "wish-fulfilment" type, to find temples and altars everywhere. In 1899 Bliss and

Macalister dug up at Tell eṣ-Ṣâfi a building about sixty by forty feet in the court of which were three rough stone pillars averaging about six feet high. This structure was not unnaturally taken to be a sanctuary, though no objects of cultic type were discovered in it.[94] For many years it was regularly reproduced in handbooks as an example of the pre-exilic Jewish sanctuary. At Tell Beit Mirsim in 1926 we found a number of such alignments of pillars projecting above the surface of the ground when we began to dig, and at first we considered them likewise to be cultic in character. But continued excavation showed that practically every house of the period 800-589 B. C. was characterized by precisely similar rows of three or four rude stone pillars, which supported the ceilings of the first story. In other words the supposed shrine of Tell eṣ-Ṣâfi was merely a typical house of the age, though a little larger than most.

In 1927 W. F. Bade discovered the foundations of a substantial house, about forty feet in length (12 by 10 metres) at Tell en-Naṣbeh, north of Jerusalem. The partition walls were three in number, dividing the house into four nearly equal parts, three running parallel to the axis and one occupying one end at right angle to the other three. The extraordinary regularity of the plan made archaeologists think at once of a possible sanctuary.[95] A structure of similar plan had been excavated before the First World War at Jericho, where it was taken to be a fortress and compared to the so-called *ḫillâni* type of residence in northern Syria. Later Badè discovered other houses of the same type at Tell en-Nasbeh, and additional examples have turned up at Gerar (Tell Jemmeh), Shechem, Beth-shemesh, etc. In none of these was any evidence for cultic use discovered, so Watzinger, Wright and the writer are entirely justified in regarding them as residences, probably built by officials or by wealthy persons.[96] Where they can be dated approximately, as at Beth-shemesh and Gerar, they fall into the period between 1000 and 800 B. C.

All over Palestine and Transjordan have been found groups of standing pillars which do not fit into the Tell eṣ-Ṣâfi and Tell Beit Mirsim picture. Some of these groups of pillars have been shown to belong to stables for chariot-horses, built by Solomon and his successors between 950 and 750 B. C. The most remarkable of these stables have been excavated by the Oriental Institute at Megiddo, where several hundred pillars, one for each horse, have been found. The Megiddo discovery showed that previously discovered groups of pillars at Tell el-Ḥesi and Taanach must also belong to stables; Sellin had considered a Taanach stable as a "high place." When Garstang subsequently discovered similar pillars at Hazor he correctly recognized their profane significance.[97] The alignment of rude pillars at Gezer remains, however, authentically religious; in Chapter IV we shall deal with their significance for the history of Palestinian religion. Also religious in character was the row of much higher pillars at Ader in Moab, probably contemporary with the adjacent temple, which dates from the latter part of the third millennium. A group of fallen pillars found in the middle of an empty plain, several hundred metres from the great open-air enclosure of Bâb edh-Dhrâʿ in Moab, belonging to the end of the third millennium, must also represent an ancient open-air sanctuary, since it cannot have had any conceivable utilitarian purpose. The pillars of Lejjûn belong in the same picture.

To illustrate the necessity of careful and critical investigation in dealing with the interpretation of unwritten documents, we may say a few words about the religious meaning of the motifs on Palestinian bronzes, ivories, seals and gems. The fact that some of these objects bear short inscriptions with the name of the maker or (usually) of the owner does not affect our problem, except where the inscription throws light on the nationality and religion of the maker or owner. It has been maintained that the elaborate scenes on Phoenician ivories and metal objects of the period 1200-600 B. C. reflect Phoenician myths.[98] This theory is rendered very questionable by the fact that nearly all the motifs and often entire scenes have been borrowed directly or indirectly from foreign sources, generally Egyptian. The Egyptian scenes and motifs are usually of mythological nature, representing the infant Harpocrates on the lotus, Isis and Nephthys protecting the *djed*-pillar of Osiris, etc., etc. Moreover in the seventh century we find a tendency to copy whole *tableaux* from the triumphal relief paintings of Egyptian pharaohs. Occasionally Mesopotamian and Hittite motifs and *tableaux* are reproduced in the same way by the Phoenician artists, employing their own conventions and techniques in such an obvious way that the Syro-Phoenician origin of the designs is never in doubt.[99]

On seals with Israelite or Jewish names, which have been found by the score in Palestine, are often carved emblems or symbols of various kinds. We find, for example, a lion, a young bull, a ram, a fighting cock, two gazelles, a standing human figure, a griffin with the crown of Upper and Lower Egypt, a four-winged cobra (also Egyptian), as well as more complex scenes, sometimes drawn from non-Israelite mythology or cult. Among miscellaneous symbols may be mentioned palmettes, winged solar discs, winged rolls(?), either with two or with four wings, four-winged scarabs, etc. To what extent these representations possessed religious significance is very obscure; [100] the writer tends to reject such meaning in the majority of cases, on the analogy of Phoenician art as well as of synagogal Jewish art in the Roman-Byzantine period, but there must be a residue of cases where we are dealing with authentic religious symbolism. Each case or category of motifs must be analyzed by itself, but results can seldom or never be considered as more than tentative, in the present state of our knowledge.

Chapter III

ARCHAEOLOGY AND THE RELIGION OF THE CANAANITES

1. The Sources and Scope of our Knowledge

Since we have already described the principal archaeological sources for our reconstruction of the religions of ancient Palestine and Syria, we need not recapitulate them here. In order to utilize the archaeological data to the fullest advantage we must supplement them by reference to literary sources such as the Bible and the Graeco-Roman authors. It is interesting to note that we now supplement archaeological information by the use of literary sources, whereas only twenty years ago we still had to base any study of Canaanite religion on surviving literary sources, which could at best only be illustrated by the use of archaeological data.

In dealing with the Canaanites and their religious ideas we must never forget that Canaanites and Phoenicians were one people, so far as language and cultural tradition went.[1] The Phoenicians called themselves " Canaanites " down to the end of Phoenician cultural life in Syria, and their colonists, the Punic Carthaginians, still called themselves by the same name in the fifth century A. D., as we are told by St. Augustine. We can trace Canaanite language and religion backward to the beginning of the second millennium B. C. through Egyptian sources of information, and there is no serious reason for denying that their ancestors had already lived in Phoenicia and Palestine long previously. At all events, we can prove that Palestine was inhabited by people speaking Northwest-Semitic (of which Canaanite, as we know it, is a later dialect or group of dialects) in the early third millennium.[2] But there was a

major break in the continuity of Canaanite history in the thirteenth and twelfth centuries B. C. In the course of not over
half a century the Israelites occupied Palestine, the Philistines
and other Sea-peoples seized most of the Palestinian coast, and
the Aramaeans began the movement which was to deprive the
Canaanites of extensive tracts previously held by them in southwestern Syria and along the coast north of Arvad. In this brief
period the Canaanites must have lost a good nine-tenths of the
territory once belonging to them, or at least to groups sharing
their culture. During the twelfth century the Canaanite remnant
made a fresh start under the hegemony of Sidon, with a political
capital on the island of Tyre.[3] This Sidonian state reached its
climax under Hiram I about the middle of the tenth century;
flourishing emporia and colonies were established about that
time in Cyprus, Sicily, Sardinia, North Africa and Southern Spain.[4] Assyrian pressure and Greek competition weak-
ened the Phoenicians so much in the eighth century that they
were no longer able to hold their commercial empire together,
and finally after cir. 600 B. C. they lost even their cultural pre-
dominance in the Mediterranean. However, several Phoenician
cities maintained a shadowy political autonomy through the
Persian period, and Sidon still had its own kings under the
Ptolemies in the third century. Meanwhile Aramaic had supplanted Phoenician as the language of the people and Phoenician ceased entirely to be used for public documents shortly
before the Christian era. How much longer Phoenician was
taught in the temple-schools we cannot tell; it certainly continued as a learned language even down to the third or fourth
century A. D., as proved by coins from the time of Gordian.

Not far from 100 A. D. Philo of Byblus, a native Phoenician
scholar of good family, collected extensive data for a work
which is variously called " Phoenician Matters " (*Phoinikiká*)
and " Phoenician History " by later Greek scholars. According

6

to Porphyry and Eusebius, Philo translated the books of an earlier Phoenician named Sanchuniathon, supposed to have lived at a very remote age and to have handed on matter originally collected by Hierombalus (Ierembal?) under Abibal, king of Berytus, who is said to have flourished before the Trojan War. This is all very obscure; we can only say with confidence that Philo attributed his sketch of Phoenician cosmogony and mythology to Sanchuniathon and apparently mentioned Hierombalus as a source of the latter. The name *Sanchuniathon* appears in Phoenician as *Sakkun-yaton,* known from inscriptions of the Persian period. Eissfeldt has made it probable that Sanchuniaton flourished not later than the sixth century, and we may reasonably connect his activity with the renaissance of Canaanite literature about this time which recent research has disclosed. A date between 700 and 500 B. C. is at present most reasonable for Sanchuniathon, and Hierombalus, if authentic, may have lived not long before.[5]

The abstract of Phoenician mythology which Eusebius drew from Philo used to be regarded with suspicion by many critical scholars, who were inclined to think that it was mostly an invention of Philo's, without any independent value as a source for our knowledge of Phoenician religion. This pessimistic attitude has been disproved rather completely by the discovery and decipherment of Ugaritic mythological literature since 1930. We now know that the gods of Philo bear in large part names familiar from Ugarit as well as from other contemporary and later Canaanite sources. The myths reflect precisely the same combination of primitive barbarity with fondness for descriptive names and personifications that we find at Ugarit. It would seem that there was little change in the content of Canaanite mythology between cir. 1400 and cir. 700 B. C. Since not only the names of gods and the mythological atmosphere, but also many details of Philo's narrative are in complete agreement with Ugaritic and later Phoenician inscriptions, we are fully justified in accepting provisionally all data preserved by him, though we may often remain in doubt as to the exact meaning of a passage or the original name underlying Philo's Greek equivalent. We must, of course, also allow for mistakes in interpretation made by Philo or his precursors.

2. THE CANAANITE PANTHEON

Two things strike the student at once when he deals with the Canaanite deities. The first is the extraordinary fluidity of personality and function, a fluidity which makes it exceedingly hard to fix the domains of different gods or to determine their relation to one another. Physical relationship and even sex change with disconcerting ease. The second is the extent to which the gods receive etymologically transparent names and appellations. We have, to be sure, several archaic Semitic divine names which we cannot explain, as well as a number of names taken from Sumero-Accadian, Hurrian and Egyptian, but the majority of divine names are quite intelligible. Since this is not true of Greek or Roman divine names, nor of Accadian and Egyptian names of gods, it would appear that Canaanite religion was in this respect, at least, more primitive and nearer its fountain-head than the others. The same relatively primitive state of Canaanite religion may be deduced from its mythology, as we shall see below.

From miscellaneous epigraphic and literary sources we learn the names of the chief gods and goddesses of many Canaanite cities in different periods. We know the deities of Ugarit best, thanks to the sacrificial rituals and related texts which were discovered in 1929. Since there is, in general, only a vague relation between the divinities which figure most prominently in the mythological tablets found at Ugarit and the most popular deities worshipped in the city itself, we can scarcely be far wrong in supposing that the myths were more or less common to all Canaanites and were in no way peculiar to Ugarit.

The generic Canaanite word for "god" was originally *'ilum*, which later became *'el*; it was almost certainly an adjectival formation (intransitive participle) from the stem *'wl*, meaning "the strong, powerful one." The gods were called either *'elîm* or *benê 'el*, literally "the sons of god," meaning "members of the *el*-group," i. e., "gods," following a widely attested Semitic expression for members of a class or guild. The *el, par excellence*, was the head of the pantheon, El, whose name meant originally precisely that: "*the* god," just as "the priest" may mean "the high priest" in Hebrew. El was generally a rather remote and shadowy figure, like Sumero-Accadian Anu, god of heaven, or Egyptian Rê', the sun-god, but like them El sometimes stepped down from his eminence and became the hero of exceedingly earthy myths. In the Ugaritic epics El is represented as living at a great distance, "a thousand plains, ten thousand fields," [6] from Canaan, "at the source(s) of the (two) rivers, in the midst of the fountains of the two deeps." [7] The sense of these poetic expressions is undoubtedly that El was believed to dwell in a cosmic paradise, just as the Babylonian flood-hero was translated to "the source of the two rivers." In Genesis the Garden of Eden is also situated at the source of the four great rivers.[8] To this remote spot the gods invariably had to travel when they wished to consult him. El was called "the father of years" (*abu shanîma*), "the father of man" (*abu adami*); he was also called the "father bull," i. e., the progenitor of the gods, tacitly likened to a bull in the midst of a herd of cows and calves. Like Homer's Zeus, El was "the father of men and gods." Following old Graeco-Phoenician syncretism, Philo applied the name "Cronus" to El, because of various parallel features. For instance, both gods had been dethroned by their successors on the throne of the gods, Zeus in Greece and Baal in Canaan. However, El retained a position of influence which was never attributed to Cronus, at least in historical times, and he was the nominal head of the Byblian pantheon. According to Philo, El (Cronus) had three wives, Astarte, Asherah (Rhea) and Baaltis ("my lady," the goddess of Byblus), all three his sisters. The Ugaritic texts also make Asherah wife of El (see below). Philo portrays El as a brutal, bloody tyrant, whose acts caused "all the gods to be terrified by the decision(s) of Cronus." For example, he dethroned his own father, Heaven (Uranus),[9] and castrated him; he slew his own favorite son, probably Iadîd ("Beloved"), with the latter's iron weapon; he cut off his daughter's head; he offered up his "only begotten son" as a sacrifice to Heaven (Uranus). The tablets of Ugarit furnish other illustrations. El seduces two women, whose names are not mentioned, and allows them to be driven into the desert after the birth of two children, "Dawn" (Shaḥru) and "Sunset" (Shalmu).[10] The description of the act of seduction is one of the frankest and most sensuous in ancient Near-Eastern literature.

The figure of the great storm-god Baal, king of the gods, dominates the Canaanite pantheon. Since the word *ba'lu* meant simply "lord," it could be applied to different gods. In practice, however, from an early period (not later than the fifteenth century B. C.) the ancient Semitic storm-god Hadad (Accadian *Adad*) became "the lord" *par excellence.* As reigning king of the gods, Hadad was enthroned on a lofty mountain in the far northern heavens; he was sometimes considered as being himself the "Lord of Heaven" (Baal-shamêm) and sometimes distinguished from the latter (as in Philo). Baal is called in the tablets of Ugarit "the One who Prevails" (Al'iyân),[11] "the Exalted, Lord of the Earth,"[12] etc. He alone reigned over gods and men; his kingdom was "eternal, to all generations."

As the god of the storm, whose voice resounded through the heavens in the form of thunder, he was the giver of all fertility; when he was slain and fell into the hands of Death all vegetation languished and procreation ceased. He was also the god of justice, the terror of evil-doers. In the tablets of Ugarit Baal is called " the son of Dagon," the grain-god, who was the chief god of Ashdod (I Sam. 5: 1-7), and who had temples at Ugarit and Gaza (Jud. 16: 23). In Hebrew the name of Dagon came to be used as a poetic word for " grain," and in Philo the name is explained in the same way. Actually, Dagan was one of the oldest Accadian deities, who was worshipped all through the Euphrates Valley as far back as the 25th century B. C.; Dagon was undoubtedly a vegetation-deity, but the original meaning of the name is unknown. Baal's consort was his sister Anath, who is said by Philo to have been the daughter of El. Anath appears as Baal's consort both at Ugarit (fifteenth century) and in Egypt (thirteenth century), but at Samaria in the ninth century B. C. Asherah seems to appear in that role (I Kings 18: 19). We must always remember that different places and different periods arranged the pantheon differently, though the picture is as a whole relatively stable. We shall describe the contents of the great epic of Baal and Anath below.

The three goddesses, Astarte (Ashtaroth), Anath and Asherah, present the most complex pattern of relations. The goddesses Ashtaroth and Asherah seem to interchange repeatedly in the Hebrew Bible, where both are mentioned with Baal. In contemporary Egypt Anath and Astarte are even fused into one deity 'Antart, and once they are identified with Asherah, while in Syria they later became 'Anat-'Ashtart, Aramaic 'Attar'atta (Atargatis).[13] Astarte was goddess of the evening star, and originally she must have been identical with a male figure, 'Ashtar, god of the morning star, known to us from South Arabia, Moab, Ugarit and Roman Syria (see below). The original character of Anath is still obscure,[14] and Asherah was originally goddess of the sea, as we shall show below. All three goddesses were principally concerned with sex and war. Sex was their primary function. In an Egyptian text of the thirteenth century B. C. Anath and Astarte are called " the great goddesses who conceive but do not bear," i. e., the goddesses who are perennially fruitful without ever losing virginity. They are therefore both mother-goddesses and divine courtesans. In the former capacity Asherah is called in Ugaritic literature the " Creatress of the Gods," [15] while Anath bears the appellation " Progenitress of the Peoples." [16] In Biblical Hebrew the plural of the name *'Ashtart* (Astarte) is used repeatedly (Deuteronomy) in the sense of " (sheep) breeding," just as the name of the god Dagon was transferred to grain (see above).

The other aspect of sexual life illustrated by these goddesses was sensuous rather than maternal. Anath is generally called " the Virgin Anath " in the Ugaritic myths, employing the word *batultu,* which also means " virgin " (*bethûlah*) in Hebrew. Philo Byblius refers to the virginity of Anath (Athena) and Astarte. Sacred prostitution was apparently an almost invariable concomitant of the cult of the Phoenician and Syrian goddess, whatever her personal name, as we know from many allusions in classical literature, especially in Herodotus, Strabo and Lucian. As sacred prostitute the goddess was, strangely enough from our point of view, called " the Holy One," literally, " the holiness (*qudshu*) of (Asherah, etc.)." [17] The Egyptian representations of Qudshu, "the Holy One," show her *en face* as a naked woman in the prime of life, standing on a lion, with a lily in one hand and a serpent (or two serpents) in the other. Her hair is particularly characteristic, falling down on her shoulders in two elaborate spiral locks. Posture, nudity, spiral locks and lilies or serpents identify the Egyptian representation, labelled with the name *Qudshu,* with the clay plaques of the Syrian goddess, which appear so constantly in all Bronze-Age sites of Palestine during the period 1700-1300 B. C. While it is true that these plaques have been influenced artistically by the form of the Hathor wig which was fashionable in Egypt during the Middle Empire (cir. 2000-1800) and which was early transferred to representations of the goddess Hathor, it is now certain that they were originally imitations of the Ishtar plaques of the same type which were popular in Babylonia between 2000 and 1600 B. C.[18] Since the type in question does not appear in Syria or Palestine until the eighteenth century or a little later, whereas it goes back in Babylonia through successive stages into Sumerian times, there can be no doubt that the iconographic form was borrowed from Mesopotamia. However, the Canaanites lost no time in substituting carnality for the grace of the Babylonian originals. Both in these plaques and in later ones the female organs are accentuated in various ways, nearly all of them more direct and less restrained than was true of Babylonia. Moreover, in Mesopotamia the plaques nearly all obviously represent a mother-goddess, whereas in Canaan most of them just as clearly portray a sacred courtesan. The lily and serpent are characteristically Canaanite; the former indicates the charm and grace of the bearer—in a word, her sex appeal—and the latter symbolizes her fecundity. It was only natural that the Phoenicians should attribute to Astarte two sons, named (according to Philo) "Sexual Desire" (Pothos) and "Sexual Love" (Eros). The original Canaanite names escape us, but Ugarit has provided many analogies for such etymologically transparent names of minor deities At its best there can be little doubt that there was a certain amount of aesthetic charm about Canaanite literary and artistic portrayal of these goddesses; in the Keret Epic, for instance the hero's betrothed is poetically described as having "the charm of Anath" and "the beauty of Astarte." At its worst however, the erotic aspect of their cult must have sunk to extremely sordid depths of social degradation.

Besides being patronesses of sexual life these interesting ladies were also goddesses of war. Anath or Astarte is depicted in Egyptian representations of the New Empire as a naked woman astride a galloping horse, brandishing shield and lance in her outflung hands. In the Baal Epic there is a harrowing description of Anath's thirst for blood.[19] For a reason which still escapes us she decided to carry out a general massacre: " With might [20] she hewed down the people of the cities, she smote the folk of the sea-coast, she slew the men of the sun-rise (east)." After filling her temple (it seems) with men, she barred the gates so that none might escape, after which " she hurled chairs at the youths, tables at the warriors, foot-stools at the men of might." The blood was so deep that she waded in it up to her knees—nay, up to her neck. Under her feet were human heads, above her human hands flew like locusts. In her sensuous delight she decorated herself with suspended heads, while she attached hands to her girdle.[21] Her joy at the butchery is described in even more sadistic language: " Her liver swelled with laughter, her heart was full of joy, the liver of Anath (was full of) exultation(?)." Afterwards Anath " was satisfied " and washed her hands in human gore before proceeding to other occupations. One is reminded of the words of Mesha, king of Moab about 840 B. C., " And I slew all the people of the (Israelite) city in order to satiate Chemosh and Moab."

The career of the goddess Asherah is even more curious. The goddess is called *Athiratu-yammi* in the Ugaritic litera-ture; since the stem *'-th-r* (Heb. *'-sh-r*) means " to walk " in Ugaritic and Biblical Hebrew, and since the first element has the vocalization of an intransitive participle, we must obviously render, " She who Walks on the Sea," or perhaps " She who

Walks in the Sea." This appellation reminds one strikingly of the similar appellation of the modern Syrian patron-saint of the sea, el-Khadhir (Khiḍr), who is called today *khauwâḍ el-buḥûr*, "The One who Wades in the Seas." The abbreviated form, *Athir(â)tu,* was early substituted for the full appellation, as in so many cases in the ancient Near East.[22] We find the shorter form of the name for the first time as *Ashratum* in a Sumerian inscription set up by an Amorite official in honor of Hammurabi, about 1700 B. C.; she is there called " the bride of Anu (god of heaven)." In the roughly contemporary canonical list of Babylonian deities she is also called the spouse of Anu, who was closely related to Canaanite El in function. As we have seen, Asherah was uniformly considered as wife of El in Ugaritic mythology. Since the Canaanites associated El most closely with the underground source of living fresh water in the far west or north, it is scarcely surprising that his consort was preëminently a sea-goddess. Asherah was the chief goddess of Tyre in the fifteenth century, with the appellation *Qudshu,* " holiness." [23]

In the Bible Asherah appears as a goddess by the side of Baal, whose consort she appears to have become, at least among the southern Canaanites. As has already been observed, we find the goddesses Asherah and Astarte alternating in the Bible rather disconcertingly. Most of the biblical allusions to the name, however, indicate that it was then applied to a cult-object of wood, which might be burned or hewed down like a tree, and which was set up in high places beside altars of incense (*ḥammânîm*) and stone pillars (*maṣṣebôth*). In the Authorized Version the word *asherah* is usually translated " grove," following the Greek and Latin versions, which were presumably based on old tradition. Just what the cult object was we cannot say; some kind of wooden emblem, like contemporary Babylonian examples, is perhaps most probable. That it was originally a tree appears from her appellation, *Elat*, " the goddess," which became Heb. *ēlāh*, " terebinth," planted in high places.

Many other deities were worshipped by the Canaanites. Since we seldom have any detailed descriptions of their myths or cults, we cannot safely define their character in most cases. Their names are often transparent appellatives. E. g., the Canaanite figure which appears in the Bible as Resheph, mentioned as an angel of pestilence in Hab. 3: 5, is found in the inscriptions as *Rashap, Rushpân,* and *Rashpôn* (which is the later Canaanite equivalent of the older *Rushpân*); *Rashap* is " the burner," and the longer form *Rushpân,* from which *Rashpôn* is derived, means etymologically something like " the one connected with burning." [24] Similarly, we have the names *Shalim, Shulmân* and *Shalmôn* (Canaanite derivative of *Shulmân*), as well as the derived Phoenician *Eshmûn*; *Shalim* meant " the healthy, well one," and *Shulmân* was " the one connected with welfare" (*shulmu* = " welfare, well-being ").[25] From the names alone we should at once gather that Resheph was somehow connected with pestilence, whereas Shulmân-Eshmûn was the god of healing. Artistic representations and references in inscriptions prove that both deductions are correct: Resheph was the lord of the underworld, the god of war and pestilence, whose associated animals were the vulture and the gazelle, and who was, therefore, closely related to the Babylonian Nergal and was identified by the Greeks with Apollo; Eshmun was the god of healing, *par excellence,* who was identified by the Greeks and Romans with Aesculapius.[26] How complex the situation was, moreover, appears from the fact that about 1300 B. C. Resheph was identified with Shulmân, as the composite deity Rashap-Shalmôn. This combination is particularly interesting when we consider the identification in later Cyprus of Resheph with Mukal, known nearly a thousand years earlier as the god of Beth-shan.[27] In view of the exceptional unhealthi-

ness of Beth-shan, we may well suspect that Mukal was an exaggerated form of the god of pestilence, but we cannot be sure.
The god who brought death through disease was also best fitted
to heal the ills which he had inflicted.

Actually, the opposition between the god of death and destruction and the god of life and healing was no more difficult
to reconcile than was the character of Anath as goddess of life
and procreation and as the destroyer. Such polarities are universal and were felt instinctively to be part of the nature of
things. What was more natural than to pray to the god of
pestilence for healing from the disease which he controlled?
Similarly, the mighty storm-god was also the dying and reviving deity, whether in the name of Al'iyân Baal (at Ugarit), of
Hadad-Rimmon (at Megiddo), or of "my lord," *Adonî*
(Greek Adonis), at Byblus and in Cyprus. In no religion of
antiquity was there such a strong tendency to bring opposites
together as in Canaanite and Phoenician belief and practice.

We cannot illustrate the problems that face us any better
than to sketch the material now at our disposal for the reconstruction of the beliefs about the god Ḥaurôn (originally
Ḥaurân, whence *Ḥôrân* and *Ḥaurôn*).[28] This god appears as
an Asiatic divinity in three different Egyptian sources: on a
number of faience plaques from the fifteenth century; on a statue
of the young pharaoh as the god Ḥaurôn from the early thirteenth century; in several passages in the Magical Papyrus
Harris. The monumental representations identify the god consistently with Horus, while the magical papyrus calls him "the
valiant shepherd," who protects his worshippers from wild
beasts. Here he is associated with Anath. At Ugarit Ḥaurôn
appears, cir. 1400 B. C., in association with Astarte. In a Phoenician incantation from Arslan Tash, dating to the seventh
century B. C., Ḥaurôn is mentioned with Baal and said to have
a number of wives; his chief consort is given the appellation

"whose utterance is true." Finally, on a Greek inscription from Delos in the Aegean, about the third century B. C., Ḥaurôn (*Hauronas*) is invoked, along with Hercules, by men of Jamnia in the land of the Philistines. Moreover, the name of the god appears in Canaanite personal and place-names (*Bêth-ḥôrôn*, etc.) from cir. 1900 to cir. 600 B. C. Yet the existence of this deity in the Canaanite pantheon was unknown only twenty-five years ago. The interpretation of the name is obscure, but the most likely rendering is "the one belonging to the depths," i. e., god of the underworld. In this case his figure was closely related to that of Resheph. His close association with Hercules at Jamnia suggests that he was the god who was adopted by the Tyrians as their chief deity, under the name of Melcarth (Phoenician *Milk-qart*, "King of the City," i. e., of the underworld, which was called "the city," in Ugaritic, just as in Accadian).[29] Since Melcarth was called "Hercules" by Greeks and Romans, this suggestion is entirely reasonable. The god of the underworld was at the same time a chthonic deity, that is, he was lord of the ground and of its productive faculties. So we can scarcely be surprised to find that the annual festival of the resurrection of Melcarth was celebrated in the early spring at Tyre.

One of the most interesting Canaanite gods was Kauthar (later pronounced *Kôshar* and still later *Kûshōr*), who was virtually unknown until the decipherment of the Ugaritic tablets made it possible to interpret other available data.[30] Koshar, as we may call him for convenience, was the Canaanite Hephaestus or Vulcan, the wise craftsman and the inventor of tools and weapons, as well as of the arts. In particular Koshar was the discoverer and the patron of music. Both the Ugaritic myths and Philo Byblius outdo themselves in attributing varied skills to Koshar. In Philo Chusor (Koshar) appears as the originator of poetry, magic and incantations, as well as the inventor of all fishery appliances and the first to employ boats; he was also the archetype iron-smith. In the Ugaritic myths Koshar appears whenever the arts and crafts are required; he is described as the artificer of the gods, their goldsmith, the "Master of Handicrafts," the "Skilled Workman," the "fisherman of Asherah," etc. It is Koshar who makes the first composite bow.[31] Women singers are called after him, just as in the Bible, where they appear as *kôsharôth* (Psalms 68: 7 [6]). There can be no doubt that the name *Kôshar* means something like "highly skilled."

It is interesting to note that Koshar, with his complex and specialized characteristics, caught the imagination of men more than did many other deities. He was, at least in later times, considered to be the father of Adonis, as we know from pagan Aramaean mythology, where Kautar is father of Tammuz, and from Cypriote sources, in which the god of the lyre, Cinyras, plays the same role. In view of the name of the latter, which is Canaanite *kinnôr* (later *kinnûr*), "lyre, harp," it is very significant that Cinyras was regarded by the Greeks as having been the archetype musician, a magician, metal-worker, inventor of the art of fishing, etc.[32] The Canaanites, on their part, identified Koshar with Egyptian Ptah, the artificer god of Memphis. As a result of this identification a temple of Ptah was built at Ascalon,[33] and we read in the Ugaritic texts that Koshar's favorite residence was precisely in Egypt—then called *Hikupta(h)* after its early capital, Memphis.[34]

In comparison with these personifications of natural forces and patrons of culture, such deities as sun-god and moon-god play a surprisingly small part in Canaanite religion. In part this situation is perhaps due to the fact that solar and lunar aspects were attributed to other divinities. For example, Baalhammon (later the chief god of Carthage), of whom we know very little, may have been primarily solar in character and one or more of the female deities may have had lunar attributes. However, the evidence on which Baal was formerly asserted by some scholars to represent the sun and Astarte the moon, has faded away into insignificance and must be disregarded by the serious student. From the mythological tablets of Ugarit we learn that Yarakh (also *Yarikh, Yarkh*) was moon-god, though the only text in which he plays an effective role has been proved to be a translation·or adaptation in Canaanite of a Hurrian (Horite) original.[35] In personal and place-names from the third and second millennium the god Yarakh figures often, but it would seem that his popularity decreased greatly between cir. 2000 and cir. 1000 B. C.[36]

The question of the solar deity among the Canaanites is even more obscure. Since the name *Shamash* (*Shemesh, Shamsh*) appears in several place-names and a number of personal names in the course of the second millennium, a sun-god was evidently worshipped. On the other hand, the god Shamash is never mentioned at all in the documents from Ugarit, which substitute a goddess, named *Shapash* (or *Shapsh*), who is regularly called "the Luminary of the Gods." It is not surprising to find that the solar deity was feminine among the early Canaanites, since the lunar deity was masculine and since we find moon-god and sun-goddess among the Arabs, both northern and southern, for more than a thousand years (cir. 700 B. C.-600 A. D.). The name *Shapash* does not seem to be etymologically related to *Shamash,* though it was obviously selected in part because of its similarity in sound; it may mean "the Radiant." [37]

In connection with our account of Astarte we have referred to the Canaanite god of the morning-star (the planet Venus), 'Ashtar, who is called by the older form *'Athtar* in Ugarit and South Arabia. To judge from Accadian evidence, this god was originally androgynous, being male in the morning and female in the evening. As evening-star 'Ashtar became the feminine

Ishtar in Mesopotamia and the feminine ʿAshtartu, Greek Astarte, in Canaan. It is interesting to note that ʿAshtar, in the Phoenician form ʿAshtōr (Greek Astōr), was still revered in northern Syria in Roman times. In Moab ʿAshtar was identified with the national god, Chemosh, and in the Bible (Isa. 14: 12) we have a quotation from Canaanite poetry in which the god appears as Helel, " son of Dawn."

3. CANAANITE MYTHOLOGY

The great Baal Epic of Ugarit, incomplete as it is, gives us a good conception of Canaanite mythology. Some 1500 lines of the cuneiform text have been published hitherto by Virolleaud and there is said to be more material unpublished. While many of these lines are badly broken or are still unintelligible, the extant lines are so well distributed that we can form an excellent idea of the character of the epic, though the sequence of episodes often remains uncertain. The Baal Epic lacks the unity of movement which characterizes the great Accadian epics; it concerns itself not only with the death and resurrection of Baal but also with minor myths which do not seem to have any organic relation with the main theme. However, no really comprehensive judgment can be pronounced until we know more about the course of the epic and the exact relation between successive episodes.

An episode which forms the theme of a single tablet with three columns, deals with Baal and his sister Anath.[38] At the beginning of the preserved part Baal is said to have taken his bow and sling and to have gone out from his temple to hunt wild bulls (called "unicorns" in the King James Version of the Bible). His sister Anath learns about it and spreads her wings in pursuit. Apparently she could be pictured as winged. Baal meets her with the words, " The horns of thy might, O virgin Anath, the horns of thy might let Baal stroke (or anoint)." The text is not quite clear, but it seems that Anath had transformed herself into a wild-cow, in which form she yielded to Baal's embrace [39] and bore him a wild bull. The text ends with the words, " And hear the good tidings, O thou offspring of Dagon, for a bull is born unto Baal and a wild bull to the Cloud-rider! "

In another tablet we learn how Baal was destroyed by his foes.[40] Baal's bitter enemy, the goddess Asherah, consort of El, was commanded by El to go out into the desert and to give birth there to ferocious monsters, entitled the " Devourers " and the "Renders." How she had conceived such beings we are not told in the extant portion of the text, but the preparations for their delivery are recounted in some detail. The monsters were horned like oxen. with humps like bulls; they possessed super-human powers. In the course of his hunting, Baal came upon them and was filled with desire to hunt them down. A break in the tablet prevents us from learning the details of the battle and his ultimate defeat and death. " Thus Baal fell like an ox and Haddu (Hadad) collapsed like a bull." His death was to a certain extent vicarious: " El completed seven years, eight yearly cycles, while he (Baal) was clad with the blood of his brethren as a garment, with the blood of his companions as a cloak." During this time "the king ceased to give judgment, women ceased to draw water from the spring, the well of the temple ceased to yield water, and the sound of work ceased in the workshop." In other words, all activity ceased.

The first of two large tablets, partly preserved, begins by describing the grief of Baal's friends at his death.[41] Anath in particular is overcome with sorrow: " she was sated with weeping, she drank tears like wine." Then the sun-goddess Shapash placed the body of Baal on Anath's shoulders, and she carried him up to his home in the northern heavens, where he was duly buried, together with burial offerings consisting of seventy each of different kinds of animals: wild bulls, oxen, sheep, stags, wild goats, deer. Then Anath made her way to the palace of El in the Canaanite Elysium and announced the death of Baal to the assembled deities with the words, " Let Asherah and her children rejoice, Elat and the band of her companions; for triumphant Baal is dead, the prince, lord of the earth, has perished! " Asherah, delighted at the death of her adversary, responded at once to the demand of El for a successor to Baal by nominating 'Ashtar, god of the morning-star, to the vacant post. The text breaks off at this point, but it would appear that 'Ashtar was too small to fill the empty throne of Baal. His subsequent fate is perhaps described in the passage quoted in Isa. 14: 12 ff. (see above).

Anath, however, was full of grief and desire for revenge: " Like the heart of a cow toward its calf, like the heart of a ewe toward its lamb, so was the heart of Anath attached to Baal." Mot, god of death, challenged her insultingly, proclaiming his own destructive power in the following terms: When he goes forth, Death tramples the mountains into the ground, all life ceases among men, the earth becomes a desert. Baal has become as a lamb in his mouth; as a kid Mot crushes him. Even the sun-goddess Shapash is helpless in the grasp of Mot. Thereupon Anath's patience came to an end; she attacked Death like an avenging fury, " cutting him off with her sword, winnowing him with the sieve, burning him in the fire, grinding his ashes with the hand-mill, sowing what was left of him in the field, in order that the birds might eat their portion, utterly destroying the sprouts." [42] The importance of this passage for comparative mythology has often been stressed in the past few years. No other mythology has so explicitly described the sympathetic ritual by which the god of grain is restored to life. The ritual was intended to revive Baal by sympathetic action, not to bring the god of death himself to life. However, in view of what we have said above about the fluidity of mythological conceptions among the Canaanites, as well as about the dual functions of such gods as Resheph, we may safely infer that Mot is also treated as though he were a god of fertility. The grain-god is harvested by cutting the stalk with the sickle; he is then threshed, winnowed, ground in the mill or sown in the field, either giving his life that men may eat immediately, or dying in the ground in order that he may later come to life again and sustain mankind.[43]

With Anath's destruction of Death it would seem that Baal came immediately to life again. We read in the next column, after a break of over forty lines, the following words, addressed to El by a deity whose name is broken off:

> " In a dream, O gracious One, compassionate(?) El,
>   in a vision, O Creator of Creatures,
> The heavens rained oil,
>   the valleys ran honey;
> So I know that triumphant Baal lives,
>   that the prince, lord of the earth, exists! "

At this good news El " rejoiced, he put his feet on the footstool, and he put away grief and he smiled."

After Baal's release from the underworld begins a mighty combat between Baal and Mot, in which Baal is aided by the sun-goddess, Shapash. Mot threatens Baal with all the successive woes which Anath has visited on him: cutting in two with the sword, winnowing with a sieve, burning in the fire, grinding in a hand-mill, etc. Then they attack each other, burning like hot coals (?) with zest for the fight. " They gore one another like wild bulls, they bite one another like serpents "—but neither yields. Then " they kick (?) one another like chargers " and both fall to the ground. The sequel to the conflict has been lost.

The best preserved part of the Baal Epic may be described

succinctly at this point, though it is by no means clear whether it precedes or follows the tablet just described—or indeed whether it stands in any organic relation to it at all.[44] At the outset we hear that Baal had no house or temple like the other gods. It would seem that the words *bêtu,* "house," and *hêkalu,* "temple," refer both to a residence in heaven and to temples on earth; proto-logical ambivalence must frequently be assumed in mythology. Apparently El and his consort Asherah were in accord with Baal and his sister Anath on the desirability of providing this residence. Preparations were immediately begun. The god of craftsmanship, Koshar-and-Khasis (also called *Hiyyân*), "went up to the bellows, in his hand he grasped the tongs, he melted silver, he hammered out gold."

For some reason, however, Asherah decided to oppose the plans of Baal and Anath, as we may gather from an obscure fragment of Col. II. In the next column a bitter argument seems to have arisen between Asherah and her followers, on the one side, and Baal and Anath, on the other. However, in Col. IV Asherah accompanied Anath to the palace of El, and in the ensuing colloquy she apparently supported Baal's plea for a residence of his own. Asherah's entreaties seem to be motivated by her fear that Baal will withold the rain unless his desires are fulfilled. Anath was instructed to inform Baal that his request had been granted; he will receive houses like his brethren, the other gods. Baal thereupon lost no time in despatching an expedition into the mountains for the purpose of procuring gold, silver and precious stones. The craftsman-god Koshar now entered the scene; a feast was prepared for him, in which he sat at the right of Baal and devoured a fat ox. Koshar then proposed that windows be included in the temples of Baal, but his suggestion was rejected by Baal. In the face of his continued insistence on windows, Baal finally gave in. An allusion in the next column indicates that the windows in

Baal's residence correspond to the lattices of heaven, through which rain was supposed to fall (cf. Gen. 7: 11; 8: 2).[45] Some of the preparations for construction are unusual. After the choicest timber had been brought from Lebanon and Antilibanus (Canaanite Sirion, as in Deut. 3: 9), Koshar ordered Baal to set fire to the existing temples (whose ownership is left obscure) for seven days, after which the silver was found to be changed to bars and the gold to bricks. The temple thereupon arose, built of gold and silver, and Baal gave his brethren, "the seventy children of Asherah," a great eight-day feast.[46]

Now that his palace is complete, Baal decides to throw down the gauntlet to his old enemy, Mot, with the ringing declaration: "It is I alone who shall reign over the gods, in order that gods and men may grow fat; (it is I alone) who will satisfy the inhabitants of the earth." He sends his faithful retainer, Vineyard-and-Field (Gapnu-wa-Ugâru),[47] to bear the challenge to the god of death. His instructions to his envoys are preserved in Col. VIII, but they are none too clear as yet. Apparently the envoys are warned not to direct themselves toward two mountains with strange, non-Semitic names, which are said to be "at the bourne (?) of the underworld," but to descend into the underworld by stealth, concealed beneath a mountain and forest (?).[48] By thus concealing themselves, they "will be counted among those who go down to the underworld," [49] i. e., they will be treated as though they were ordinary shades on their way from the upper world to Hades. Vineyard-and-Field is further warned not to approach too close to Death, but to pay him obeisance at a great distance. Here our tablet breaks off. Another tablet takes up the story somewhat later, and we learn that Vineyard-and-Field had to pay dearly for carrying out the instructions of Baal. In this text he appears after his return from the lower world and tells the goddess Anath that he must die, as the penalty for having "gone down into the throat of Death." [50] In vivid terms he describes the contrast between his former vigor and the remorseless approach of death. As god of vegetation Vineyard-and-Field must, of course, die like his master, Baal.

Other tablets and fragments describe the victory of Anath over a whole series of dragons and monsters, including Yam (Sea), Tannin and Leviathan (*Lôtân*) of the Bible, and the seven-headed dragon Shalyat.[51] Baal also fought the dragon Yam (Sea) in a bitter duel, as a result of which Yam was dethroned and Baal took his place, " in eternal dominion." [52] Above we have alluded to Anath's massacre of mankind, described in close connection with a sympathetic ritual by which Anath brought back the dew and rain which had been withheld, either because of Baal's death or for some other reason. Lack of space, however, prevents us from going into further detail with regard to the contents of the Baal cycle, which must have been very extensive in its original form.

The epics of Keret and Dan'el are much less purely mythological in character than the Baal Epic, and they may have a nucleus of legendary history, heavily embroidered with myth and folk-tale. They are, accordingly, more important for comparative literature than for comparative mythology. Good synopses of their contents have recently been published, though much remains to be done in detail. During the War Virolleaud published two more tablets of the Keret Epic, both in very fragmentary form; all three tablets have now been admirably edited by H. L. Ginsberg.[53]

In reading the foregoing pages, the student has doubtless received a number of general impressions. The first is undoubtedly that there is little resemblance between sketches of Canaanite religion written before 1932 and since that date. The interpretation of the Ugaritic documents has not only given body and spirit to what was merely a collection of more or less related items, but it has also enabled us properly to utilize the extensive material from other sources which was already available as well as what has been found during the past decade. Before 1932 it was of little use to describe the Canaanite pantheon, since we knew too little about the functions and the personalities of its component elements. The absence of mythological texts and hymns made it quite impossible to reconstruct the Canaanite attitude toward their gods.

Now all this has changed. Canaanite mythology can be described; mythical stories can be retold and the characteristics of the more important divinities can be defined. Canaanite mythology stands just about where one might have placed it a priori, in an intermediate position among Mesopotamian, Egyptian, Anatolian and Aegean. The Canaanite pantheon reminds one almost equally of Mesopotamian and of Homeric conceptions. Baal corresponds to Ellil or Marduk or Adad in the East and to Zeus in the West. The three goddesses Astarte, Anath, and Asherah correspond to Innini-Ishtar in Mesopotamia and to Aphrodite, Athena, Hera, and other Aegean figures. Resheph and Haurôn are parallel to Nergal and Ninurta in the East, to Apollo in the West. Shulmân corresponds to Apollo or in his later form Eshmûn to Aesculapius (Asklepios). Kôshar is Hephaestus (Vulcan). The mythology of Ugarit strikes a happy medium between Babylonia and the Aegean, scarcely resembling the former any more than the latter. Canaanite theogony, especially in its later, Phoenician form, resembled early Greek theogony much more closely than Babylonian. As we learn more about Horito-Hittite (Anatolian) religion we note that it had even more in common with Canaanite religion than had either Aegean or Mesopotamian.

What can we say about the evolution of the Canaanite pantheon? Some indications have already been given with regard to the chronological vogue of certain deities. For example, to judge from Canaanite place-names of the earliest period, such as " Jericho " and *Beth-yerah,* as well as from Northwest-Semitic personal and place-names of the second millennium, the cult of the sun-god and moon-god (or goddess) was at its height in very early times and steadily declined thereafter. In the first millennium B. C. we find scarcely any personal names formed with these divine elements. Some of the early figures in the pantheon disappeared in later times; others, such as Eshmûn and perhaps Sakkûn, emerged and became very popular.

4. SOME ASPECTS OF CANAANITE RELIGIOUS PRACTICE

We are now in a position to say something definite about the religious cult of the Canaanites in the second millennium and to compare it with what we find later. Canaanite sacrificial ritual was much more diversified than Israelite. Many more animals were employed as offerings. The sacrificial ritual of Ugarit, in so far as it has been preserved, mentions various bovides (especially bullocks) and small cattle (rams, ewes, lambs, kids, etc.), as well as birds (small birds) and doves. Excavations in Palestine illustrate this picture very well; the temples of Beth-shan and Lachish have yielded quantities of bones of large and small cattle, to which the Gezer " high place " adds bones of deer. A mythological text from Ugarit adds wild bulls, stags, wild goats, fallow deer, etc. Essentially the same picture is found in the sacrificial tariffs of Carthage, dating from about the fourth century B. C.; they add young deer, showing apparently that the list of animals offered to Baal in the Ugaritic myth was not purely imaginative, however rare it may have been in practice, especially after large game had become less abundant in Canaan.

The extent to which human sacrifice was practiced among the Canaanites has not been clarified by the discoveries at Ugarit, which nowhere appear to mention it at all. That it was

prevalent in the early first millennium is certain from numerous biblical allusions, as well as from the fact, attested by many
Roman witnesses, that the Carthaginians, who migrated from
Phoenicia in the ninth and eighth centuries B. C., practiced
human sacrifice on a large scale down to the fall of Carthage.[54]
The degree to which the practice was rooted in Punic religion
is illustrated by the fact that it had not died out completely in
the third century A. D., in spite of repeated Roman efforts to
suppress it. According to Quintus Curtius (IV, iii, 23), the
historian of Alexander's campaigns, the Tyrians thought seriously during the siege of their city in 332 B. C. of renewing
the old custom of offering freeborn children to Saturn (El),
though the practice had then been discontinued for "many"
centuries (*sacrum . . . multis saeculis intermissum*).[55] Philo
Byblius is said by Porphyry to have cited many examples of
human sacrifices in early Phoenician history. We may safely
suppose that human sacrifice was gradually abandoned by the
Phoenicians after their country had been absorbed into the
Assyrian provincial system in the early seventh century, since
the Assyrians did not practice it themselves in later times and
presumably objected to its practice by others, just as the Romans
did when confronted with it in North Africa. It was perhaps
not entirely abandoned until the impact of Iranian and Hellenic
cultures on Phoenicia during the sixth and fifth centuries had
changed the traditional attitude of the people of the land
toward it.

It is also probable that sacred prostitution, to which we have
referred above in connection with the cult of the goddesses of
fertility, declined in late Phoenician times. Direct evidence for
this view is wanting. However, there can be no doubt that there
was increasing decency in the treatment of Astarte figurines,
vividly illustrated by comparison of the sensuous nudity of these
figurines in the Bronze Age with the restraint shown in Iron-
Age examples. It is also evident that the mythology of Ugarit

was much cruder in such respects than Sanchuniathon's account as preserved by Philo Byblius. We may be sure that Eusebius would not have toned Philo down, since Christian writers were interested in presenting the worst aspects of paganism. Furthermore, the trend toward decency in these matters appears very clearly when we compare Assyro-Babylonian literature and practice in the early second millennium with corresponding phenomena of the seventh century B. C. and later.

It is very improbable that the evolution which we have indicated had seriously begun when the Israelites conquered Palestine. The sedentary culture which they encountered in the thirteenth century seems to have reflected the lowest religious level in all Canaanite history, just as it represented the lowest point in the history of Canaanite art.[56] Against this religion the Israelites reacted with such vigor that we find only the scantiest traces of it surviving in Yahwism—many of these traces belonging, moreover, to later waves of Canaanite (Phoenician) influence.

In the preceding pages we have made no attempt to give an exhaustive sketch of Canaanite religion. We have not tried to list all known deities nor to describe all the elements of mythology which are now available. We have omitted all detailed treatment of places of worship and cult-objects, since we shall have occasion to deal with these subjects below. Enough, however, has been said to accentuate the significance of Israel's borrowings from Canaanite religion. These adaptations lay almost entirely in the domain of religious architecture, cultic symbolism and sacrificial practice, poetic language and temple music. But the God of Israel was so far superior to the gods of the pagans, both conceptually and ethically, that theological borrowing from Canaanite sources was scarcely thinkable—at least until much later times, when the elements in question had become dissociated from their crude polytheistic background.

Chapter IV

ARCHAEOLOGY AND THE RELIGION
OF EARLY ISRAEL

In this chapter we shall restrict ourselves, as far as practicable, to a survey of the religious history of Israel from the Conquest to the end of David's reign. Since the construction of the First Temple brought new elements into the practice of Yahwism, elements which were to influence its future decisively, we shall postpone consideration of the reign of Solomon to the following chapter. We shall focus our attention on the religious side of early Israelite history; but since religious practice is seldom intelligible without adequate understanding of social, economic and political history, it will be necessary to go into more detail than in Chapters IV and V of *From the Stone Age to Christianity*, where emphasis was laid on the development of monotheism, other aspects of religious history being strictly subordinated. Where any subject has been adequately treated in that volume we shall dispense with a detailed discussion here. In Chapter V we shall follow the same principles as those we have just outlined.

1. Israel and its Religion after the Conquest

Archaeological discoveries have compelled us to modify the standard tradition of the Conquest, as reflected in the book of Joshua. They have not, however, yielded results which conflict with the older traditions, which we find imbedded in the Deuteronomic narrative in the books of Joshua and Judges (chap. 1), supplemented by scattered data elsewhere. At present we cannot propose any safe reconstruction of the actual course of events during the period of the Israelite settlement in Palestine. What we already know from archaeological sources is, however, enough to disprove any radical reconstruction. The Mosaic period certainly preceded the age of Joshua and the Israelite conquest of Canaan reached its climactic stage during the second half of the thirteenth century, probably about 1230 B. C. The writer's point of view has been adequately stated elsewhere and need not be repeated here.[1]

We are in a more favorable position with reference to Israelite religion just before the invasion of Canaan than we are with regard to its external history. The Mosaic tradition is so consistent, so well attested by different pentateuchal documents, and so congruent with our independent knowledge of the religious development of the Near East in the late second millennium B. C., that only hypercritical pseudo-rationalism can reject its essential historicity.[2] We need not dwell here on the monotheistic character of Mosaic Yahwism; nor need we repeat our arguments on behalf of the Mosaic origin of other aspects of Yahwism.[3] We shall, accordingly, presuppose the historicity of Moses and of his role as founder of Yahwism. Instead of dealing here with these questions, we shall describe some of the social aspects of early Israel before they became modified in detail by the exigencies of sedentary life and by influences from pagan Hebrew and Canaanite sources.

There has been so much misapprehension of the function of nomadism in the formative stage of Israel that a clear statement of the situation, as we may reconstruct it with the aid of archaeology and human ecology, is badly needed. In the thirteenth century B. C. the domestication of the camel had not yet progressed to a point where it could have any decisive effect upon nomadism; no traces of domestic camels have been yet discovered in any contemporary record or excavation. It is not until the eleventh century that camel-riding nomads first appear in our documentary sources. It is quite possible that pressure from camel-riding nomads may partly explain why the Israelites invaded Canaan just when they did, but it is certain that the Israelites themselves were not camel-nomads, but ass-nomads. In other words, the nomadic Hebrews cannot be compared exactly to any modern Arab society, whether Bedouin, or semi-nomadic (modern ʿArab), or travelling tinkers (gypsies, Sleib).⁴

The true Bedawi differs from the Hebrew nomad in his ability to cover great distances on camel-back, to live during the dry season in parts of the desert where the shepherd could not possibly exist, and to derive his subsistence almost entirely from the camel. The camel eats desert shrubs and bushes which grow without a direct supply of water and which sheep and goats will not touch. The Bedawi drinks camel milk, eats camel curd and camel flesh, if necessary slits open a camel and drinks the fluid stored in its " stomachs." He uses camel skin and camel hair to make tents and equipment. The ass-nomad does not dare move more than a day's slow journey (about twenty miles) from water; his asses yield too little milk to be of any appreciable value as food and they are practically hairless; their flesh was eschewed by Hebrew and Arab alike, though it might be eaten to ward off starvation. Sheep and goats are even more dependent than domesticated asses on pasturage and water.

The semi-nomadic Arab lives in tents or temporary houses (which become villages as he settles down); he owns sheep, goats and camels, but also raises crops of grain and sometimes gardens of vegetables. His sphere is limited much more sharply by the extent of his tribal territory than is that of the true Bedawi. The semi-nomad engages constantly in inter-tribal warfare if left to himself without pressure from an organized state, but seldom makes long razzias like the true Bedawi. In short, he is a Bedawi settled in semi-arid or fertile land but not entirely sedentary like his peasant neighbors. Many of the semi-nomadic tribes wander around and between peasant villages, especially in Galilee and (formerly) in the Coastal Plain of Palestine. Thanks to his camels the semi-nomad can supplement his agricultural earnings by engaging in caravan trade or freight transport; in dry years he can exist in semi-arid districts which would not support him otherwise. The early Hebrew tribes of the Negeb, south of Palestine proper, must have been forced to abandon their country in pre-Israelite times, both during the dry season and during long arid periods. This state of society is reflected by the Patriarchal stories of Genesis, which picture the forefathers of Israel as shifting back and forth between the Negeb and the hill-country of central Palestine in what must have been a regular seasonal movement. A similar movement still takes place in dry years, especially when they are prolonged over several seasons.

The travelling smiths or tinkers of modern Arab Asia, whether Sleib or Nawar (Gipsies), follow more or less regular trade-routes. With their asses and their tools these groups depend for their livelihood on their craftsmanship, supplemented by music and divination, in which the women excel. It is probable that the Kenites of the Bible, with a name derived from qain, " smith," resembled these groups somewhat in their mode of living.[5] It can scarcely be accidental that Cain's descendant Lamech had three sons, each of whom is credited with originating one of the three occupational specialties of this form of society: tents and herds, musical instruments, copper and iron working.[6] The famous party of Asiatics depicted on a tomb at Beni Hasan, belonging to the early nineteenth century B. C., probably represents just such a group; the number of individuals (thirty-seven) which constituted it, is about right. In keeping with the character of the group is the fact that it is represented as possessing asses, weapons, musical instruments and portable bellows for use in working copper.[7] While the Kenites were in later times a rather highly specialized class of the population, there is some reason for thinking that the ancestral Hebrews were in part, at least, composed of groups belonging to the same or related types.[8] At all events, travelling craftsmen were closely associated with the Mosaic movement and held a recognized place in Israelite society until much later times.

It is a serious error in method to assume that the " Israelites " of the period immediately preceding the Conquest were a homogeneous body, illustrating a fixed social type of known character. In the first place, they formed a body of very mixed origin, as explicitly admitted by Israelite tradition. In the second place, their remarkable history and their religious zeal were undoubtedly the principal cohesive forces in their organization. Under no circumstances must we underestimate the power of the religious factor. Mosaic Yahwism was a missionary religion, still in its first and most active phase, when compromise between faith in the jealous God of Israel and pagan practices was unthinkable. We may safely suppose that some of the groups which joined in the Mosaic movement were entire clans, each with a normative patriarchal tradition behind it. Other elements must have been quite without such organization. These elements are obviously referred to in Ex. 12: 38 and Num. 11: 4, where different, equally derogatory Hebrew words are employed.[9] The clans and groups which had escaped from the Egyptian corvée were certainly not typical ass-nomads. On the other hand, such Negebite clans as Caleb and Kenaz were probably ass-nomads of normal character. It is, accordingly, unlikely that the latter were actually part of the main Israelite body, since we have good reason to suppose that they invaded Canaan from the south. In view of the tenacious Kadesh tradition, it is most unreasonable to deny their Yahwism.

Leaving these historical considerations aside for the moment, we have ample reason for not attributing fixed nomadic traditions to early Israel. It must never be forgotten that true camel nomadism was still unknown in the thirteenth century, since the domestication of camels was then at best only of recent date. Under the conditions of nomadism previously existing, it was not possible for nomadic hordes to pour out of the Syrian desert or out of the Ḥejâz as has occurred innumerable times during the past three thousand years. Small groups might trickle from the southern oases, but mass movements were not possible for the simple fact that the true desert could not sustain large numbers of tribesmen simultaneously, while long-distance treks from Yemen or Nejd were impossible without camels. Archaeological exploration has demonstrated that there was no appreciable difference in hydrographic conditions along the edge of the desert between the late third millennium, the early first millennium and subsequent periods: the boundary between the desert and the sown ran approximately along the same line then and now. It is true that the boundary between sedentary and semi-nomadic zones oscillated with slow, but pendulum-like, regularity; but there are no important ancient town-sites along the edge of the desert except in places where water is still available.[10] We may except certain cases, especially in the Negeb of Palestine, where caravan towns arose in the Roman period though there had never been any previous occupation; but these exceptions do not affect the period which we are discussing. In Midian no trace of any sedentary occupation before the Roman age has yet been discovered.

It is, therefore, extremely dangerous to assume close parallelism between social organization and customary law of the early Israelites, on the one hand, and of the Bedouin Arabs, on the other. The Arabs are the heirs of over thirty centuries of camel-nomadism and of some thirteen centuries of Islam. They reflect the most highly developed pride of race and family. The most ignorant and the wildest Bedawi may be capable of displaying courtly manners and unexpected eloquence. The Bedawi tradition of freedom and culture is so high that the humblest tribesman considers himself immeasurably superior to the peasant and even to the semi-nomad—who in his turn despises the peasant. On their part the peasants may hate the Bedouin and call them " wild beasts " (*wuhûsh*), but they admire them all the same, and Arab oral literature is full of their praise. Consequently we cannot be surprised to find Bedouin institutions persisting tenaciously, even two or three hundred years after a given tribe has settled down to sedentary life. In the day of ass-nomadism on the fringe of Palestine everything was different. All really arable or irrigable land was already occupied by peasants or semi-nomads, and any wandering group had to eke out its existence in the uncertain zone between the desert and the sown. The list of the forty-two stations visited by the Israelites during their wilderness wanderings may be incomplete and in part artificial, but it strikingly illustrates the kind of country to which their mode of life limited them—Sinai, the southern Negeb of Palestine, the Arabah, and the region east of Edom and Moab proper. This is still the land of disoriented groups and of individual fugitives, where organized semi-nomadic Arab tribes alternate with the flotsam and jetsam of sedentary society, with runaway slaves, bandits, and their descendants, like the Ghawârneh and the Budûl of today.[11] The nomads of that day were despised by their wealthy and cultured neighbors, as we know from many passages in Sumero-Accadian and Egyptian literature. There was then no such exaltation of the Bedouin ideal as we find in Arab literature, from the fifth century A. D. to our own day.[12] Under such conditions nomads and semi-nomads, destitute of cultural traditions, must have borrowed continuously from their sedentary neighbors. Sharp differentiation between sedentary and nomadic culture would, therefore, be quite impossible, in religious matters as elsewhere.

8

That the Israelites were not typical nomads appears also from what happened at the Conquest. Their tradition represents them as settling down almost at once, with only the briefest interval following the destruction of Canaanite towns. Excavations have confirmed this tradition most remarkably in such cases as Kirjath-sepher (Tell Beit Mirsim?), Beth-shemesh and Bethel, and have proved that fresh settlements such as Beth-zur and Gibeah were founded very soon after the Conquest. Such rapid resettlement could not be expected in the case of nomads with fixed traditions and habits, but we should expect it of a heterogeneous congeries like earliest Israel. The stereotyped filiation which we find in the Israelite tribal organization of subsequent centuries, where all the tribes are neatly divided into clans, each with its patriarchal subdivisions, is undoubtedly of later origin. It must have arisen after the whole of Israel had been systematically grouped under twelve tribes and had been assigned to clans within the tribes, each descended from its putative founder, according to very ancient Northwest-Semitic patriarchal formulas. This tendency is well illustrated by the fact that Canaanite cities such as Shechem, Hepher, Tirzah and Zaphon, were absorbed into the tribal system by the time of David, each becoming a " clan " or " sub-clan " in the genealogical lists. It is quite possible that the framework of twelve tribes antedates the Conquest, but the variations in the biblical lists, though slight in themselves, prove that the individual names were never so important as the framework—a deduction which other evidence renders virtually certain.[13]

The central religious institution of Israel after the Conquest was the system of twelve tribes grouped around a central shrine. The close parallelism between this institution and the amphictyony which characterized other Mediterranean lands a few centuries later has been emphasized effectively by Noth, whose work is now standard.[14] Numerous amphictyonies and groupings of amphictyonic character are reported by classical writers from both Greece and Italy; a number of them are explicitly stated to have had twelve tribes. The best known is the famous Pylaean or Delphic amphictyony, which may be traced back at least to the eighth century B. C., but which may easily have been several centuries older. Characteristic of these systems was the fact that the central sanctuary formed the bond by which the political structure was held together. Among the Etruscan colonists from Asia Minor there was, for example, a cultic league centering about the temple of the goddess Voltumna, to which the representatives of the Etruscan communities assembled once a year, in the spring, to attend games in honor of the goddess.

The uniform biblical tradition places the central sanctuary of Israel at Shiloh. To substitute Shechem for Shiloh or to suppose that Shechem was replaced by Shiloh, as thought by Sellin and Noth,[15] is unwarranted. Shiloh is stated repeatedly in Joshua to have been the place where the Tabernacle was set up and where the Israelites were assigned their future homes by lot. In Judges 21 it figures as the place where an important annual festival of Yahweh was celebrated. In Samuel we find the Tabernacle and chief magistracy of Israel established there at the beginning of Samuel's career. In Judges 21: 19 and repeatedly in Jeremiah the abandonment of the site for centuries after a destruction—which was evidently the destruction suggested in I Sam. 4: 10 ff.—is presupposed.

The Danish excavations at Shiloh, directed by Kjaer, Schmidt and Glueck,[16] have demonstrated conclusively that there was a very extensive settlement at Shiloh in the days of the collared store-jar rim, which was characteristic of all central Palestine in the twelfth and the early eleventh century. This period of occupation came to an end before the introduction of a new type of store-jar rim, characteristic of the Gibeah of Saul as well as of contemporary deposits at Bethel.[17]   In several places the excavators found that houses of this period had been destroyed by a great fire. Since the Ark of the Covenant was later moved to Nob and eventually to Kirjath-jearim, it follows that Shiloh must have been destroyed by the Philistines, either immediately after the battle of Ebenezer or a little later. Dead reckoning on the basis of estimates derived from passages in Samuel indicates a date not far from 1050 B. C.—rather earlier than later.[18]

Two passages seem to prove that Shiloh was regarded by the Israelites as their inter-tribal focus in the first quarter of the eleventh century: Jud. 20: 26-28, where the priest Phinehas appears as leader of Israel, which was then encamped at Shiloh (Jud. 21: 12) ; I Sam. 1: 3 ff., where Hannah, Samuel's mother, goes up to Shiloh once a year to worship Yahweh there. It is true that in Jud. 20-21 Bethel (which was also a cultic center) appears ·repeatedly as the Israelite base of operations against Benjamin (20: 18, 26, 31; 21: 2), but we are not warranted in assuming that Phinehas appeared there more than temporarily. The Ark was, of course, taken occasionally to the scene of a battle or at least to the base of operations, so that it may well have been in Bethel for the time being. Yet the reference to Shiloh in 21: 12 cannot be dismissed lightly. The story in Jud. 21: 16 ff. has such strong folkloristic tinge that we can safely deduce from it only the important fact that there was a well-known festival of Yahweh which was celebrated there annually.[19]   This agrees strikingly with I Sam. 1: 3, and so may be taken as certain.

It may be observed in this connection that it would be very strange if Israel were the only country in the ancient Near East without its great central sanctuary, to which pilgrimages were made. Nippur in Babylonia and Nineveh in Assyria played this role in their respective countries during the third quarter of the second millennium, as we know from contemporary documents. The Mari tablets prove that the temples of Sin in Harran and of Belit-ekalli in Qatna enjoyed great renown in surrounding countries in the eighteenth century B. C.[20] The importance of the latter temple is confirmed by du Mesnil's excavations there; votive offerings included gifts not only from Syria but also from an Egyptian princess of the late twentieth century and from a Hyksos (?) king of the late eighteenth.[21] The temple of Baaltis in Byblus received votive offerings in great quantities from Egypt all through the Bronze Age. The cultic image of the Tyrian goddess Asherah seems to have been reproduced in amuletic form and distributed over all Palestine in the Late Bronze Age.[22]

However, it is quite certain that Shiloh was by no means the only sanctuary of Yahweh in the time of the Judges. Other shrines of more than local renown existed at Gibeon (called "the great high place" in the time of Solomon), at Bethel, at Gilgal near Jericho, at Dan, and presumably also at Beersheba, etc. Every Israelite town probably had at least one place where sacrifices might conveniently be offered to Yahweh and where the people of the community might meet on special occasions to eat the sacrificial animals which they had vowed. The name given to these special meeting-places was *bamah*, a word which meant "back, ridge," in Canaanite.[23] There is no extra-biblical indication of this use of the word in the extant Canaanite inscriptions. The most probable basic meaning of the word in the cultic sense is "cairn, tumulus," erected over graves in Sinai and Arabia. Burial cairns were sometimes later changed into altar platforms,[24] which occur with one or more memorial steles (*masseboth*), such as were common in the ancient Near East, e. g., at Gezer, Ader, Byblos, and Hazor. In these cases Eduard Meyer seems to be right in explaining them as stelae erected in honor of defunct princes or other notables.[25] At Assur the German excavators discovered some 140 such stelae, with or without inscriptions and dating between 1400 and 614 B. C.—mostly in the latter part of the second millennium.[26] Nearly thirty may be assigned to Assyrian royalty; the rest belonged to nobles and high officials. The Gezer alignment of pillars was a living shrine between 1500 and 1200 B. C., to judge from Macalister's data.[27] Since some of the Assur stelae are just as crude in form as the better Gezer stelae, they are definitely comparable. Moreover, two stelae (*siknu*) [28] erected by individuals to the god Dagon in commemoration of mortuary offerings (*pagru, peger*, which means "corpse" in Accadian, Aramaic and Hebrew) [29] about the fourteenth century B. C. have been found at Ugarit;[30] they have nearly the same form as a number of Assur stelae. A passage in the Dan'el Epic illustrates this practice: "(his son) who sets up the stelae (*siknu*) of his hero-ancestors in the sanctuary (*q-d-sh*)." [31] In Hebrew tradition this practice is illustrated only occasionally; cf. II Sam. 18: 18, where Absalom is said to have erected a funeral stela (*massebah*) for himself because he had no son to commemorate his name. Since Absalom was the son of a Geshurite princess, it is not necessary to suppose that the practice was widespread in Israel; the emphasis put on it in our passage suggests the contrary.

While the *bamoth* we have been describing were certainly intended for the cult of heroes, this is not certain of other high places, like those of Petra. The Conway high place, excavated by the writer in 1934, belongs to the circular processional type and is comparable to pre-Islamic sanctuaries recorded in Arab literary tradition.[32] The others, though different in detail, were undoubtedly meant as places for sacrificial feasts, where the animals vowed to a god might be eaten in an appropriate sacred place. The so-called Great High Place of Petra, discovered by George L. Robinson in 1900, and a number of other less impressive sites were clearly intended for sacrificial feasts in the open; several of them possess rock-cut triclinia (dining rooms with three couches) which will not admit of any other explanation.[33] Details of their planning and construction must have diverged very widely from Israelite examples, which presumably branched off from a common pre-Israelite prototype more than a thousand years earlier. However, such characteristic features as the festal court, rock altar, cistern or reservoir for water-supply, etc., were doubtless common to both, however differently the sanctuary complex may have been laid out. Rustic *bamoth* were generally located on hills or under trees, unquestionably for the purpose of catching the cool west wind in summer and of obtaining shelter from the sun. In this respect the *bamoth* of ancient Palestine have been justly compared to the modern Islamic *welis*, or shrines of saints.[34] There is no reason to suppose that the religious usages in vogue at the *bamoth* in the time of the Judges differed in essential respects from the practices described by Hosea three centuries later, which included festal gatherings on such occasions as new moons, sabbaths and annual feasts, sacrifices of sheep, goats and large cattle, offerings of grain, wine and oil, of flax and wool, figs and raisin-cakes, etc.[35] Gifts were made either to the priests or Levites who had charge of the place, or they were consumed in picnic fashion by the worshippers. Other questions connected with the Israelite high place will be treated below, in Chapter V.

The problem of early Israelite cultic personnel has been sadly complicated by unnecessary assumptions. It has been assumed, for example, that because the role of the high priest in the preexilic Jewish monarchy was insignificant, there was no high priest at all in the time of the Judges and all contrary biblical statements are erroneous.[36] If institutional evolution in Israel had to proceed in a straight line this extrapolation might be justified, but an oscillating development is at least as probable, *a priori*.[37] Moreover, contemporary neighbors of Israel laid great stress on a priestly head. In Egypt from the fourteenth century onward for several hundred years the high priests of Amûn at Thebes held a position of the greatest political importance. In the early eleventh century the high priest Hrihor established a priestly state in Upper Egypt, which eventually became amalgamated with the Tanite dynasty of the north.[38] During the following century and a half the high priests of Amûn retained their prestige. R. de Vaux [39] and J. Begrich [40] have recently shown that the Davidic state owed its administrative organization largely to Egyptian models of the New Empire. It would be only natural to find similar Egyptian influences operating even earlier, especially since every temple priesthood in Egypt had a head, whose prestige was by no means limited to his city or district. Moreover, we now know that the land of Ugarit had a high priest (*rabbu kâhinîma*, "chief of the priests," like Aramaic *kahnâ rabbâ*, "the [Jewish] high priest ") in the fourteenth and thirteenth centuries.[41] The same title, *rab kôhanîm*, is still used for the chief priest in late Phoenician inscriptions. Difficulty has frequently been caused by the fact that our older biblical sources generally refer to the putative high priest as simply *hak-kohen*, "the priest," not *hak-kohen hag-gadol*, "the great (high) priest." This usage is, however, perfectly natural and has many excellent ancient parallels; cf., for instance, the general Accadian practice of calling the prince of a city or land simply *awîlu*, "man."

While the sanctuary at Shiloh was the religious focus of the amphictyony, it was only natural that its chief priest should enjoy very considerable prestige in Israel, which tradition recognized in the case of such outstanding personalities as Phinehas and Eli, both of whom were remembered as important political figures. After the establishment of the monarchy the position of the high priest rapidly declined, for reasons which will be explained in Chapter V. Then again, after the fall of the monarchy, the religious head of the state rapidly regained the prestige which he had lost under the monarchy.

The question of the Levites is still obscure and involved. It is probable that the Hebrew term *Lewî*, " Levite," is derived from * *lawiyu*, " person pledged for a debt or vow," and refers to a class of such persons, just as *Qênî*, " Kenite," comes from *qain*, " smith," *hophshî*, " free-man," from *ḫupshu*, *'Ibhrî*, " Hebrew," from *'apiru*, or the like.[43] All these words were coined to designate classes or groups of people by the addition of the same grammatical ending. The classical illustration of a " Levite " of this type in the Bible is Samuel, who was vowed to Yahweh at Shiloh by his mother before he was born.[44] In later times Samuel, though an Ephraimite of the Zuphite clan (I Sam. 1: 1; 9: 5), was actually assigned to the tribe of Levi. There seems to be no reason why the origin of the class in question should not go back to pre-Mosaic times, just as in the case of the Kenites; in those remote times the name was presumably applied already to persons vowed to the cult of a deity, much as was the case in Dedan (North Arabia) nearly a thousand years later.[45] The Levites were thus a class or " tribe " which was kept distinct from other tribes because of its function. In practice we may safely suppose that the Levites were constantly being increased in number by the addition of children vowed by their parents to Yahweh, but that the total number was kept down by the defection of Levites scattered through the country, either through intermarriage or because of inability to make a living as sanctuary attendants. Seen from this point of view the question of whether Moses and Aaron were members of the tribe of Levi loses all significance; they were Levites by virtue of their priestly function. In other words, one could either be born into the Levite tribe or one could be adopted as a full member of it.

There is no reason to regard the priestly function in early Israel as being radically different from what it was in later times. The priests of Shiloh were descendants of Aaron, and both Saul (at first) and David continued to treat their line as legitimate. Zadok was not a descendant of Eli, but there is no adequate reason to consider him as not an Aaronid.[46] The priests of Dan were believed to be descendants of Moses [47] and the priests of Bethel apparently claimed descent from Aaron, though this claim was rejected by the Deuteronomist.[48] Some priestly families may well have been promoted from Levitic standing and it is quite possible that laymen may have become priests in a generation or two by being vowed to Levitic status and by functioning in priestly capacity at some local sanctuary. In short, we are not justified either in throwing overboard the standard Israelite tradition regarding priests and Levites, or in considering these classes as hard and fast genealogical groups.

2. THE CONFLICT BETWEEN YAHWEH AND THE GODS OF CANAAN

The period of the Conquest, in the narrow sense, began somewhere around the middle of the thirteenth century and continued until about 1195 B. C. In the latter year Nakht-seth and his son Ramesses III reëstablished the Egyptian state after a generation of weakness which reached a nadir with the usurpation of the throne by an unnamed Syrian. This interregnum was providential for Israel, since it enabled the latter to establish itself firmly in the conquered Canaanite towns. In it we may perhaps date the first oppression, attributed to the enigmatic Chushan, king of Aram.[49] The restoration of Egyptian power in Asia might have had very serious consequences for Israel. That it did not may safely be credited to its brevity. At first Ramesses III seems to have swept through Syria and Mesopotamia as far as the Tigris without serious opposition, since the Hittite Empire had disintegrated and Assyria was extremely weak.[50] The important fortress of Beth-shan, commanding the road from Esdraelon to Transjordan and Syria, was rebuilt by his order.[51] Then came shattering attacks from the north, partly through Libya and partly through Syria and the coast of Palestine, beginning in his fifth year and reaching a climax in his eighth, when he defeated a coalition of the Peoples of the Sea on the borders of Egypt.[52] The northern danger was finally removed by a great victory over the Libyans and their allies in the eleventh year of Ramesses III. Egypt was, however, no longer strong enough to drive the invaders out of the districts they had occupied, and Libyans, Philistines and Tsikal were allowed to remain, under nominal Egyptian rule. This state of affairs meant that the Egyptian empire in Asia became increasingly futile after about 1190 B. C. After the middle of the twelfth century Egyptian control ceased entirely to be effective, and about 1080 B. C. we find that Byblus, once as Egyptian as Memphis (according to its prince Rib-Hadda),[53] had long since rejected all vestige of allegiance to Egypt. Under these circumstances it is scarcely surprising that Israelite tradition should completely forget the few years after the accession of Ramesses III when the Egyptian empire in Asia was restored.

The twelfth century left little impression on the national memory of Israel. Of all the material found in Judges we can safely date to this century only the oppression of Eglon, the episodes of Shamgar and Jabin, a few scattered notices and, above all, the Song of Deborah. The hero Shamgar was a Canaanite from Beth-anath in Galilee,[54] and his victory over the Philistines must either go back to the time of the original invasion or have been a local triumph over an otherwise unknown northern group. The triumph over Jabin of Hazor became associated either with the earlier period of Joshua (Jos. 11: 1) or with the later time of Deborah (Jud. 4: 2).[55] The story of Samson is perhaps the most instructive of all the stories recorded in Judges, since it has passed from history into folk-lore, with corresponding modifications in the process. In other words, the present form of the story of Samson offers colorful scenes of life on the Philistine border in the period of the earlier Judges, as well as characteristic examples of early Hebrew story-telling, with comparatively few definite names or occur-rences. It is accordingly more valuable to the historian in many respects than is, for example, the Mesha Stone, with its bald lists of places conquered, historically accurate but colorless.

It must not be inferred, however, that the twelfth century was a period without particular historical importance. On the contrary, it was precisely during this century that Israel was transformed from a congeries of groups and tribes, some still typical ass-nomads, some in the process of settling down, into a confederation of worshippers of Yahweh. It would be interest-ing to know how many Hebrews were already in Palestine before Moses, pursuing a semi-nomadic existence in the hill-country; in any case the proportion must have been considerable. The first occupation of central Palestine by Hebrew tribes must go back to much earlier times, probably to the Patriarchal Age, but details escape our control.[56] These older Hebrew tribes seem to have accepted Yahwism almost immediately, but the actual process of discarding pagan practices required genera-tions. Early in the eleventh century we hear of the conflict between Yahweh and Baal at Ophrah of Manasseh, near the edge of the hill-country of central Palestine. Characteristic of the involved situation is the fact that Gideon's father, who bore the Yahwistic name " Joash " (It is Yahweh who has given), had built an altar to Baal and had set up an Asherah, to say nothing of calling his son " Jerubbaal " (probably " May Baal give increase ").[57] Gideon himself, however, supported the new faith and destroyed his father's cult objects.

The story of Abimelech, Gideon's Shechemite son, provides a drastic illustration of the persistence of paganism in a Canaanite town which had been taken into the Israelite confederation. The short reign of Abimelech, which lasted only two or three years (he died in his third year), may be dated in the third quarter of the eleventh century, not long before Saul; [58] since it can scarcely have extended beyond Western Manasseh, it possessed only slight significance in itself. However, the circumstantial account of his career in Judges is exceptionally important for the light it sheds on conditions in central Palestine at that time. The Shechemites seem to have carried on the tradition of an early Amorite [59] tribal confederacy, since their principal deity was called " Baal-berith," literally " Lord of the Treaty (Covenant)," and since they traced their origin back to Hamor, literally " Ass." The Mari documents from the eighteenth century have proved that the expression " killing (the) ass "was synonymous with " making a treaty " among the Amorites.[60] The designation " Sons of (the) Ass," applied to the Shechemites several times, might possibly, it would seem, be a picturesque expression for " Members of a Confederacy." What the personal name of the deity in question was, escapes us. According to the Canaanite incantation from Arslan Tash contracts were under the supervision of the god Haurôn, " whose utterance is true," so Baal-berith may be an appellation of this deity, whose cult in Palestine is amply attested.[61]

We may, therefore, reasonably expect to find traces of older Canaanite paganism still surviving a few years later in the time of Saul. One of Saul's sons was called " Esh-baal " (Baal exists) [62] and another son, as well as a grandson, was named " Merib-baal " (Baal defends [my] case). We cannot indeed push deduction from personal names too far, remembering that many Jews bore pagan theophorous names in Babylonian, Persian and Greek times, but the relative frequency of such names is none the less significant. On the other hand, archaeology can now give a negative answer to the traditional view that the teraphim of I Sam. 19: 12-17 were an " image " or images of idols. That the word sometimes had this sense is undeniable, but the context absolutely precludes it in this passage. No " idols " of comparable size have ever been found in Palestinian excavations, and the representations of divinity from Canaanite temples are all carved outlines on stelae; all known copper or clay plaques and figurines are much too small. Since neither the true meaning of the word " teraphim " nor the expression translated " pillow of goats' hair " in the Authorized Version [63] is clear, there is no reason to suppose that any cult object is referred to.

It is very significant that no Astarte plaques or figurines have hitherto been discovered in any early Israelite levels in central Palestine. This is true of the four phases of Iron I which the writer excavated at Bethel; it is equally true of the excavations at Gibeah, Tell en-Nasbeh and Shiloh. To be sure, such figurines may be found at any time, since it would be very rash indeed to say that they were never used in Israel proper. However, their absence so far from these levels is in striking contrast to their frequency in corresponding deposits of the Late Bronze and Iron II (from the ninth century onward), and requires an explanation. The explanation can scarcely fail to be connected somehow with the aniconic character of Yahwism, which was, especially at first, bitterly opposed to human representations of all kinds, especially to representations of pagan idols or amulets.

This was not true, however, on the periphery of Israel, where contact with non-Israelites was more frequent and where Yahwistic tradition was not so strong. In stratum B of Tell Beit Mirsim (cir. 1200-920 B. C.) some eight plastic representations of nude females were discovered, mostly fragmentary.[64] One was part of a perfume juglet representing the Cyprian goddess with a dove clutched to her breast; the piece was certainly imported and there is nothing to suggest any cultic connection with Palestine. Two others were nude Astarte plaques, neither of them belonging to any known type and thus being isolated—possibly belonging originally to the Bronze Age, since both were broken and were found in Iron-Age debris. The other five plaques undoubtedly come from stratum B; and since they all belong to the same type but were struck from five different moulds, it is certain that the type enjoyed rather widespread popularity, in spite of the fact that it has not hitherto been found elsewhere. It seems to be related to pregnant types known from Shechem and Megiddo.[65] The type in question represents a nude woman in travail, with her hands clasped over her abdomen and a distended hypogastric condition, suggesting the imminence of parturition. Her only ornaments are three bracelets on each wrist and there is nothing whatever to indicate copying of any feature from a cultic image of the mother-goddess. It is very significant that neither this type nor the later Israelite " nursing mother " (*dea nutrix*) has any connection with the characteristic Canaanite types of preceding centuries, most of which represent the goddess of fertility as a sacred harlot. What the Israelites read into these plaques we cannot, of course, say, but there is absolutely no reason to treat them as anything but amulets designed to help expectant mothers to pass safely and successfully through labor. The amulets may also have been employed for the purpose of sympathetic inducement of fertility or even to ensure satisfactory flow of milk in nursing. In no case can we label them with the name of a goddess. Incidentally, it may be pointed out that the artistic crudity of the moulds is in keeping with the general decline of artistic standards in this age.

From various fragmentary sources we may reconstruct, in

very broad lines, a rough picture of what Yahwism was like in the eleventh century B. C., after the process of consolidation had reached a relatively stable phase. Periods of violent impact of social and cultural forces usually produce rapid change, followed by much longer periods when change is almost imperceptible to the close observer.[66] We begin with the concept of Yahweh Himself, presupposing the monotheistic point of view which we have described elsewhere as consisting essentially of the following elements: belief in the existence of only one God, who is the Creator of the world and the giver of all life; the belief that God is holy and just, without sexuality or mythology; the belief that God is invisible to man except under special conditions and that no graphic nor plastic representation of Him is permissible; the belief that God is not restricted to any part of His creation, but is equally at home in heaven, in the desert, or in Palestine; the belief that God is so far superior to all created beings, whether heavenly bodies, angelic messengers, demons, or false gods, that He remains absolutely unique; the belief that God has chosen Israel by formal compact to be His favored people, guided exclusively by laws imposed by Him.[67]

The collision with Baalism was not likely to reduce the stature of Yahweh in Israel. In the first place, the Canaanite Baals were all high gods in their own right. The Baal *par excellence*, undoubtedly intended whenever the singular noun " Baal " is mentioned, was the storm-god, who ruled over the world from his home in the northern heavens (see Chap. III). Compromise could result only in turning Yahweh into a form of Baal, a process which we may safely assume in different districts and periods, though we have no positive evidence of it. The problem of henotheism is in this connection wholly academic, since there is not the slightest hint anywhere that Baal was less than cosmic in his scope. Like the contemporary

Babylonian Marduk, Baal was *ex officio* lord of everything " as far as the earth extends and heaven spreads and the sun shines and fire glows and water flows and the wind blows." [68] On the other hand, the Early Iron Age, from the twelfth to the ninth century B. C., was unquestionably characterized by increasing particularism, when contrasted with the universalistic and international tendencies of the Middle and Late Bronze Ages. Local cultures tended to become isolated and to develop national pecularities, as may be illustrated by comparison of institutions, languages and even of pottery.[69] Under such conditions it might be expected that the Israelites would become increasingly conscious of their peculiar religion, which set them and their land apart from other, surrounding nations.

If we turn to early Israelite tradition, we find that this tendency is vividly illustrated, even in our scanty source-material. In the Song of Deborah, from the early eleventh century, the universality of Yahweh's power is stressed: He marches north to the help of His people from His favorite terrestrial abode in the southern mountains; in heaven the stars leave their appointed orbits to join in the battle against Sisera. He is addressed by His name as " Lord of Sinai " [70] at the same time that He is considered to dwell on the mountains of Edom and to marshal the celestial hosts to His aid in northern Palestine. We must remember that Edom was then a separate nation, with its own god Qaus, lord of the bow [71]—yet Yahweh is there. It has been urged repeatedly that the words of Jephthah to the king of Ammon, " Wilt thou not take possession of what Chemosh thy god divests of a possessor for thee, and let us take possession of whatever Yahweh our God divests of a possessor before us? (Jud. 11: 24)," imply that the Israelite regarded Chemosh as on a par with Yahweh. This deduction is wholly unwarranted. In the first place, the passage can scarcely be older than the late seventh century B. C. in its present form, since Chemosh was

9

regarded in previous centuries as the chief deity of Moab, not of Ammon. The Bible agrees elsewhere with Moabite and Ammonite inscriptions, as well as with cuneiform sources, in this point. The Moabites certainly began to decline as a nation in the eighth century, and there is reason to suppose that northern Moab passed into Ammonite hands early in the seventh century,[72] after which there may well have been increasing confusion as to the primary home of Chemosh. In the second place it is so obviously a typical argument *ad hominem*, where Jephthah couches his appeal in terms best suited to impress the Ammonites, that no inference as to Jephthah's own beliefs is admissible.

At the end of the eleventh century the story of David's adventures provides a striking illustration of the particularistic tendency which had been spreading through Israel in the generations since the Song of Deborah. In I Sam. 26: 19 David is quoted as saying to Saul: . . . " May they be accursed, for they have driven me out today, so that I can no longer be attached to the inheritance of Yahweh, (for) they say, ' Go, serve other gods! ' " Later passages in the Bible [73] make it clear that the particularistic trend which we have mentioned led to increasing correlation between the land which Yahweh had given to Israel, and the worship of Yahweh by Israel. This is so universal a tendency that it should not occasion any surprise. Similarly the increased concentration of sacrificial ritual in the Temple of Jerusalem led finally to the prohibition of sacrifices outside of the latter. In the same way, again, in the Christian church of the West Rome gradually became the Holy City, *par excellence*, and many features of ecclesiastical polity became restricted to it. In practice it was in those days nearly impossible for an Israelite to remain faithful to Yahweh in a foreign land, where there was no cultic organization or social environment to assure his loyalty. However, it is entirely unwarranted to deduce the existence of a henotheistic attitude toward Yahweh's power from such passages. An Egyptian or Babylonian in a strange land had no trouble in remaining a faithful votary of Amûn or Marduk; he simply took for granted that foreign deities were part of the same pantheon and that his deity was either identical with one of them or was actually more powerful than any of them. In Solomon's day the royal princesses of Ammon, Moab and Sidon could worship their own deities in sanctuaries in and around Jerusalem. For them there was no such problem. But Yahweh was *El qannô*, " the jealous God," who brooked no rival,[74] who could not be identified with any other god, and whose nature was radically different from all figures of pagan mythology. Hence the tendency to restrict the cult of Yahweh to Israel, at the same time that He remained uniquely superior to all possible competitors and continued to be the God of all nature and all mankind.

3. DAVID AND THE RELIGION OF ISRAEL IN THE EARLY TENTH CENTURY

The fall of Shiloh about 1050 B. C. (see above) put an end to the old amphictyonic organization, which had so greatly contributed to the cultivation of Israelite nationalism for the first century and a half after the Conquest. The Aaronid house of Phinehas and Eli was more or less discredited by the catastrophe at Ebenezer and the loss of the Ark. Since there is no mention of the family of Eli in connection with the subsequent career of Samuel, it is probable that it played a minor role, wholly overshadowed by the impressive figure of Samuel. After Saul had become king (cir. 1020 B. C.) he gave the site of Nob, on the Mount of Olives, three miles southeast of Gibeah,[75] to the family of Eli as their residence, but they can scarcely have lived there more than a few years before the king's insane rage was directed against them and they were massacred almost to

a man. Meanwhile the Ark, sent back to Israel by the super-
stitious Philistines, reposed at Kirjath-jearim; apparently the
Israelites were just as afraid of it as the Philistines after the
episode of Beth-shemesh (I Sam. 6: 19 ff.).

But for the new movement of ecstatic prophetism which
appeared in Israel after the middle of the eleventh century,[76]
there might have been a very serious decline in Yahwistic zeal
during this priestly interregnum. The enthusiasm of the prophets
and their followers saved the day, and organized Yahwism
emerged under David as a more powerful force than perhaps
ever before. The moral and ethical tradition of Yahwism was
so strong that the ecstatic element in prophetism soon became
little more than a powerful tool in the campaign for religious
reform, just as has happened so many times in the history of
Christianity, from the Apostolic Age to the Methodists and
some of the Pentecostal sects of the past half-century. The
books of Samuel contain many instructive references to the role
then played by prophetism and make it clear that David was at
least as much influenced by Nathan and his prophetic colleagues
as by Abiathar and other priests.

David's vivid personality and brilliant military exploits have
distracted attention from his administrative achievements,
which are nowhere chronicled as such. To understand something of what he did to consolidate the new state and to
introduce political and ecclesiastical innovations we must utilize
other sources of information. Elliger, de Vaux and Begrich
have shown that David organized his officialdom, at least in
large part, according to Egyptian models. Of course, it does not
necessarily follow that he copied these models directly; he may
have obtained them through Phoenician or other intermediaries.
Among the Egyptian official institutions which he copied were
the division of functions between the *sôpher* and *mazkîr*, and
the council of thirty—though naturally in modified form.

We may rather confidently attribute to David the allocation of Levitic cities, substantially as preserved for us in Jos. 21 (= I Chron. 6: 54 ff.). It has been emphasized already by Löhr [77] and Klein [78] that there is no reason whatever why we should reject the substantial authenticity of the list of priestly and Levitic towns, with which the list of cities of refuge is intimately bound up.[79] Löhr pointed out that the cities of refuge may best have been instituted in the time of David and Solomon, while Klein made out a very strong case for assigning both lists to the reign of David. The writer had independently come to the same conclusion.

With the aid of the Greek (especially the Vaticanus readings), which Klein has entirely neglected, we can eliminate nearly all the differences between the lists in Joshua and Chronicles.[80] The two or three remaining apparent divergences may be plausibly excised by simple textual changes of well-known types.[81] We thus arrive at a form of the list which must be older than cir. 400 B. C. Careful analysis of the corrected list with the aid of all now available documentary, topographical and archaeological data makes its attribution to the time of David a mere matter of chronological elimination. The following illustrations must suffice us here. It was impossible before the time of Saul or David for most of the Canaanite cities mentioned in Jud. 1 and in our list to have been Levitic towns, since they were not Israelite at all; this applies to towns like Gezer, Taanach, Ibleam, Rehob in Asher, Jokneam and Nahalal. The towns of Eltekeh and Gibbethon, both recently identified with high probability,[82] belonged to the Philistines until the time of David. It is highly improbable that such insignificant hamlets as Anathoth and Alemeth in Benjamin can have become Levitic towns before the removal of the Tabernacle to Nob in the time of Saul. This follows from the fact that they cannot have been founded at all before about

David's time,[83] and that Gibeah of Saul, Nob, Anathoth and Alemeth were all inside an equilateral triangle with each side only about four kilometres (cir. 2½ miles) long! It is more likely that they were assigned to the Levites after the Jebusite city of Jerusalem had become the capital of Israel early in David's reign. Since Anathoth was only an hour's walk from Ophel and since Alemeth was only half an hour beyond it, this deduction is inevitable. On the other hand, the list cannot well be later than cir. 900 B. C., since Golan and Ashtaroth were lost to Israel in the reign of Baasha, remaining thenceforth part of the kingdom of Damascus,[84] and since Bezer was in ruins when it was occupied by Mesha of Moab cir. 850 B. C., as he tells us in his stela. Jahaz was also taken from Israel by Mesha, and Mephaath, which lies nearly due south of Rabbath-ammon, must have become an Ammonite town in the same general period. These last facts only reinforce our obvious deduction from the character of the list that it must date from a time when Israel was united, not later than the reign of Solomon. Davidic rather than Solomonic origin follows from a number of cogent historical considerations. In the first place the tribal boundaries which are indicated in this list are much closer to the standard tradition as preserved in Joshua than they are to Solomon's political redistribution of administrative districts. Yet they are not identical with the tradition as found in Joshua; Shechem is assigned to Ephraim instead of to Manasseh as in the tribal genealogies, whose antiquity is established by the eighth-century Ostraca of Samaria.[85] Of still greater significance is the fact that Heshbon, which is assigned to Reuben in the standard tribal lists, appears in our list as Gadite. It must be remembered that the Reubenites vanished from the political scene for practical purposes not later than the tenth century and that the process, which reached a climax in the ninth century as we know from the Mesha Stone, must have begun considerably earlier, with Gad gradually replacing Reuben in northern Moab and southern Gilead.[86]

Klein has effectively demonstrated that other references to these towns strongly sustain the authenticity and the Davidic date of our list.[87] Thus we know from other sources that there were Levites or priests at Gath-rimmon, Anathoth, Gibeon, Shechem, Tabor, Jazer, etc. We must not assume that the Levites formed the majority of the population of all these towns, but merely that there were larger or smaller groups of Levites or priests already in most of them and that David assigned quarters to other groups in a number of recently conquered Canaanite towns and in villages near Jerusalem.

Our argument for Davidic date of the list of Levitic towns receives important additional support from other considerations. There can be no doubt that David planned some kind of administrative reorganization of the Israelite confederation. We know that David sent his military officers out to make a complete census of the land, which is said to have been accomplished in nine and two-thirds months. This innovation was bitterly resented by the liberty-loving Israelites, who explained a plague which followed as a demonstration of Yahweh's wrath at David for his lack of piety in ordering the census. As we have shown elsewhere, two parallel lists of the population of each tribe, both preserved in Numbers, are recensional variants of a single original list, which is almost certainly to be connected somehow with the Davidic census—the only one recorded and the only possible census embracing all Israel.[88] The individual and total numbers have been corrupted in the process of transmission, but the total Israelite population originally listed was probably about 600,000. The detailed census was necessarily accompanied by a description of the boundaries of each tribe, in order to fix the exact scope of each tribal enumeration. The writer has long held that the description of the boundaries of the tribes in Joshua goes back to the reign of David.[89] However, Alt and Noth are quite justified in maintaining that it reflects the tribal boundaries at the end of the pre-monarchic period, toward the end of the eleventh century.[90] This correct observation does not compel us to date it before David's reign—quite the contrary, since the purpose of the census was surely to fix the correct tribal boundaries and determine the total population within these boundaries. The "correct" boundaries were, of course, the boundaries which had been regarded as valid during the previous two or three generations, i. e., at the very beginning of the monarchy.

As Löhr has pointed out, there was a very real need of some such institution as the cities of refuge in the time of David.[91] During the age of the Judges private, clan and tribal vendettas ran their normal course, which might be very destructive, as illustrated by the stories of Jephthah and the war with Benjamin. No stable monarchy has ever tolerated blood-feuds, though many attempts to suppress them, whether by the Turks and the British in Palestine or by the French in Corsica, have been only partly successful. The idea of having places of asylum to which the unjustly accused might flee, was familiar throughout the ancient Mediterranean world. It is significant that all three of the cities of refuge in Western Palestine are known to have been towns containing important temples or sanctuaries. But the selection of six Levitic towns which were so admirably suited for the purpose and so convenient of access, demands a statesman as well as an administrative plan. After cir. 900 B. C. two of the towns, Golan and Bezer, were no longer Israelite, as pointed out above. We may safely, therefore, attribute this idea to David's sagacity, along with the associated plan for forty-eight Levitic cities. Both institutions were probably quite ephemeral, since the Division of the Monarchy and later administrative changes must have made them increasingly impractical. We may reasonably doubt whether they were ever much more than an ideal plan. Our view is, however, far sounder from the standpoint of historical method than the current one that they were post-exilic schemes which never had anything but an existence on paper. Noth, for example, dates the list of Levitic cities after the sixth century B. C., a date to which he is forced by the theory of the development of priests and Levites which he follows.

The Chronicler, writing not far from 400 B. C., attributes to David the organization of the guilds of temple musicians. The current critical theory is that the formal establishment of classes of temple musicians is strictly post-exilic and that the attribution of their founding to David is aetiological in origin. Until the past year or two this position was difficult to refute, since external evidence was totally lacking. The subject is too complex to be treated here in detail, and we shall restrict ourselves to a few indications, reserving a full discussion for another place.

A priori there is nothing to be said against the Davidic origin of temple music. Syria and Palestine were noted for their musicians in the ancient Near East, as we know both from Egyptian and from Mesopotamian sources.[92] The band of travelling Semitic craftsmen depicted in the early nineteenth century B. C. at Beni Ḥasan in Egypt brought musical instruments with it, and the antiquity of music among the early Hebrews is attested by the story of Jabal, Jubal and Tubal-cain (cf. above). In the New Empire we have a good many references to Canaanite music and many representations of Canaanite musicians and instruments. Hezekiah sent male and female singers to Sennacherib as part of his tribute, according to the latter's account. Moreover the Greeks borrowed several Canaanite musical instruments along with their names; in Cyprus they also took over the figure of the archetype craftsman-musician, Cinyras, from the Phoenicians.[93] There is, accordingly, no reason why the institution of temple musicians might not go back to an early date.[93a] Furthermore, so many distinct biblical traditions mention David's musical prowess that scepticism would be thoroughly unwarranted. In the story in I Sam. 16:14-23 David is " a skillful player on the lyre." The theme of David's playing before Saul appears repeatedly. In II Sam. 1: 17 ff. David appears as the composer of a beautiful lament over Saul and Jonathan; in those days there was no clear distinction between poet, composer and player. In II Sam. 6: 5, 14 David is said to have played musical instruments and to have danced before the Ark. Even if the long psalm in II Sam. 22 should be wrongly ascribed to David, it is going much too far to deny him authorship of the short psalm at the beginning of II Sam. 23, which begins:

> The utterance of David, son of Jesse,
>> and the utterance of the man whom the Most High hath inspired,
> Of him who was anointed by the God of Jacob,
>> and of the singer of Israel's songs.
> The spirit of Yahweh hath spoken to me
>> and His discourse is on my tongue . . .

The antiquity of this little poem is sufficiently established by the fact that it begins exactly like the two archaic poems of Balaam in Num. 24.[94] The significance of these passages is not obscured, but heightened, by the persistent later tradition that a large proportion of the Psalms was composed by David. The memory of his musical prowess and of the musical institutions which he founded, was so strong in later generations that many hymns were erroneously attributed to him.

Moreover, we have incontrovertible external evidence for the antiquity of the musical guilds themselves. The Chronicler mentions their names repeatedly as Asaph, Heman and Ethan or Jeduthun. Now, as well known, Ethan and Heman also appear in the lists of traditional wise men in I Kings 5: 11 (4: 31) and I Chron. 2: 6, along with Chalcol and Darda. In the former passage, which is older, Ethan is called " the Ezrahite," that is, " member of a pre-Israelite family," [95] and the other three, Heman, Chalcol and Darda, are called " sons of Mahol," i. e., " members of the orchestral guild." [96] It must be remembered that a great musician was also a seer (I Chron. 25: 5, II Chron. 29: 30, of Heman and Asaph) or a prophet (I Chron. 25: 2-3), as well as a wise man. All the founders of these guilds were called " Ezrahites " in the tradition underlying I Chron. 2: 6, as illustrated by the heading of Psalm 88, where Heman is an " Ezrahite." In other words, at least one tradition regarded all these guilds as Canaanite in origin. The names prove the correctness of this tradition, as we can now say, thanks to the archaeological discoveries of the past few years. " Chalcol " appears on several ivories found at Megiddo in the hieroglyphic form *Kurkur,* that is, *Kulkul,* since there was no *l* in Egyptian.[97] According to the accompanying inscription, which dates probably from the thirteenth century B. C., Kulkul was a female singer of the god Ptah-prince-of-Ascalon, i. e., she was attached to the temple of Ptah in the Canaanite city of Ascalon (Ashkelon).[98] Since names of men and of women constantly interchanged in Canaanite and Hebrew, the difference of sex need arouse no surprise. The names " Ethan " and " Heman " may be closely paralleled by scores of abbreviated names found at Ugarit and elsewhere in the late second millennium B. C.[99] The type of name which they represent, with an ending in *ān* which appears elsewhere in Semitic as diminutive, was characteristically Canaanite in the Late Bronze Age, but seems never to appear in any later Hebrew lists of contemporary names. It may also be added that " Chalcol " and " Darda " both seem to reflect a class of plant-names or flower-names applied to musicians.[100] Henceforth it is to be hoped that the alleged " Edomite " origin of these names will disappear from scholarly literature, along with related speculations about the supposed wisdom of legendary North Arabians.

The foregoing comparisons prove only that Hebrew temple-music as such was recognized in Israel as going back to early, pre-Israelite, sources; they do not prove that David organized the first religious music in Israel. Still less do they show that any of the Psalms go back to the time of David. However, the literary texts of Ugarit do demonstrate that many of the Psalms are saturated with Canaanite stylistic and verbal reminiscences, and even with direct quotations from passages found in Ugaritic sources already known to us. In view of the fact that the passages in question all come from epics and that no genuine Canaanite hymns or psalms have yet been discovered, we may rest assured that the number of parallels would be many times what it is now if we possessed the latter. There does not appear to be much difference between the amount of Canaanite matter utilized in each of the five collections which make up our Psalter. Some of the Psalms which do contain recognizable Canaanite matter are undoubtedly post-exilic in date, just as we should expect from the abundance of Canaanite material in other exilic and post-exilic books, such as Job, Proverbs, the exilic parts of Isaiah and Deutero-Isaiah, Ezekiel and Habakkuk.[101] In principle we cannot, therefore, establish any definite correlation at present between the date of a Psalm and its Canaanite content. To judge from the fact that Canaanite parallels abound in the Song of Deborah and the Lament of David over Saul and Jonathan, that they cease almost entirely in the prophetic literature of the eighth century [102] and emerge in great abundance not far from 600 B. C., we should be inclined to attribute most of the Psalms with Canaanite coloring either to the sixth-fourth centuries B. C. or to the eleventh-tenth centuries. Approximately to the tenth century we may provisionally attribute such Canaanizing Psalms as 18 (= II Sam. 22), 29 (a hymn to Baal which has been only slightly modified), 45, and especially 68.[103] It is very significant that two Psalms both of which swarm with Canaanitisms, 88 and 89, are expressly attributed to the Canaanites Heman and Ethan in their headings, which reflect post-exilic tradition. Actually many of the Canaanizing Psalms may, either in whole or in part, antedate the tenth century, but it is scarcely probable that any of them were taken over by the official cult of Yahweh until the time of David or later. Early Hebrew psalms presumably failed to measure up to later standards of taste and were forgotten; it is significant that scarcely one of the fragments of hymns preserved in the Pentateuch is repeated in the Psalter.

Chapter V

ARCHAEOLOGY AND THE RELIGION OF LATER ISRAEL

1. The Economic and Political Background of the Age of Solomon

Attention has often been called to the rare opportunity for Israelite expansion provided by the period of Egyptian and Assyrian weakness in the tenth century B. C. Egypt had not recovered political strength since the middle of the Twentieth Dynasty, about 1150 B. C., and was not to be a strong state again until the reign of Shishak (cir. 935-915 B. C.).[1] Assyria declined slowly after the great reign of Tiglath-pileser I (1114-1076 B. C.),[2] but did not reach her lowest level of power until the long and feeble reign of Asshur-rabi II (1012-972 B. C.), during which the Assyrian outposts along the Upper Euphrates fell into the hands of the Aramaeans, as we know from recent discoveries. The eclipse of Assyrian power continued under the helpless Tiglath-pileser II (966-935 B. C.), who was Solomon's contemporary, and it was not until after 875 B. C. that the Assyrians regained the Upper Euphrates Valley.[3] The reigns of David (cir. 1000-960) and Solomon (cir. 960-922)[4] could not possibly have fallen in a period more suitable for Israelite expansion.

There has been a tendency, inaugurated by Hugo Winckler and best illustrated by Hermann Guthe,[5] to reduce the extent of the Davidic empire to Israel itself, Edom, Moab, Ammon and Ḥaurân, excluding even Damascus. Zobah, the land of Hadadezer, whom David conquered, was located by these scholars in Ḥaurân, biblical Bashan. However, the analysis of the Assyrrian provincial organization, which was constructed on older foundations, has demonstrated conclusively that Zobah, Assyrian Subatu,[6] lay north of Damascus, not south of it, and almost certainly included the region east of Antilibanus and southeast of Hums.[7] It follows that the biblical narrative is perfectly reasonable geographically, in spite of its chronological dislocation in the form in which we have it. The principal towns of Hadad-ezer, king of Zobah, as given in the text of the Chronicler, are undoubtedly to be identified with Tubikhu and Kunu of the Egyptian list of Syrian cities conquered by the pharaohs of the New Empire; both were certainly located in the region south of Ḥumṣ, since Kunu cannot be separated from Roman Conna (now Râs Baʻalbek) and the Amarna Ṭubikhu is in the same general region.[8] David's empire then extended from the Gulf of ʻAqabah in the south to the region of Ḥumṣ in the north, and it remained, at least nominally, in Solomon's hands until his death or shortly before.

The expansion of Israelite territory could scarcely fail to be the signal for unprecedented commercial development, especially under a man of Solomon's versatility and need of money. The time was just ripe for it, since both sea and desert were then the scene of extraordinary new activity. In the sea the Sidonians were engaged in launching one of the greatest seafaring enterprises of history. After the disruption of the Mycenaean " empire " by the Sea-peoples in the late thirteenth and the early twelfth centuries, chaotic conditions prevailed in the eastern Mediterranean, with piracy dominant. The Egyptian account of Wenamûn's adventures early in the eleventh century gives a vivid idea of the anarchic situation at that time; Byblus and Sidon were still the leading Phoenician ports and Tyre is not mentioned. From their rebuilt capital on the island city of Tyre the Canaanite Sidonians (Phoenicians) rapidly extended their sea-power after cir. 1050 B. C. until by the end of the tenth century they controlled the Mediterranean highways as far as Spain and possessed trading colonies and mining settlements in Cyprus, Sicily, Sardinia, and probably also in North Africa and Spain.[9] Hiram I (cir. 969-936 B. C.) appears in Phoenician records as a conqueror and builder, victorious over colonial revolts[10] and builder of several temples at Tyre. It was probably Hiram I to whom the great expansion of the Phoenicians in the Western Mediterranean was due, since we cannot go back very far before his time and since we now know that there were at least two well-organized Phoenician colonies in Sardinia less than a century after him.[11] The Israelites cannot fail to have been profoundly impressed by the tales of maritime adventure and the wave of commercial prosperity which the northernmost tribes, Asher, Naphtali and Dan, must have shared to some extent with their Sidonian neighbors. It must not be forgotten that the Israelite towns of Abel and Dan were less than twenty-five miles due east of Tyre and that the Danites are said to have taken service in ships as early as the third quarter of the twelfth century (Song of Deborah).[12] Moreover, the Sidonian strip of territory along the sea south of Râs en-Naqûrah was directly contiguous to Asher. An illustration of the close physical relationship in which the two peoples stood, is provided by the statement that Solomon's master-architect, sent him by Hiram of Tyre, was son of a Tyrian coppersmith and an Israelite woman of Naphtali.

Turning from the sea to the desert, we find the same situation, *mutatis mutandis*. The effective domestication of the Arabian camel, which took place not long before the eleventh century B. C., brought with it a tremendous increase in nomadic mobility.[13] Caravans could now travel through deserts whose sources of water might be two or three days' journey apart. The first known razzia of camel nomads is the Midianite invasion in the early eleventh century, which was successfully repelled by Gideon. In the ninth century the Arabs first appear in contemporary sources (cf. I Kings 10: 15), and in the eighth we find the Sabaeans already emerging on the Assyrian horizon. This means that caravan trade between the Fertile Crescent and South Arabia was already well developed and probably that the Sabaeans had extended their sphere of influence as far north as the central Hejâz. It must have required generations for this evolution to take place, and we are probably justified in tracing its start back to the twelfth century B. C., during the Aramaean movements which led to their occupation of nearly all Syria. Tiglath-pileser I's occupation of the oasis of Palmyra (Tadmar) about 1100 B. C. points to nascent expansion of caravan trade in the Syrian Desert, since the oasis can scarcely have had much importance otherwise. Even in the Syrian Desert camels were a great improvement on the asses of earlier days, making it possible for caravans to travel there at all seasons of the year without troubling over-much about food and water. Further south we may say that true caravan trade was impossible before the days of domesticated camels. Solomon's control of the frontier districts of Zobah, Damascus, Haurân, Ammon, Moab and Edom meant that he monopolized the entire caravan trade between Arabia and the north from the Red Sea to Palmyra.

With these marvelous new opportunities for lucrative trade at Solomon's disposal, we can scarcely be surprised at his prosperity, as described in Israelite tradition and further illustrated by archaeological discoveries. Two specific examples of Solomon's trading enterprises are mentioned in Kings: his expeditions to Ophir every three years and his trade in horses and chariots. The voyages to Ophir, which was apparently on the African coast in the general region of Somaliland,[14] were undertaken in coöperation with Hiram of Tyre, perhaps following the Phoenician system of joint maritime enterprises which we find already attested at the time of Wenamûn, about 1080 B. C. The trading fleet is called 'onî tarshîsh, which probably means "refinery fleet,"[15] copied after similar fleets which plied the

Mediterranean, connecting the mines and refineries of Sardinia and perhaps already of southern Spain with Phoenicia. The African products brought back to Ezion-geber were all among those which figure in Egyptian voyages to Punt (the same general region as biblical Ophir) : gold, silver, ivory, and two kinds of monkeys.[16]

The voyages to Ophir are said in Israelite tradition to have taken three years, i. e., one entire year and parts of two others.[17] For example, the fleet may have sailed from Ezion-geber about November or December of the first year, returning in May or June of the third year, thus avoiding as much summer heat as possible. The total duration of the voyage need not have been over a year and a half, in our terms. Similarly the Babylonians of the late third millennium allowed three years for a voyage to Melukhkha, which was probably in southwest Arabia, though it may have included Somaliland, since the Babylonians identified it with Ethiopia as early as the fourteenth century B. C.[18] It must be emphasized that such a prolonged voyage cannot have been restricted to the African coast but must also have extended to the Arabian, unless we are to assume a highly adventurous voyage to East Africa, for which there is not a shred of evidence. In the time of the Tenth Chapter of Genesis, which was probably composed in the tenth or possibly the ninth century B. C.,[19] the South Arabians were already settled on both sides of the Red Sea, as we must infer from the fact that the South Arabians are considered as descendants both of Cush (Ethiopia) and of Eber (the Semitic nomads). With such an ethnic relationship, which favored active sea-traffic across the southern Red Sea, closer commercial relations by sea with South Arabia could scarcely fail to develop. We may safely connect the famous visit of the Queen of Sheba to Solomon with these voyages to Ophir and suppose that they had stimulated the Sabaeans to extend their incipient caravan trade far to the north. The great expansion of Arabian camel trade in the early first millennium would then be the direct result of competition with the sea-trade of the Red Sea, a competition made possible by the domestication of the camel.

The second specific instance of Solomon's trading enterprise is found in I Kings 10: 28-29, which describes Solomon's trade in horses and chariots, though in enigmatic terms which have only lately become clear, thanks to archaeological discoveries. We can now translate the passage as follows: " And Solomon's horses were exported from Cilicia: [20] the merchants of the king procured them from Cilicia at the current price; and a chariot was exported from Egypt at the rate of six hundred shekels of silver and a horse from Cilicia at the rate of a hundred and fifty; and thus (at this rate) they delivered them by their agency to all the kings of the Hittites and the kings of Aram." [21] According to Herodotus (iii, 90), strikingly confirmed by unpublished contemporary documents,[22] Cilicia was the source of the best horses which were used by official Persian couriers. It is well known that the Egyptians of the New Empire became experts in the manufacture of chariots, for which they imported hard wood from Syria.[23] The passage in Kings states clearly that Solomon's merchants obtained a practical monopoly of the trade in horses and chariots, since they controlled all the trade-routes between Egypt and Syria; the Egyptians were dependent on Israel for their best horses and the Syrians were dependent on Israel for their finest chariots. Whatever the original price may have been, a standard exchange rate of four Cilician horses for one Egyptian chariot was established.[24]

Any doubt about the correctness of the tradition that Solomon was himself interested in chariots and horses, and that he built up a powerful standing army, is removed by the discovery of the royal stables of the tenth and ninth centuries at Megiddo. The excavators have estimated that these stables were intended to hold some 450 horses and perhaps about 150 chariots. Since Solomon is stated (I Kings, 4: 26; 9: 15-19; 10: 26) to have built a number of chariot-cities (of which Hazor is also attested archaeologically) and to have had 1400 chariots and apparently 4000 horses,[25] we have full agreement between tradition and archaeological discovery.

Archaeological finds have recently brought to light a new and very significant phase of Solomon's industrial activity—his development of copper mining and refining. Nelson Glueck's excavations at Tell el-Kheleifeh, ancient Ezion-geber on the Gulf of ʿAqabah, have brought to light an extensive copper refinery, first built in the tenth century B. C. and rebuilt at various later periods.[26] The earliest refinery stood in the middle of a fortified rectangle, surrounded by a casemate wall of typical Early-Iron type. To the same period belongs a triple gateway of characteristic plan. The construction of the refinery is extraordinarily good and shows, as Glueck has pointed out, practical knowledge which can have come only from long experience. Glueck has also shown that the laborers in the copper refinery must have been slaves or prisoners, since it is incredible that freemen would have consented to work under such trying conditions.[26a] These facts point irresistibly to Phoenician models and to imitation of Phoenician refinery methods, just as in the somewhat parallel case of the construction and arrangement of Solomon's Temple. We have shown elsewhere that the word *tarshîsh* must have meant approximately " refinery " in Phoenician; Tell el-Kheleifeh was then presumably a *tarshîsh*, something like Phoenician stations with the same name in Sardinia and Spain.[27] It must be bracketed with the Temple of Solomon and Solomon's stables at Megiddo as an example of Syro-Phoenician (Canaanite) influence on Israel about the middle of the tenth century.

The discovery of the copper refinery at Tell el-Kheleifeh

makes it practically certain that the Early-Iron-Age mines found by Glueck in the 'Arabah, south of the Dead Sea and north of Ezion-geber, must also have been worked, at least to a considerable extent, by Solomon.[28] This datum is paralleled by the statement in I Kings 7: 40-46, that the copper cult-objects and utensils used in the Temple were cast in the Jordan Valley between Succoth and Zarethan, that is, in the valley east of the Jordan and north of the Jabbok. Near by are ancient copper workings in the precipitous hills which line the Jordan Valley on the east, but which have not yet been explored by archaeologists.

To the wealth which all this industry and commerce brought to Israel must be added the regular tribute paid yearly by the subject states, which included the Philistines[29] as well as the border states in Transjordan and the new Aramaean states in southern and eastern Syria. However, as wealth grew the royal expenditures for building operations and fortifying towns, for maintaining an increasingly expensive standing army (for the first time in Israel consisting primarily of chariotry), as well as a constantly swelling harem and entourage of dependents, grew even faster. Solomon was forced to resort to direct taxation, apparently for the first time in Israelite history, as well as to levying compulsory military and other services from the native Israelite population. The narrative in I Kings 11-12 is very significant in this respect. At the same time it is only reasonable to assume that private Israelite enterprise was enormously stimulated by the prosperity of the state and by the new forms of consumption which had been introduced into the country, as well as by the previously untapped channels of trade with Mediterranean regions and Arab tribes (cf. I Kings 10: 15). Morgenstern has recently described the probable impact of the new opportunities on Israel in the most vivid terms;[30] our principal correction would be that foreign trade was essentially a royal monopoly, just as it had been in many Near-Eastern lands. In Accadian, for instance, no distinction in name is made between trading expeditions and military adventures; both are called *kharrânu* and *gerru*.

As Alt has clearly demonstrated, the history of the Israelite state under David and Solomon was fundamentally a conflict between the tribal separatism of early Israel and the centralizing tendencies of the crown.[31] Despite the different geographical situation, we are justified in drawing a general analogy with the corresponding state of affairs in the first eighty years of the United States. The colonies of the American union were, it is true, much more widely separated from one another and usually formed more sharply defined geographical units. On the other hand, they lacked, in general, the compensatory sense of tribal and clan solidarity which was characteristic of Israel in the time of the Judges. When David fixed the capital of the united monarchy at Jerusalem, he deliberately selected a town near the geographical center of Israel which had not previously formed part of any tribe.[32] Here he installed his officials, retainers and mercenaries, who by entering into royal service had become juridically "slaves of the king" and had ceased to belong to specific tribes.[33] Down to the end of the Israelite state the term "slave" (*'ebed*), which had been inherited from the Accadians of the third millennium and was employed by Edomites and Ammonites as well as by Israelites, continued in regular use as the class designation of royal officials.[34] During the united monarchy Jerusalem was thus a symbol of the superiority of the crown to the old tribal amphictyony.

The most important single step taken by David and Solomon to supplant the amphictyonic tradition was the former's action in attaching the chief priest and his family directly to the court. Abiathar, as legitimate high priest of the Shiloh line, headed the provisional cultic establishment in Jerusalem. When he was removed by Solomon for suspicious political activity, Zadok took his place as head of the priestly organization of Israel. As has been shown by Alt and Möhlenbrink, the temple of Solomon was *primarily* a royal chapel, attached to the palace much as were the royal temples of Nineveh and Khorsabad.[35] This view is confirmed by R. B. Y. Scott's convincing demonstration that the names of the two columns Jachin and Boaz, which stood before the Temple of Solomon (see below), represent the first words of dynastic oracles which were inscribed upon them.[36] The Jachin formula may have been " Yahweh will establish (*yakîn*) thy throne for ever " (or the like) and the Boaz formula may have run " In the strength of Yahweh shall the king rejoice," or something similar. The writer long ago proposed somewhat similar formulae as the sources of the abbreviated names Jachin and Boaz (APB 217, n. 87), but failed to recognize the fact that these formulae must have had dynastic connotations. Additional support, if any is required, is derived from the fact that the sanctuary of Yahweh at Bethel was regarded in a similar way two centuries later; the chief priest of Bethel, Amaziah, said to Amos: " Thou shalt not continue to prophesy at Bethel, for it is a royal sanctuary (*miqdash*) and a dynastic temple (*bêth mamlakhah*)." By identifying the religious focus of the tribal confederacy of Israel with the court of the king, David and Solomon forestalled the most serious threat to national unity, and prevented the high priest from setting himself up as the head of the state. How effective an element in the constitutional tradition of Judah their innovation became, may best be illustrated by the fact that the house of David continued to occupy the throne for four centuries and remained the center of Jewish national aspirations for many centuries more. In the Northern Kingdom, without a comparable tradition, no attempt to establish a dynasty proved long successful, and even the house of Jehu survived for only a century. Of course, it stands to reason that the religious factor could scarcely have been enough without other elements, such as the tremendous prestige attached to the memories of David and Solomon, and the high average standard of capacity shown by the Davidic kings of Judah.

Solomon profited by David's experience with the centrifugal tendencies of the tribes and reorganized the administrative divisions established by his father which, as seen in Chapter IV, closely followed the old tribal units. It is entirely possible that David himself planned some such move before his death, and the Solomonic reorganization may actually represent the execution of a plan formed by David. However this may be, the new system, described in the valuable document preserved in I Kings 4: 7-19, diverged in at least half of the twelve new administrative districts from older tribal boundaries.[37] This was partly forced on the king by the addition to Israel proper of extensive new territory, such as the Mediterranean coast from south of Joppa to Carmel, much of the Plain of Esdraelon and tracts in Transjordan, but was partly a deliberate attempt to break up larger units in Northern Israel. For example, the tribe of Manasseh was divided into three parts—or four if we count the district of Dor (included in Manasseh according to the tradition of Joshua 17: 11). Since the earlier Israelite " king," Abimelech, was a Manassite and since Manasseh later became the focus of Jeroboam's rebellion and the district in which the latter's three successive capitals were located, this arrangement was evidently a sound move politically. Solomon further cemented the loyalty of his new district-officers by marrying at least two of them to daughters of his; it may be significant that the two sons-in-law who are mentioned by name were in the most remote parts of the kingdom.

Our list is unfortunately not quite intact: the upper right edge of the document from which the redactor of Kings or a precursor copied it was torn off, as we can prove by the fact that all the personal names of the first four officers are missing, only their patronymics having survived. Moreover, as the writer pointed out in 1925, the entries in verses 13 and 19 are obvious doublets.[38] The probable explanation of this situation is that the name of the district officer of Judah had somehow been lost (perhaps the bottom of the document had also been torn off) and was replaced (in order to make up the total of twelve) by the variant doublet in verse 19. Just after this doublet, at the end of the list, the significant addition was made: " and a district officer (*nṣb*, just as in verse 7), who was in the land of Judah" (4: 19-20). In our judgment these facts speak for themselves, and it is impossible to accept the view of Alt that Judah was excluded from the system of twelve administrative units into which all Israel (v. 7) was divided. If David and Solomon really wanted to give Judah a privileged place in the state, why did they select a new capital which, as Alt himself has so convincingly pointed out, was entirely outside the old tribal system? Moreover, why did Solomon undertake to attach the northern district-officers so closely to himself by ties of marriage? Dussaud is evidently correct in pointing out that in some ways it was the Northern Kingdom which continued the Solomonic tradition.[39] It is not likely that the marriage of two northern governors to daughters of Solomon would have been mentioned in our document unless later Israelite noble families traced their origin back to them. Judah continued the priestly tradition of older Israel, but it was the Northern Kingdom which consciously carried on the political traditions of the Solomonic state. Incidentally, as the writer has pointed out,[40] the Ostraca of Samaria, coming from the reign of Jeroboam II in the first half of the eighth century,[41] clearly define an administrative unit of the Northern Kingdom which agrees topographically with Solomon's third district, thus indicating that the Solomonic system of administrative districts was continued, at least in principle, for a century and a half after his death. Moreover, the three provinces which Tiglath-pileser III created out of the annexed portions of the Northern Kingdom in 733 B. C., Megiddo, Dor and Gilead, correspond closely to the fourth, fifth and seventh districts of Solomon.[42]

2. THE PLACE OF THE TEMPLE OF SOLOMON IN THE HISTORY OF ISRAELITE RELIGION

Few subjects in biblical research are so tantalizing as the Temple of Solomon. In spite of the space devoted to it in our sources, many points still remain obscure. Until recently the architectural plan and decoration of the Temple could not be related with confidence to any archaeological discoveries. Now, thanks especially to the recent treatments of Temple architecture by Möhlenbrink, Watzinger and Wright,[43] this problem is largely settled, as we shall see below. We shall also deal below, though all too briefly, with the related question of the character and purpose of the cultic installations described in Kings. Details of cult, however, must remain in many cases doubtful, because the Priestly Code restricts itself in principle to an account of the Tabernacle service in so far as it could be reconstructed from tradition in the late seventh and the sixth centuries B. C. There can be little doubt that many elements of liturgy and sacrificial practice were continued with relatively little change in the Temple of Solomon and that the practice in the latter profoundly influenced the tradition with regard to the former; but many uncertainties remain, as we shall see in selected instances.

For a long time there was no general agreement as to the type of national architecture to which the Temple of Solomon might best be attributed. The total absence of comparable Iron-Age building remains in Phoenicia and Syria made it difficult to assign it to Phoenician inspiration, and the closest parallels remained Greek. The latter were in part so close as to suggest some kind of reciprocal dependence, and more than one authority on Greek architecture felt himself forced to disregard the description of the Temple of Solomon entirely, on the ground either that it was unique and incommensurable or that it was to be dated after the sixth century B. C., when Hellenic influences were beginning to be felt throughout the Near East.[44] Discoveries of roughly contemporary buildings at Sham'al (Zendjirli) and Carchemish modified this attitude slightly; in 1933 Watzinger came out vigorously for a Phoenician or Syrian source, from which both Hebrews and Greeks drew their inspiration. In 1936 the Oriental Institute of Chicago excavated a small temple of about the ninth century at Tell Tainât in northern Syria; when the plan was published by C. W. McEwan in 1937 it became immediately certain that the missing Syrian parallel had been discovered.[45] This building was rectangular in form, divided into three connecting rooms: the portico, with two columns in front; the main hall; and the cella, with a raised platform in the rear. In length it was about two-thirds the size of the Temple of Solomon (omitting the side-chambers of the latter); in floor space it was also about two-thirds as large, since the width was proportionately greater. A very important respect in which the Temple of Solomon resembled Syrian structures of the Iron Age was in the practice of lining the interior walls above the orthostates with wood. Recent finds of carved ivories at Megiddo (early twelfth century), Samaria (ninth century) and elsewhere, together with the discovery of proto-Aeolic pilaster capitals at Megiddo (tenth century on), Samaria (ninth century) and elsewhere,[46] have thrown a great deal of light on the interior decoration of the Temple, which turns out to have been characteristically Phoenician, just as one might expect from the fact that it was built by a Tyrian architect.

Much light has already been shed on the two enigmatic columns of Jachin and Boaz. Such columns or pillars, flanking the main entrance to a temple, were common in the first millennium B. C. in Syria, Phoenicia and Cyprus; they spread eastward to Assyria, where they occur in Sargon's temples at Khorsabad (cir. 710 B. C.), and westward to the Phoenician colonies in the Western Mediterranean.[47] Some of these pairs of columns were used to support the roof of the portico, in megaron fashion, others were free-standing, without constructional relation to the building. There can be no reasonable doubt that the pillars Jachin and Boaz were of the latter type. There are a number of theories as to their function and significance:[48] they are supposed to have been sacred obelisks or massebôth with phallic associations; others regard them as cosmic pillars (like the pillars of Hercules) or as representing the twin mountains between which the sun was believed to emerge each morning; some think that they reflect stylized sacred trees; Robertson Smith regarded Jachin and Boaz as gigantic cressets or fire-altars.[49] Robertson Smith's view has been treated by more recent scholars as fanciful, but the writer considers it essentially correct as applied to the two pillars before the Temple of Solomon. Since this question has not been discussed for many years and since the writer has unpublished material of vital significance to present,[50] a more detailed treatment is in order, especially since the problems involved are characteristic of similar problems in the field.

In 1920 the writer visited the painted tombs of Marisa (south of Beit Jibrîn in southern Palestine) in company with their discoverer, the late J. P. Peters. In the second tomb, the so-called Tomb of the Musicians, dating from the late third century B. C., two paintings of candelabra were found on the two opposite piers leading from the vestibule into the main tomb-chamber. In a subsequent visit with C. C. McCown photo-

graphs, tracings and measured sketches were made. All trace
of the painted candelabra has long since disappeared. Both
candelabra are painted yellow, indicating that the originals
were gilded or painted to imitate gold; the flaming wicks at the
top were painted red. The height of the prototype represented
by the paintings may be approximately deduced from the height
of the accompanying worshippers, two of whom are shown
standing with upraised hands beside each candelabrum. Since
the worshippers are about one-third as tall as the cult-objects,
the latter must be from fifteen to twenty feet high.

We have referred to these objects as candelabra, in order not
to anticipate our conclusions. Actually, however, they cannot
have been simple candelabra, like the two metal candelabra
from the tomb of Tabnit king of Sidon, which date from the
late fourth century B. C. [51] The latter are entirely different in
shape, stand on a tripod and are only a third as high. Moreover, our objects were worshipped, which can scarcely have
been true of simple light-giving cressets or candlesticks. They
thus belong with a large class of incense-burners, also characterized by several horizontal projections of identical type (often
replaced or supplemented by lily knobs), represented on Phoenician, Punic and Etruscan seals, coins and monuments dating
chiefly from cir. 800-300 B. C. [52] Most of the known examples
have been collected by Karl Wigand, who applied the Greek
term *thymiateria*, "stands for burning incense," to them.[53] The
type in question undoubtedly originated in Phoenicia, from
which it spread westward to Cyprus, Greece, Etruria, Carthage,
and eastward to Mesopotamia. Representations show them
either standing before a deity or priest, or flanking the entrance
of a temple. In the latter case they are shown as slender free-
standing shafts on either side of the main portal, characterized
by the same horizontal projections, bowls and cones of incense
or tongues of flame; their height, to judge from the adjacent

building, was comparable to that of the portico of the temple. It is naturally quite impossible to separate these objects from the similar shafts in the Tomb of the Musicians at Marisa, which have the same general form and the same immediate function, stood in pairs on either side of a portal, and were objects of adoration. The painted tombs of Marisa belonged to a Sidonian colony, as we are expressly told by an inscription commemorating its founder, Apollophanes, a statement amply confirmed by many specifically Phoenician names borne by deceased colonists. There is, accordingly, no possible doubt that these very un-Hellenic objects go back to Phoenician practice.

Another significant point illustrating the character of the incense-stands of Marisa is that they, like many other known objects of this class, incorporate the three or four horizontal projections which were peculiar to the Egyptian " djed " pillar, the sacred emblem of Osiris.[54] There is ample archaeological evidence for the popularity of the sacred symbol of Osiris in Palestine and Phoenicia. Locally made amulets in this peculiar form begin to appear before 1800 B. C. at Byblus.[55] A terra cotta mould from Israelite Samaria exhibits the same form.[56] Moreover, it is highly probable that the Phoenician god Ṣid, the vocalization of whose name is established by Greek and Latin transcriptions of theophorous names containing it, was originally identical with Egyptian Djid, the personified Osiris pillar.[57] The lily knobs were presumably decorative in origin, but they became characteristic elements of small incense-stands about the beginning of the Iron Age and continued in use for centuries thereafter. It is not at all probable that this class of metal incense-stands was called by the name ḥammôn (Heb. ḥammân), applied to incense-burning braziers and altars.[58] It is, however, instructive to note that the latter were associated in name with the god Baʿal-ḥammôn and were perhaps regarded as symbols of him.[59]

As noted above, Robertson Smith suggested more than half a century ago that the pillars Jachin and Boaz were really lofty cressets. In support of this view he noted that the shafts of the two pillars were crowned with *gullôth* (I Kings 7: 41), and that *šebakôth* were added to cover the *gullôth*. Since *gullah* is the word used in Zech. 4: 3 for the basin of a lamp-stand with seven wicks,[60] and since *šebakah* means "network," hence "grating," this argument is very strong. Moreover, the crown of the shaft was adorned with lily-work, i. e., with lily knobs, just as in the case of the Megiddo incense-stand and of many later examples of Phoenician origin. Nor is it indifferent that the shafts were of copper or bronze, just as is attested in the case of the two shafts at Gades in Spain and just as must be inferred with regard to other such objects, including the prototypes of the incense-stands of Marisa (which seem to have been gilded). In height, too, the objects are comparable; the pillars at Gades are said to have been twelve cubits high, which is approximately the height of the prototypes of the Marisa paintings. The shafts at Jerusalem are said to have been eighteen cubits, or about twenty-seven feet, in height; the breadth attributed to them was about 3.8 cubits (cir. 5 ft. 9 inches), which scarcely seems probable. It may be that the original document from which the various biblical passages referring to the two pillars are derived, gave a circumference of two cubits, inadvertently reproduced by a copyist as "twelve," through one of the commonest types of scribal error (*homoioarkton*). Since the proportion of height to diameter of the shafts at Marisa was about 40: 1, the suggested ratio of 28: 1 is in no way abnormal. Whether the formulae from which the two names were abbreviated, were actually inscribed on the shaft or were transmitted by tradition is naturally an insoluble question.[61]

Since the two shafts of Jachin and Boaz thus go back to Phoenician models, there is reason to suppose that their symbolic interpretation was influenced by Canaanite conceptions. As in the case of other cult-objects in the Temple (see below), they were presumably given a cosmic interpretation, i. e., they may have been regarded as the reflection of the columns between which the sun rose each morning to pour its light through the portico of the Temple into its interior.[62]   Like the Egyptian " djed " symbol they may also have denoted " endurance, continuity," in which case their dynastic role would become self-evident.   A third possibility is that they were interpreted historically to commemorate the pillar of cloud which accompanied the Israelites by day and the pillar of fire which went with them by night during their wanderings in the desert. At night the burning wicks of the *gullah* and in the day the smoking incense might well be associated with Israelite traditional history.   However this may be, we may be sure that Jachin and Boaz possessed rich symbolic meaning to the men of Judah during the time of their existence.

Archaeological finds have thrown a great deal of light on the furnishings and cult-objects of the Temple.   Thus the portable lavers,[63] fire-shovels, flesh-hooks, etc., are now well known.[64]   The cherubim have been discussed elsewhere;[65] in any case they were inherited from the Tabernacle and cannot figure among cultic innovations in the Temple.   We shall, accordingly, restrict our attention to the copper Sea, as well as to the altar of burnt offering and the portable platform, since the symbolic meaning of the latter two has been practically disregarded.   Since the first two and probably the third were invested with cosmic symbolism of great interest, they are particularly instructive.

The Sea (I Kings 7: 23-26) has been universally recognized as having cosmic significance of some kind.[66]   In function it cannot be separated from the Mesopotamian *apsû*, employed both as the name of the subterranean fresh-water ocean from which all life and all fertility were derived and as the name of a basin of holy water erected in the temple.[67] All these cosmic sources of water were conceived in mythological imagery to be dragons, as we know from Accadian, where *ti'âmtu*, "sea," and *apsû* were both portrayed in art and myth as dragons,[68] from Canaanite, where the same is true of *yammu*, "sea," and *naharu*, "river,"[69] and from Biblical Hebrew, where we find *tehôm* (etymologically identical with *ti'âmtu*),[70] *yam*, "sea,"[71] and *neharôth*, "rivers,"[72] all described as dragons. In Hebrew the word *yam* means "(large) river" and "fresh-water lake" as well as "sea" in the English sense. In our case we cannot, however, be sure whether the designation *yam* came originally from inland, referring to pure fresh water as the source of life, or from the coast of the Mediterranean, in which case it referred to the Mediterranean as the main source of Canaanite livelihood. In view of the ease with which motifs can be transferred and of the highly syncretistic character of Phoenician culture, the question is not vitally significant; either or both alternatives may be correct. The relation between the Sea and the portable lavers was like that between the *apsû* and the *egubbê*, "portable basins of holy water," in Babylonian temples.[73] Scholars of the pan-Babylonian school have falsely interpreted the Sea as the heavenly ocean and the twelve oxen (properly bulls) which supported it as the twelve signs of the zodiac. Unfortunately cuneiform evidence is increasingly opposed to the idea that the twelve signs of the zodiac had come into astrological use so early. The oldest known list of twelve zodiacal signs is much more recent, as has been pointed out by Weidner; the Babylonian proto-zodiac had seventeen signs.[74] It is much more probable that the twelve bulls (which the "oxen" must have been intended to represent) are partly symbolic, partly decorative in origin.[75] The bull was one of the most popular symbols of fecundity in the ancient Near

11

East; the animal was almost invariably associated with the rain-giver Hadad (Baal), but also appears in connection with the life-giving water of rivers and the underworld.[76] The four-fold arrangement in groups of three clearly represents the four seasons of the year, well attested in Jewish and Arabic calendars, and traceable at least as far back as the third century B. C.[77] In connection with the circular arrangement of the twelve oxen, it is interesting to note that the Hebrew word for "season" is etymologically connected with the Ugaritic word for "year," and that it originally meant "cycle, orbit" (Psalms 19: 6) from a common Semitic verb meaning "to encircle."[78] The arrangement in four groups was presumably also connected with the four directions. From the decorative point of view it may be noted that the use of animal supports for sacred objects and pieces of furniture became very common in the Iron Age, and is found in the case of images of deities, thrones, beds, etc.

It was shown more than twenty years ago that the altar of burnt offering, a description of which, with valuable details of terminology, has been handed down to us from Exilic times, reflects Mesopotamian cosmic ideas.[79] Subsequent treatments of the altar by de Groot and Galling [80] have missed this point. According to the description in Ezekiel 43: 13-17 [81] the altar of burnt offering was built in three square stages, each with a side two cubits shorter than the stage below it; the sides of the three stages were, respectively, twelve, fourteen and sixteen cubits long. The lowest stage was set on a foundation-platform called the "bosom of the earth" (ḥeq ha-'areṣ).[82] This foundation-platform was set in the pavement, its upper surface being apparently level with the surrounding pavement, but distinguished from it by a "boundary." The total height of the three stages was ten cubits, agreeing thus exactly with the height of the altar recorded in Chronicles.[83] The "twenty cubits" stated by the Chronicler to be the length and breadth of the altar, may either be a round number, or it may reflect the side of the foundation-platform, which is not easy to reconstruct with certainty from the present text, but seems to have been between 18 and 20 cubits. Galling has recently noted that the dimensions of the Temple of Ezekiel are substantially the same as those of the Solomonic Temple as given in Kings, and that the differences may readily be explained if we assume that the ruins of the Temple were actually measured by the Exilic prophet, who lacked precise information from a documentary source.[84] In the case of the altar we may suppose either that the "twenty cubits" of Chronicles is a round number, or that Ezekiel's figures are given from memory and do not coincide precisely with the original dimensions. It stands to reason that any priest who had been a member of the Temple staff would know the approximate dimensions of the altar from memory, simply by relating them to the height and limbs of a man. The summit of the altar, which was crowned by four "horns" at the four corners, is repeatedly given the curious name *'ar'el* or *har'el*, erroneously explained by most scholars as "hearth of God," or the like.[85] Actually this *'r'l*, the vocalization of which is rather uncertain, can be shown to mean "underworld, denizen of the underworld," [86] and is almost certainly derived from Accadian *Arallu* or *Arallû*,[87] which has the dual sense of "underworld" and "mountain of the gods," the cosmic mountain in which the gods were born and reared according to an Assyrian text.[88] The expression *har'el* actually means "mountain of God"; it is thus a slight popular etymology of the Accadian loan-word. Such borrowing from Sumero-Accadian is no more remarkable than the fact that the Canaanites borrowed the Sumerian *egal*, "temple, palace," with which several names of Sumerian temples begin,[89] or the Sumero-Accadian word *kiuru* (*kîyôr*), on which see the discussion below. Moreover, there is a still more unexpected borrowing from Accadian in the name of the foundation-platform, "bosom of the earth," since exactly the same expression, *irat erṣiti* or *irat kigalli*, "bosom of the earth, bosom of the underworld," was employed in the inscriptions of Nebuchadnezzar for the foundation-platform of the royal palace and of the great temple-tower of Marduk in Babylon, Etemenanki, the "Tower of Babel." [90] Lest a wholly unwarranted lowering of dates be based on this parallel with the texts of the early sixth century, it must be emphasized that the latter archaize very strongly and that the expressions are much older.

These parallels become intelligible as soon as we recall that the Mesopotamian temple-tower was also built in stages and that its summit was similarly called *ziqquratu*, literally "mountain-peak," while Sumerian names of temple-towers very often refer to them as cosmic mountains (*khursag* or *kur*). Moreover, the summits of temple-towers were also adorned with four "horns," as we know both from inscriptions and from monumental representations.[91] It is, accordingly, not surprising that the foundation-platform (Accadian *temennu*) should also receive the same unusual designation "bosom of the earth" in both the Mesopotamian temple-tower and the Israelite altar. In any case we may safely regard the form of the altar, together with its symbolism, as derived from Phoenicia, where it went back to older Canaanite borrowings from Mesopotamia.

The Chronicler has preserved another very interesting tradition, omitted in Kings, according to which Solomon stood before the altar on a copper *kîyôr*, five cubits square and three high, while he prayed to Yahweh (II Chron. 6: 12-13). Otherwise the *kîyôr* appears frequently, especially in the description of the Tabernacle and Temple, as the name of a portable laver of copper. The dimensions of the latter *kîyôr* are given as four cubits (in diameter); in the Temple of Solomon it stood on a wheeled carriage four cubits square and three high. Name, material and dimensions show that we are actually dealing with comparable objects. We may perhaps infer that the lavers were square instead of being round like the similar portable lavers of Late-Bronze Cyprus. There can be little doubt that the portable platform on which Solomon stood to pray before Yahweh must be compared with two Syrian monumental representations to which attention was called by the late Heinrich Schäfer in 1937.[92] In a limestone stela found at Ugarit in 1932 a king is shown praying to the storm-god Baal; the stela may be dated about 1400 B. C.[93] The king is shown standing on a chest or tub, apparently of metal and provided with a lid. His hands are upraised in the attitude of prayer. A stela from Lower Egypt in the Cairo Museum, published many years ago by W. Max Müller,[94] portrays a Syrian bearded god standing on a lion, with the Egyptian divine scepter in his hand. Before him stands a votary, perhaps a priest, with upraised hand; an altar of incense stands at one side. This votary also stands on a chest, this time a square or oblong box on legs. Here also the chest has a lid, as indicated by a short handle projecting in front. Judging from relative heights, the chest on which the king stands at Ugarit was about a cubit high, whereas the chest in the Egyptian stela was about two cubits high (counting the legs). It is rather obvious that the Biblical account refers to the same practice, though it may have been quite differently motivated. Whether the copper platform was designed merely to lend resonance to the speaker's voice or whether it also contained sacred objects on which the votary relied to add efficacy to his prayer,[95] we cannot say.

The name kîyôr is very significant. In Accadian it occurs in the inscriptions of Sargon II of Assyria repeatedly as a word for "copper caldron" (of unknown shape, but sometimes large enough to hold fifty measures of liquid) ; it is regularly spelled *kiuri* in one text, *ki-ùr* in the other.[96] But the latter spelling is found repeatedly in cuneiform vocabularies and Sumerian texts with the meanings " foundation-platform " (*durushshu* [with synonyms *ishdu* and *temennu*] and *kigallu* [see above]) and " entrance to the underworld " (*nêrib erṣiti*). The phonetic form of the Sumerian word is fixed by the fact that the spelling *ki-úr* alternates with *ki-ùr*.[97] Hebrew *kîyôr*, " platform " and " laver," thus goes back to a Sumerian word meaning literally " foundation of the earth," with cosmic significance (it is employed also in temple-names, as in *E-ki-ùr-ra*, " House of the Foundation of Earth "). There is not enough material available to enable us to go farther [98]—the implications are clear.

Our survey of the hitherto unrecognized or misunderstood cosmic significance of various parts of the construction and paraphernalia of the Temple of Solomon proves that the latter possessed a rich cosmic symbolism which was largely lost in later Israelite and Jewish tradition. Its existence is very important for correct understanding of the religion of Yahweh in the early monarchy. That Yahweh was universal deity in the time of the Judges we have already seen in Chapter IV, though increasing particularistic tendencies might occasionally dim the cosmic significance of Israel's God. But in the time of David and especially of Solomon there was no longer room for any doubt as to the universal character of Yahweh's dominion. For a good sixty years Israel was a state with imperial pretensions. As we have seen above in this chapter, David and Solomon controlled virtually all Palestine and Syria except the kingdoms of Sidon and Hamath; all the deities of the conquered lands were therewith eliminated from serious competition with Yahweh. In the Temple Yahweh was enthroned as the sole ruler of the entire cosmos; heaven, earth and underworld were all subject to him; all functions of all pagan deities were gathered into his hands. The Temple further symbolized the permanence of the Davidic dynasty, which was expected to stand as long as the two cosmic pillars Jachin and Boaz. It cannot be emphasized too strongly that there is no room here for territorial henotheism. The cosmic monotheism of Solomon's Temple makes Mosaic monotheism a *sine qua non* for the comprehension of early Israelite religious history, since there is no suggestion in any of our sources that a paramount spiritual leader had arisen between Moses and David.

At the same time there was a serious spiritual weakness in the new Temple, with its elaborate organization and its heavy indebtedness to Syro-Phoenician religious architecture and practice. The danger of syncretism became very great—so great that the following centuries were, to a considerable degree, characterized by bitter intermittent conflict between religious assimilators and religious separatists. The first official concessions were made by Solomon himself when he allowed shrines and altars of foreign deities to be built in the immediate vicinity of Jerusalem itself. Whether this concession was only political or tinged with syncretistic practice we cannot say. However, there were still undoubtedly many vestiges of Canaanite cult which survived among the people, and Solomon's concessions can only have encouraged the partial relapse into paganism with which Deuteronomic tradition credits the next two generations.

3. ARCHAEOLOGY AND THE RELIGION OF THE DUAL MONARCHY

The paganizing movement which may be said to have been inaugurated with the building of the Temple and to have been accelerated by Solomon's tolerance of pagan cults within the very shadow of the Temple, continued and developed to dangerous extent during the next two generations. In the

North Jeroboam I tried to counteract the political influence of the Temple by reviving earlier Israelite practice and by founding two shrines of Yahweh at Bethel and Dan, where Yahweh was represented as an invisible Presence standing on a young bull. Elsewhere we have briefly explained this conception and cited archaeological parallels from the earlier and contemporary Near East.[99] Two very early stories reported in I Kings 13-14 illustrate the hostility of the nascent prophetic movement toward the shrines of Jeroboam I.[100] Nothing is said about them in the pericope of Elijah and Elisha, as we have it in Kings, but this is easily explained by the fact that far greater danger to Yahwism was involved in the spread of the cult of the Tyrian Baal and Asherah. Similarly, little is known about the conflict between the precursors of Sadducees and Pharisees in early Maccabaean times, when the opposing factions were temporarily united by a much greater peril in the form of the Hellenizing movement.

Some confusion has been caused by Alt's contention that the Baal of Elijah's crusade was the local Baal of Carmel [101] and by Eissfeldt's view that it was not the Tyrian Melcarth but Baalshamem, the Syrian " Lord of Heaven." [102] Both interpretations are partly correct: Alt is clearly right in stressing the antiquity and importance of the sanctuary of Baal on Mount Carmel; Eissfeldt is emphatically correct in protesting against the current scholarly belief that the " Baals " of the Old Testament were merely local vegetation deities and in stressing the cosmic sweep of Baal's power, but there is nothing concrete to justify his identification of the Baal against which Elijah contended with Baal-shamem. It is quite possible that the Israelites identified the Canaanite Baals with which they came into contact with Baal-shamem, perhaps following Canaanite usage, but this view is only one of several possibilities. We do not yet know to what extent the Canaanites themselves syncretized their various Baals. On the other hand, Eissfeldt is not warranted in suggesting that the Tyrian Baal was a deity of local rather than cosmic significance, since all high gods possessed cosmic scope and cosmic functions among the Canaanites, as we have seen in Chapter III.[102a] The decisive proof that the Baal whose cult was propagated by the Tyrian princess Jezebel was really the Baal of Tyre, is furnished by a comparison of I Kings 18: 19, which mentions 450 prophets of Baal and 400 prophets of Asherah, with the Ugaritic epic of Keret, lines 198, 201, which refer to the goddess " Asherah of the Tyrians." Many other references to Asherah in the books of Kings, once together with Baal (II Kings 23: 4), suggest that the Canaanite Baal of the Israelite Monarchy was formally identified with the Tyrian Baal, though it is still quite impossible to say just how this Baal differed in myths and attributes from the great storm-god of the second millennium. In view of the enormous commercial influence and cultural prestige of Tyre and its nearness to Israel, there is nothing at all surprising in the diffusion of the cult of its principal deity through Israel.

Unfortunately much less is known about the situation in Judah which led to the drastic reformation of Asa. The traditions preserved in Kings, together with the still later version of the events given by the Chronicler, enable us to form a partial idea, somewhat obscured by our uncertainty as to the extent of the revision of tradition by the Deuteronomic editor. It is clear that the tradition was correct in emphasizing the increasing paganism of the royal family of Judah. The inevitability of such a trend becomes obvious when one bears in mind that Rehoboam's mother was an Ammonite princess named Naamah, whose very name suggests a background of worship of the Canaanite goddess,[103] and that Asa's mother was Maachah, who belonged to the family of Absalom. Absalom, being himself son of a Geshurite princess named Maachah and having spent some time in Geshur, was presumably not a particularly loyal Yahwist. The name of Maachah again suggests pagan associations.[104] In short, on the distaff side the house of David was at that time shot through and through with pagan elements. It may be that Maachah was mother of both Abijah and Asa; the Hebrew text is less than clear on this point, since it makes her mother of both and yet calls Asa son of Abijah. The most reasonable explanation is that Asa's own mother had died and that Rehoboam's widow continued to exercise the prerogatives of queen-mother [105] during the infancy of Asa, whose father had died in the third year of his reign. At all events, a tradition preserved by the Chronicler (II Chron. 15: 8-10) places the reform instituted by Asa in the fifteenth year of his reign (cir. 899 B. C), evidently soon after he had grown to manhood. His rebellion against the dominion of Maachah would be somewhat comparable to the revolt of Tuthmosis III against Hatshepsut. Since the old queen was an adherent of the cosmopolitan paganizing party, it was only natural that the young king should have fallen under the influence of hostile Yahwistic circles.

It is not easy to determine exactly what pagan practices were current in court circles at this time. Most shocking to pious Yahwists was Maachah's erection of a "horrible thing" (*mifléṣet*) for the Tyrian goddess Asherah. The word, which occurs only in this connection, is obviously euphemistic. In Kings we are also told that Asa removed the male prostitutes (*qedeshîm*) from the land of Judah, as well as the pagan abominations (*gillûlîm*, literally "pellets of dung"?) which his predecessors had made (I Kings 15: 12). The Chronicler adds a number of items which do not alter the picture in this respect. The Chronicler's further assertion (II Chron. 14: 5) that Asa removed the high places from Judah, though not from Israel (15: 17), contradicts the statement in I Kings 15: 14, and has long been recognized as an illustration of the increasing tendency to contrast the description of good kings more and more sharply with that of bad rulers. Of course, it is possible that Asa actually made a beginning in this direction. The reference to male prostitutes ("sodomites") is confirmed by the Deuteronomic passage in I Kings 14: 24. These persons, known to classical writers as *cinaedi* or *galli*, and familiar to cuneiformists under such names as *kulu'u, asinnu, kurgarrû*, were the male counterparts of the female *qedeshah*, "sacred harlot," Accad. *qadishtu*. Their Canaanite name was, however, known only from the Bible until it was recently discovered by Virolleaud in a list of temple personnel, excavated at Ugarit by Schaeffer in 1936; in this list the *q-d-sh-m* appear immediately after the priests (*k-h-n-m*).[106] About 1400 B. C. the male prostitutes of a Canaanite temple at Ugarit were thus important enough to be listed in the second place, before temple clerks,[107] singers and janitors, etc. There was undoubtedly a distinction between *qedeshîm*, "male temple-prostitutes," and *kemarîm*, "eunuch priests," but we have ample reason to suspect that the distinction often disappeared in practice (just as did the Hebrew distinction between priests and Levites, on which cf. Chap. IV). But modern nomadic Arab ethos and Israelite religious tradition agree in their loathing for the practice of male prostitution, which the Bedouin regard as an unspeakable Turkish or Persian abomination and the Israelites considered as one of the worst features of the Canaanite culture. That this practice should have gained so much ground in Israel is a vivid illustration of the problem with which Yahwistic circles were faced in their struggle against paganism. The practice was firmly implanted among the Canaanite aborigines of Palestine and was constantly being reintroduced from the countries which surrounded Israel; it was treated by the neighbors of Israel as a "very sacred custom," to quote the words of Lucian, in describing the same practice at Hierapolis in Syria, about a thousand years after Asa.[108]

The extirpation of the house of Omri in the Northern Kingdom cir. 842 B. C. and in Judah about five years later, brought temporary triumph for prophetic Yahwism, but there is nothing to indicate that any appreciable change had taken place in the official cult of Yahweh in either kingdom. In Judah the Canaanizing ritual of the Temple continued to be in force, along with many objectionable Canaanite practices which had crept in after the time of David. In the North, as attested by both Amos and Hosea, the Bethel cult remained essentially unchanged. Thus Hosea exclaims (Hos. 8: 5-6):

Spurn thy (two) calves, O Samaria! Mine anger is hot against them.

.   .   .   .

For flames shall become   the (two) calves of Samaria! [109]

Very interesting light is shed on the popularity of the elements *Yau* (abbreviated form of *Yahweh*) and *Ba al* in personal names of this period by the Ostraca of Samaria, which date from the ninth to the seventeenth [110] year of Jeroboam II (cir. 786-746 B. C.), i. e., from about 778-770 B. C. To judge from the personal names mentioned in them, belonging to men born between cir. 840 and 800 B. C., it would seem that names formed with *Ba'al* were roughly in the ratio 7: 11 to names formed with *Yahweh* (*Yau*). It is probable that a higher proportion of the abbreviated names found in these documents contained the latter (who was, after all, god of Israel) than the former, in which case we should arrive at an approximate one-to-two ratio in favor of Yahweh. One must indeed be cautious in drawing conclusions from personal names, especially since *ba al* may have been used occasionally as an appellation of Yahweh,[111] though this is not likely in times of bitter religious rivalry. It is very significant that seals and inscriptions from Judah, which become commoner in the eighth century and are very numerous in the seventh and early sixth, seem never to contain any Baal names. Yahwism had, indeed, triumphed politically in the Northern Kingdom with Jehu's victory, but it was apparently unable to command the adhesion, even nominally, of over two-thirds of the population. This was precisely the soil from which religious syncretism was bound to emerge eventually, as in fact it did.

When Samaria fell before successive Assyrian blows in the years 734-721, Judah was left to face a pagan world which had changed in many respects. The prestige of Tyre was rapidly declining. In 814 Carthage was founded, and before the end of the eighth century the Greeks had displaced the Phoenicians as the dominant people in the Western Mediterranean.[112] The cities of Phoenicia suffered heavily at the hand of the Assyrians during the last third of the eighth century, and in the years 677-673 both Sidon and Tyre (which had been divided into separate states by the Assyrians) became Assyrian provinces. Aramaean merchants were replacing Phoenician traders and a new Aramaic culture, composed of Canaanite and Neo-Assyrian elements with the latter dominant, was spreading rapidly over the West, strongly supported by Assyrian military power. The prestige of Assyria was at its height. Henceforth the religion of Tyre was doomed to increasing loss of influence, while the closely related religion of the aboriginal Canaanites of Palestine had probably become virtually extinct as an independent factor.

In estimating the character of the pagan reaction under such kings as Ahaz (cir. 735-715 B. C.) and Manasseh (cir. 687-642 B. C.), we must not forget this significant fact, that Assyria and Syria had replaced Phoenicia as foci of influence, and that Aramaic culture had replaced Canaanite. We are told that Ahaz sent back to Jerusalem a detailed description of an Aramaean altar of bronze which he had seen at Damascus when he went there to pay homage to the Assyrian king. It is very significant, however, that he instructed the high priest to have the altar reproduced and erected in the Temple for exclusively royal use; the greater altar (which we have described above) was to continue in ritual use as before. This passage shows that even a king of Judah could not safely interfere with the time-honored religious usages of Israel.

Under Ahaz we hear for the first time—perhaps not accidentally—of the obscure pagan rite of "passing a child through fire (to 'Moloch')," an expression which is so cryptic in itself and which appears in so stereotyped a form that its literal meaning had probably long been forgotten. In 1935 it was shown by Eissfeldt that biblical *molek* (LXX: *Moloch*) cannot be separated from Punic *molok*, found in Carthaginian inscriptions of the period 400-150 B.C. as *m-l-k*, and in Latin inscriptions from near Carthage, belonging to about 200 A.D., as *molc*.[118] This word is generally followed by "sheep" or "man," and must be rendered approximately "vow" or "pledge." Eissfeldt concluded that we should render the biblical phrase "as a sacrificial vow," or the like. Philologically Eissfeldt's argument is convincing, but it now seems certain that the original conception was more complex than he was able to guess at the time. In 1938 Dossin published decisive evidence from Mari proving that a god named *Muluk* was worshipped in the Middle-Euphrates region about 1800 B.C., and that *Muluk* could alternate with the more usual form *Malik*, well attested as a divine name by Accadian texts of the third millennium and later.[114] *Muluk* is the normal form of the abstract noun *mulku*, used as a personal name of a deity. We cannot, however, simply dismiss the Punic usage as late and local, since the derived noun *mulkânâ* means "promise" in Syriac! Since the original divine appellation *Mulku* can scarcely have meant anything but "kingship," whence "king," a development from abstract to concrete for which there are many parallels, both the Punic and the Aramaic meanings must be secondary. In other words, the idea of "promise, vow, pledge" may have been derived from the name of the deity and not inversely, just as in the case of many other common Hebrew and Accadian expressions.[115] *Malik*, "king," or *Muluk*, "kingship," would thus be regarded among the early Semitic inhabitants of northern Mesopotamia and Syria as the patron of vows and solemn promises, and children might be sacrificed to him as the harshest and most binding pledge of the sanctity of a promise. The correctness of this inference is supported by II Kings 17: 31, where we are told that the men of Sepharvaim in east-central Syria [116] burned their children as offerings to their gods "Adrammelech" and "Anammelech." The former deity is now known to have been worshipped at this very time in northwestern Mesopotamia under the name *Adad-milki*,[116a] a form of the Syrian god Hadad; the latter name has not been found hitherto, but appears to be somehow connected with the Sumero-Accadian god Anu, especially since there was a joint temple to Anu and Adad in contemporary Assur. *Adad-milki* unquestionably represents an older *Hadad-malik*, since the late West-Semitic form *milk* is known to go back to older *maliku*. The name is apparently parallel in formation to Mari *Ilum-muluk* or *Ilum-malik*, though the meaning is slightly different. In Syria we thus find sacrifice of children by cremation definitely associated with the cult of two deities who were identified with the god Malik (= Muluk) [116b] Sepharvaim was still standing in the year 727 B. C., when it was attacked by Shalmaneser V; shortly afterwards its people were deported to Samaria and it became a drastic example of the fate which the Assyrians meted out to recalcitrant foes. It is thus possible that Ahaz was one of the first to borrow the Syrian custom of sacrificing children to confirm a solemn vow or pledge. We do not deny that human sacrifice was familiar to the Israelites in preceding centuries through their association with the Canaanites, nor that their ancestors had doubtless practiced it occasionally in still earlier

times, but Eissfeldt's view that the sacrifice of children was
sanctioned by Yahwism before the Deuteronomic reform, appears to be without foundation.[117] If Eissfeldt is correct in
supposing that the pagan Phoenicians abandoned human sacrifice between the eighth and the sixth century B. C.[118]—a deduction which seems exceedingly probable—it is highly unlikely
that official Yahwism had ever sanctioned a rite which even the
Assyro-Babylonians had given up.   Incidentally, II Kings 3: 27
clearly indicates that Mesha's sacrifice of his crown-prince on
the wall of a Moabite capital (cir. 850 B. C.) was considered
as a terrible thing.   The precise sense of the words " and there
was (divine) wrath against Israel " is given by Jos. 9: 20:
" This we will do to them, letting them live in order that there
may be no (divine) wrath against us because of the oath which
we swore unto them (the Gibeonites)."   The efficacy of the
Moabite king's solemn oath (whatever it may have been) was
so enhanced by the act of human sacrifice that the besiegers
were appalled by the possible consequences to themselves and
superstitiously raised the siege.

Our clearest evidence for the nature of the pagan practices
which reforming kings, like Hezekiah and Josiah, were intent
on extirpating from Israel, is derived from II Kings 18: 4,
which describes Hezekiah's activity in this direction, and 23:
3-14 (with which compare the record of Manasseh's pagan
practices, II Kings 21: 2-7), which records Josiah's drastic
reform. Hezekiah and Josiah undertook to clear away all paganizing objects and practices, from the copper serpent which
tradition attributed to Moses and the provincial sanctuaries of
Yahweh to the latest astrological and divinatory importations.
Among the victims were, of course, all surviving traces of the
Canaanite cult of the Tyrian Baal and his consort, Asherah.
Much more interesting are the allusions to post-Solomonic cult-
objects with cosmic symbolism, which were erected in the

Temple or in its immediate environs. Thus we read of " altars
for all the heavenly bodies " in the two courts of the Temple
(II Kings 21: 5) and of "horses for the sun " and "chariots
of the sun " (II Kings 23: 11). None of these objects can be
illustrated directly by archaeology. Most intriguing is the
reference in II Kings 23: 7 to the destruction of the house(?)
of the *qedeshîm* in which women wove robes(?) for Asherah.
To judge from this passage the *qedeshîm* seem to have been
removed at some past time, their house being occupied by
women votaries of Asherah.

Under these conditions, it would be very strange if various
systematic attempts to syncretize Yahwism with pagan Syrian
religion had not been made. We have two illustrations of this
syncretism about which we can speak with some degree of confidence: the rites described in Ezekiel 8 and the religion of the
Jewish colony at Elephantine in the sixth and fifth centuries
B. C. The former has just been discussed in detail by T. H.
Gaster [119] and the latter has been the subject of a comprehensive treatment by Albert Vincent; [120] we owe provocative
suggestions to both of them.

Chapter 8 of Ezekiel is a valuable description of Syro-
Mesopotamian syncretism in the priestly and noble circles of
Jerusalem. In verses 3-6 we are told of a figured slab (*semel*) [121]
which was set at the entrance of the inner north gate of the
Temple enclosure. This figured slab bears the curious designation " slab of jealousy." Gaster has proposed the combination
of this passage with lines 19-22 of the Ugaritic " Poem of the
Beautiful and Gracious Gods," but there does not seem to be
any basis for his comparison, since Hebrew *môshab*, " seat "
(verse 3) probably refers to the niche in the wall where the
figured slab was placed, while the Ugaritic word *'iqn'u* means
elsewhere " lapis lazuli " and probably " purple," [122] but not
" I am jealous," as Gaster renders it, following Virolleaud's

12

pioneer translation.[128] Carving and painting cultic and mythological scenes on upright slabs (orthostates) set against the
wall or built into it, were characteristic customs in northern
Syria, southeastern Asia Minor and northern Mesopotamia between the twelfth and the seventh centuries B. C., as we know
from the excavations at such sites as Gozan (Tell Halâf),
Carchemish, Sham'al (Zendjirli), to say nothing of Calah and
Nineveh. The "figured slab" of Ezekiel thus unmistakably
suggests Syro-Assyrian practice and cannot be squared with
Egyptian, Phoenician, or Babylonian usage in any period.

Even more curious and interesting is the practice described in
the following verses (8: 7-12), where seventy Israelite nobles
are represented as meeting in a darkened chamber beside the
Temple in order to offer incense and conduct obscure rites. On
the walls of the chamber were carved representations of reptiles
and unclean beasts, as well as mythological scenes. Gaster has
tried to explain this chamber as a marriage chamber in a mystery
cult, where the sacred marriage (*hieròs gámos*) of two deities
was celebrated. Unfortunately his Babylonian parallel is confused and misleading,[124] and there is nothing to show that the
chamber was underground, as required in the Phrygian rite
which he cites.[125] The Ugaritic passage which he quotes, instead
of meaning "When the temple-woman enters the cavern,"
almost certainly means "When the planet Venus (Venus as
evening star) sets . . ." [126] The description given by Ezekiel
points to a syncretistic cult of Egyptian origin,[127] probably containing strong magical elements, as was often true of contemporary practice in the Nile Valley. Only in this way can
the archaeologist explain the reptiles ("creeping things") and
unclean animals. One has only to examine any illustrated
manuscript of the Book of the Dead from the Bubastite or Saite
period (first half of the last millennium B. C.) to see how
often serpents, crocodiles, beetles, baboons, lions, etc., figure in

it. Late magical representations are even more instructive in this regard. It is, accordingly, most likely that the syncretistic cult in question had Osirian features and was calculated to ensure its votaries a blessed existence beyond the grave. It must not be forgotten that the name of Osiris appears as an element in Phoenician personal names at least as early as the fifth century B. C., and that the close association between Osiris and Byblus was much older.

Third in Ezekiel's list is the practice of weeping for Tammuz, especially popular among the women (verse 13-14). This reference is very significant for our purpose, since the cult of the Sumero-Accadian god Tammuz can scarcely have become popular in southern Palestine before the seventh century B. C. There were many Canaanite gods of fertility which were related to Tammuz in character, or which were the objects of similar lamentations: e. g., Baal, Eshmun, Adonis, Hadad-Rimmon. Yet there is no trace of the Babylonian god in Syria before the Neo-Assyrian period,[128] and we may safely suppose that the cult was imported into Palestine by Mesopotamian deportees in the eighth and seventh centuries. Once established it could spread rapidly through Aramaean mediation. As is well known, the cult of Tammuz became firmly rooted in Aramaean paganism, where it survived far down into the Moslem period at Harran.

Fourth comes Ezekiel's " greatest abomination " (verses 15-16): worship of the sun in the portico of the Temple, which faced eastward. Here again we may have a simple extension of the tendency toward exaggerated cosmic symbolism which we already find in the Temple. The solar orientation of the Temple and the role played by the rays of the sun at the autumnal equinox have already been stressed by Morgenstern, Hollis, May, and others; cf. above on the horses and chariots of the sun.[129] It would scarcely be surprising to find further development of this interest in the sun, along syncretistic lines. It may have been precisely Ezekiel's zeal for pure monotheism which led him to consider this practice as relatively worse than the others.

The Elephantine Papyri, published by Sachau in 1911, have introduced us to a very remarkable form of Yahwistic syncretism, entirely unsuspected before their discovery. Since a full discussion would take far too much space for the limits of the present volume, we must be content with a succinct statement of the problem, with some proposals for its solution. As is well known, the Jewish colony at Elephantine was a military garrison of Jewish mercenaries at the southern boundary of Egypt, which was entrusted with the extremely important duty of warding off attacks from the direction of Ethiopia. The Ethiopian kings of the Piankhi dynasty had overrun and conquered Egypt in the late eighth century, and their successors were still redoubtable foes in the sixth and fifth centuries. The late W. Struve, a gifted Russian Egyptologist, published a paper in 1926 in which he demonstrated with a high degree of probability that the Jewish military colony at Elephantine had been established early in the reign of Apries (588-566 B. C.) and probably in or about the year 586.[130] This study was completely overlooked by Albert Vincent in 1937. The latter contends that the foundation of the colony must be placed considerably earlier, in the reign of Psammetichus I (663-609 B. C.),[131] but Struve's arguments against so high a date appear decisive. The explicit statement of the Letter to Bagoas, dated 411 B. C., that the Temple was built before Cambyses' invasion in 525, is definite proof that the colony was already well established before the latter date.

The great list of donors to the fund which was raised in the year 419 B. C. for divine worship at Elephantine states the total contribution as 628 (or 626) shekels, which was divided between Yahweh (246 shekels), Eshem-bethel (140) and 'Anath-bethel (240).[132] The three figures are definitely correlated, and at the beginning of the list, where Yahweh is named alone, he is called " God Yahweh " (literally, "Yahu the God," following regular Aramaic word-order). In Jewish business documents from Elephantine an oath is recorded by the Sanctuary (*masgedâ*) and 'Anath-Yahu, and a man with Jewish name and patronymic challenges another man with Persian name and patronymic to swear by "the god Herem-bethel." Any lingering doubt with regard to the divine nature of the names *Bethel, Herem* and *Eshem* is removed by perusal of the lists of theophorous personal names containing the elements in question, which are conveniently brought together by Vincent (pp. 564, 593, 654). Additional names containing the theophorous element *Bethel* have been collected by Hyatt in recent papers.[133] All these names are found in the Aramaic papyri from Egypt and in Neo-Babylonian cuneiform texts, with the exception of a stray name or two from the Bible and other sources. Names formed with *Bethel* first occur in the early sixth century (reign of Nebuchadnezzar) and continue through the following two or three centuries. No examples from Assyrian inscriptions and contracts of the seventh century have been discovered, in spite of the thousands of Accadian and Aramaic names which they contain. All names, whether from Babylonia or from Elephantine, are Accadian or Aramaic. It is true that such names as *Bethel-nathan, Bethel-'aqab*, or *Bethel-nûrî* can be Hebrew, but all of these names have better Aramaic than Hebrew parallels. Of some fifteen different names containing *Bethel* which are now known, seven (or eight) *seem* Accadian (though several *may be* Aramaic), and the same number *are* Aramaic. Several of them could reflect slight alterations to adapt them to the other tongue (e. g., *Bethel-nathan* and *Bêtel-nâdin*). The two *Herem* names (belonging to four different persons) and the two *Eshem* names (borne by three different persons) exhibit the same picture, though there is reason to regard them all as Aramaic, at most employing Accadian loan-words. For instance, *Eshem-kudurrî* may be Accadian, but it may also be Aramaic, employing a loan-word * *kudurrâ*; on the other hand *Eshem-râm*, borne by a son of Nabû-nâdin, can only be Aramaic, in spite of the Accadian patronymic (which may again be a slight alteration of an originally Aramaic *Nabu-nathan*, since the god Nabû was early adopted by the Aramaeans). Another point which must be stressed is that neither the element *Eshem* nor *Ḥerem* has been reported as occurring in any Assyrian or Babylonian cuneiform text; these names cannot, therefore, be considered as of ultimately Mesopotamian origin.

Was the god Bethel of Aramaic or Accadian origin? Significant is the fact that the name did not begin to appear as an element in theophorous names until cir. 600 B. C., after all Mesopotamia had become thoroughly Aramaized. Still more striking is the fact that the name (even when it is followed by an Accadian or quasi-Accadian second element) is often spelled *ba'it-ilâni* in cuneiform, thus assimilating it to the perfectly good Accadian expression *ba'ît ilâni*, " sought by the gods." There is no evidence that the deity was of Phoenician origin; the treaty between Baal of Tyre and Esarhaddon, cir. 675 B. C., where the name first appears, mentions Baiti-ilâni among the gods of Assyria, Babylonia and Syria (Ishtar, Gula, the Seven, etc.), whereas the Phoenician deities (Melcarth, Eshmun, Astarte) are mentioned together several lines below.[134] It would appear that Baiti-ilâni (or Bait-il, as we may perhaps transcribe the name) was an Aramaic divinity listed among the gods of greater Assyria. In this connection it should be observed that the name would be pronounced *Bît-ilân* or *Bît-il* in Assyrian, *Bêt'el* in Phoenician, but *Bait'el* or *Bait'elâhâ* in Aramaic. From this analysis we may deduce the following facts.

The god Bethel did not achieve any popularity until after the middle of the seventh century B. C., as we know from the fact that the element does not occur in thousands of known names from northern Mesopotamia belonging to the period 750-650 B. C. The cult spread very rapidly during the Neo-Babylonian period, reaching its maximum diffusion in the fifth. Its secondary focus was evidently Babylonia, since we cannot otherwise explain the common use of the element in Accadian names borne by Babylonians.

If we turn to the other names of divinities worshipped by the Jewish colonists at Elephantine, we find the Aramaic origin of the cult of Bethel further illustrated and confirmed. *Ḥerem* may, of course, be either Canaanite or Aramaean; it cannot be Accadian. The divine element *Anath* (*'Anat*) may be Aramaic (in the construct state) just as well as Canaanite, since it was popular from the eighth century on in the Aramaic emphatic form *'Attâ*. The word *'eshem*, " name," instead of Canaanite *shem* and later Aramaic *shum* (which is presumably influenced in vocalization by Accadian *shumu*), appears twice in absolutely clear context in an Aramaic inscription from the early eighth century B. C. at Sham'al in northern Syria.[135] There can, accordingly, be no reasonable doubt that we are here confronted with Aramaic syncretism, arising about the seventh century B. C. in Jewish circles which were under strong pagan influence.

Where was the geographical focus of this syncretistic development? Van Hoonacker thought that it arose in Samaria,[136] a view which appeals strongly in several respects but is opposed by the stubborn fact that the colony at Elephantine always speaks of itself as " Jewish " or " Aramaean," never as Israelite. Albert Vincent has recently proposed a compromise theory, which may very well be correct, in part for reasons which he did not adduce.[137] He suggests that the colonists at Elephantine came largely from Ephraim, from the environs of Bethel, and cites various well-known biblical passages to prove that there was a strong tendency in the Northern Kingdom to employ "Bethel" as a surrogate for "Yahweh" (cf. Amos. 5: 4-6 and especially Jer. 48: 13). Both biblical tradition and archaeological discovery agree that there was some kind of renaissance at Bethel after the Fall of Samaria in 721 B. C. The excavations which the writer directed there in 1934 showed that there had been an interruption in the continuity of occupation between the early eighth century and the sixth.[138] We may safely suppose that Bethel was destroyed by the Assyrians during the years 724-722 B. C., while the siege of Samaria was in progress. That it was at least partly rebuilt is shown by II Kings 17: 28, which states that the Assyrians sent one of the deported priests of Yahweh back to Bethel in order to reestablish the cult of Yahweh in the land. It is likely that the Assyrian governor of Samaria (who may have been an ancestor of Sanballat) [139] was alarmed at the revival of Israelite interest in the Temple at Jerusalem and undertook to restore the Bethelite sanctuary as a check to this tendency. That there was growing Israelite acceptance of the claims of Jerusalem is proved by such passages as II Chron. 30: 10 ff. and Jer. 41: 5. The restored cult of Yahweh at Bethel was interrupted by Josiah's drastic eradication of it about the year 622 B. C. Some thirteen years later the battle of Megiddo put an end to Judah's brief dream of empire and the Babylonians seem to have separated the district of Bethel again from the kingdom of Judah. At least this would follow from the lack of any evidence for a destruction of either Tell en-Naṣbeh or Bethel in the early sixth century, when Jerusalem and the towns of Judah were laid waste. The excavations revealed the interesting fact that Bethel became very prosperous during the sixth century B. C. and was destroyed by a tremendous conflagration during the latter part of the Neo-Babylonian period or possibly at the beginning of the Persian.

This is proved by the pottery, which reflects the middle or latter sixth century B. C. and overlies deposits of characteristic seventh century ware. Above it again were found scanty remains of the village of the fifth and fourth centuries, referred to in Nehemiah's census (Neh. 7: 32). It would appear that the cult of the Bethel temple flourished again, even after the time of Josiah, and we may conjecture with much plausibility that refugees from Bethel played an important role in the development of the syncretistic cult of the Jewish colony at Elephantine. Whether Bethel was destroyed as a result of a rebellion against Nabonidus, in conjunction perhaps with the Syrian revolt of the year 553 B. C., or at the time of the Persian occupation of Palestine about 539/8 B. C., we cannot tell. It is quite likely that the people of Bethel already considered themselves as Jews in contrast to the people of Samaria, especially since Bethel continued to be Jewish in following centuries. It is also possible that refugees from Bethel may have joined the Jews already in Egypt and that they were absorbed by the latter. However this may be, it is difficult to separate the popularity of the cult of Bethel among the Egyptian Jews of the fifth century from the history of Bethel in the two preceding centuries.

For the nature of this syncretistic cult we may refer to previous treatments. Again we must emphasize the fact that none of the divine names can be explained simply by supposing direct adoption of pagan divinities as figures in a polytheistic Jewish pantheon. Vincent has well stressed the fact that the Jews of Elephantine still considered themselves as Jews in religion. They turned without hesitation both to the heterodox Jewish provincial court at Samaria and to the orthodox temple in Jerusalem. Their God was "God of Heaven"; their personal names were overwhelmingly of purely Yahwistic meaning. Their own priests were *kôhanîm*; the opprobrious term *kemarîm* was applied to the Egyptian priests of Khnûm, who returned their contempt with bitter hatred, culminating in the destruction of the temple of Yahweh at Elephantine. In the same year in which the list of contributors to Yahu and his companion divinities was drawn up, the orthodox Jews of Jerusalem sent the famous Passover Letter to Elephantine, exhorting the members of the heretical colony to keep the feast according to orthodox rules. It is therefore increasingly probable that the writer is correct in treating the figures of the " pantheon " at Elephantine as hypostatic forms of Yahweh.[140] These theological speculations were focused around the conception of the independent sanctity of the "House of God," developing a tendency for which there are many illustrations in Northwest-Semitic religion, as most recently emphasized by Vincent.[141] *Herem-bethel* was the " Sacredness (Consecration) of the House of God "; *Eshem-bethel* was the hypostatized " Name of God," in the still more discreet form " Name of the House of God," in accordance with a tendency found both in Canaanite religion and Judaism (e. g., *'Ashtart-shem-Ba'al* and *hash-Shem*, " the Name," as rabbinic surrogate for the ineffable Tetragrammaton). *'Anath-bethel* or *'Anath-Yahu* must be understood in the light of our observation that the first element is in the construct state, as " Sign (of the Active Presence) of God," or as " Will of God." [142] It may be that the invariable use of the abbreviated form *Yahu*, which was certainly in popular Jewish use long before the Exile,[143] instead of the full form *Yahweh*, is also an expression of the same tendency to avoid the personal name of deity and to replace it with more discreet expressions.

With the victory of Judaism over the heresies of Ezekiel's and Nehemiah's day the long conflict between the faithful followers of Yahweh and the paganizing world around them was substantially won. The history of Israel's religious evolution can be understood only in the light of this bitter century-old struggle. Every conflict with paganism brought with it new spiritual insight and new ethical rigor. The religion of orthodox Jewry had travelled a long distance since the earliest days of Yahwism. In essentials, however, orthodox Yahwism remained the same from Moses to Ezra.[144] From first to last ethical monotheism remained the heart of Israelite religion, though there were many crises through which it had to pass during the slow change from the primitive simplicity of the Judges to the high cultural level of the fifth century B. C. The foregoing pages illustrate the significance of modern archaeological discovery in reconstructing the details of this development.

POSTSCRIPT

Underlying any serious investigation of the religion of Israel is full recognition of its historical character. The Judaeo-Christian tradition is unique in this respect. No other great religion of the past can compete with Judaeo-Christianity as a phenomenon of historical order. The outstanding polytheistic systems of antiquity, together with their modern analogues, cultic Brahmanism and Shintoism, are almost totally lacking in historical orientation. Buddhism and Zoroastrianism do possess conscious historical traditions, but these traditions are almost entirely attached to the persons of their founders, and modern historians find the greatest difficulty in offering any systematic reconstruction of their subsequent early history. Islam and Mormonism are offshoots of the Judaeo-Christian stem and consequently imitate the historical tendency of the latter.

Since the Old Testament is historical in essence as well as in canonical purpose, archaeology becomes an indispensable aid to our understanding of it. Only through archaeological research can biblical history become a scientific discipline, since history can in general become scientific only by the consistent application of archaeological or other equally rigorous methodology (*From the Stone Age to Christianity*, pp. 75 ff.; above, pp. 1 ff.). There can be no doubt that archaeology has confirmed the substantial historicity of Old Testament tradition. Divergences from basic historical fact may nearly all be explained as due to the nature of oral tradition, to the vicissitudes of written transmission, and to honest, but erroneous combinations on the part of Israelite and Jewish scholars. These divergences seldom result in serious modifications of the historical picture.

Archaeology makes it increasingly possible to interpret each religious phenomenon and movement of the Old Testament in the light of its true background and real sources, instead of forcing its interpretation into some preconceived historical mould. Archaeology checks all extreme views with regard to the meaning and content of biblical tradition. Neither radicalism nor ultra-conservatism receives any support from the discoveries and the deductions of the archaeologist. In general archaeology confirms the traditional picture of the evolution of religious life and thought through Hebrew, Israelite and Jewish history.

In this book I have tried to emphasize the fact that Israelite faith was much closer to Christianity and to rabbinic Judaism than to the basically prelogical religions of the ancient Near East. Monotheism formed an essential part of Mosaic religion from the beginning. Mosaic monotheism, like that of following centuries (at least down to the seventh century B. C.) was empirico-logical; it was practical and implicit rather than intellectual and explicit. Explicit monotheism could not fully emerge until after the dawn of the logical age about the sixth century B. C., since clear definition and logical formulation are necessary to change an implicit belief or concept into an explicit doctrine or idea. To deny that men were monotheists because their monotheism remained implicit is just as absurd as it would be to assert that men could not be polytheists because their polytheism was implicit, i. e., was not yet defined and formulated in logical terms. *Mutatis mutandis*, exactly the same is true of henotheism, of democracy, feudalism or any similar abstract concept. Yet the modern scholar is entirely justified in using these terms as convenient approximations to the ancient point of view, as reflected by empirico-logical statements and expressions in any given literature. The Israelites felt, thought and acted like monotheists, even though their creed remained implicit for lack of analytic logic with which to formulate it from the raw materials which they possessed.

Another traditional element in the religion of Israel which gains in spiritual radiance by utilizing all the light which can be shed by archaeology, is the prophetic movement. My view of its nature and development has been sketched in *From the Stone Age to Christianity* (pp. 230 ff.) ; here I have gathered archaeological data from many quarters for the purpose of filling in the historical background of religious syncretism and conflict against which the prophets fulfilled their mission. Thanks to archaeology we can see more clearly that the prophets of Israel were neither pagan ecstatics nor religious innovators. In them we see the first great exponents of such profound spiritual forces as conversion after repentance and as direct communion with God, attended by an overmastering sense of personal vocation and followed by continuing personal relationship to the Almighty. The emotional reactions which accompanied these spiritual experiences did not differ in any fundamental respect from similar reactions among pious Jews and Christians, long after the dawn of the age of logic. In fact, they may often have been more powerful because of their very freshness and lack of rationalizing complications.

To the Christian Israel's religion thus remains the essential nucleus of his spiritual arsenal, still shining with the brightness of youth, still charged with latent power. Turning from its old Near-Eastern preceptors, Israel saw a vision of God at its coming of age—a vision through which man can alone be saved from the tyranny of nature and history.

NOTES TO CHAPTER I

[1] See his book *Revolutions of Civilisation*, 1911.

[2] *Von ägyptischer Kunst*, 3rd. edition, 1930; cf. FSAC 29 f. and below, § 2.

[3] FSAC 1-87, *passim*.

[4] FSAC 77 f. The overwhelming majority of "historical" data belong, I believe, to the class of judgments of typical occurrence.

[5] It is coming rapidly to be recognized by scientists and philosophers that it is precisely those aspects of natural science which are most general in their application and most subject to mathematical formulation, like the primary laws of physics, which are least subject to "objective" control. This point of view has been drastically stated by Sir Arthur Eddington in his book, *The Philosophy of Physical Science* (1939); cf. the detailed criticism by R. B. Braithwaite in *Mind*, 1940, pp. 455-466, with Eddington's reply, *Mind*, 1941, pp. 268-279. According to Eddington physical laws are of "epistemological" origin, i. e., their formulation is conditioned by the nature of the human mind. He goes so far in his contention that these laws could all have been formulated *a priori*, without the intervention of experiment and observation, that he appears to allow "objective" existence only to those relational data which have not been reduced to inclusive terms. His contention that even the physical constants can be derived *a priori* by suitable mathematical postulates and transformations, is not directly germane to the issue, and has not been accepted by any other competent physicist or mathematician, so far as I know. However, Eddington's incisive criticism of current assumptions does make it clear that there is an arbitrary character about many of the so-called natural laws which justifies their removal from the "objective" sphere to the "subjective," though they are not invalidated by this transference. The essentially *a priori* nature of all classifications which can be mathematically formulated, will be illustrated by the impending systematization of the laws governing vertebrate evolution by G. G. Simpson of the American Museum of Natural History. Simpson's paper on "Quantum Effects in Evolution," presented before the American Philosophical Society April 24, 1941, is, in my judgment, epochal in its significance. For details see his book, *Tempo and Mode in Evolution* (New York, 1944). It is time to extend his method to archaeology. Simpson quoted the late Bashford Dean as saying that he observed the same type of evolution in the development of mediaeval armor that the palaeontologists had noted in vertebrate phylogeny. It is, accordingly, probable that evolution will some day be reduced to *a priori* laws with mathematical formulation and that these laws will be found to operate regardless of the material involved. I hasten to add that these laws cannot well be derived mathematically until we know approximately how the facts work. However, since the mathematical frame of reference is itself subjectively derived, its application to a given set of data will always be conditioned by the capacity of the human mind to cognize the data and to interpret them correctly.

[6] FSAC 75 ff., 79 ff. For an excellent statement of certain aspects of the

problem see Edgar Zilsel, " Physics and the Problem of Historico-Sociological Laws," *Philosophy of Science,* 1941, pp. 567-579.

[7] FSAC 82 ff.

[8] FSAC 49 f.; JBL, 1940, pp. 95 ff.; *Science, Philosophy and Religion, A Symposium* (New York, 1941), pp. 296 ff.

[9] Cf. JAOS, 1936, pp. 139 ff.

[10] *Proceedings of the American Philosophical Society,* 84 (1941), p. 467.

[11] See *Time,* July 28, 1941, pp. 48 ff.; *American Journal of Archaeology,* 1941, pp. 509-512.

[12] On this distinction see the references in note 2. In conceptual art, which is in general more primitive than perceptual, the artist tries to portray his idea of .what constitutes an animal or other object, while the individual elements of a group or scene are arranged with a view to some special or dominant idea of arrangement, entirely without regard to perspective. In perceptual art, the figure is drawn as it would appear to an observer at a given point, all other considerations being secondary. Most developed pre-Greek art is a compromise between the two principles, which were unconsciously felt though not explicitly recognized until the logical age which began about the fifth century B. C.

[13] FSAC 98, 101 f. Examples of the ceramic art of the Halafian age may be found, e. g., in BASOR 65, pp. 3-7, and in M. E. L. Mallowan and J. Cruikshank Rose, *Prehistoric Assyria* (*Iraq,* II, part 1, 1935), *passim.*

[14] FSAC 127 f.

[15] That astral myths do go back in part to the beginnings of human myth-making has become increasingly recognized by anthropologists, especially because of the abundance of such myths among the South-American Indians, where we have some of the most archaic mythology extant anywhere in the world. A specialist in this field, Paul Ehrenreich, has stated the situation very vigorously in his study, *Die Mythen und Legenden der südamerikanischen Urvölker und ihre Beziehungen zu denen Nordamerikas und der alten Welt* (Berlin, 1905) ; cf. the review of Hugo Winckler in the *Orientalistische Literaturzeitung,* 1906, cols. 447 ff. and 488 ff.

[16] On this subject cf. J. W. and Grace M. Crowfoot, *Early Ivories from Samaria,* 1938, pp. 28 f., 50. The finding of unworked and incomplete ivories at Samaria suggests that there was a workshop there; the discovery of a hieroglyphic transcription of the Hebrew name " Eliashib " written in typical Bubastite " syllabic " fashion, would seem to prove a complex relation of some kind between Egypto-Phoenician and Israelite craftsmen.

[17] See especially Curt Sachs, *The History of Musical Instruments,* New York, 1940, and O. R. Sellers, *The Biblical Archaeologist,* IV, part 3 (1941).

[18] See Gordon, *Ugaritic Grammar,* pp. 78-87.

[19] Epic of Baal and Anath, I AB, vi: 17 ff.; for the translation see Goetze, JAOS, 1938, p. 271.

[20] For such monsters cf., e. g., the list in V AB, D, lines 35 ff.⁻ (BÁSOR 84, pp. 16 f.) and the description of the Devourers and Renders in the text published by Virolleaud in *Syria,* XVI, pp. 247 ff., col. i, lines 25 ff. Artistic

representations are equally instructive; for a particularly extravagant example from about the eleventh century B. C. see AASOR XII, p. 134, fig. 1.

[21] See Z. S. Harris, *Development of the Canaanite Dialects* (1939), pp. 50, 59 f., and chronological chart.

[22] On the recent history and present status of affective psychological theory see especially H. M. Gardiner, R. C. Metcalf and J. G. Beebe-Center, *Feeling and Emotion*, 1937.

[23] Cf. the sketch of classifications and interpretations proposed by students of affective psychology since 1900 which is given *op. cit.*, pp. 336-386.

[24] *Proceedings of the American Philosophical Society*, 1941, pp. 543-563.

[25] On the meaning of "word" in these texts cf. especially L. Dürr, *Mitteilungen der Vorderasiatisch-aegyptischen Gesellschaft*, 42, part 1, pp. 3 ff., and my brief discussion, JBL, 1941, pp. 207 f., with the references there given.

[26] See S. N. Kramer, *Lamentation over the Destruction of Ur*, Chicago, 1940, pp. 62 f., lines 370 ff.

[27] My rendering is based on the equation of *ša-ša* in this line with *ša₆* = *damâqu*, *ṭâbu*, "be favorable, gracious," and *gù-ša₆-ša₆-ga* = *suppû*, *šutêmuqu*, "to pray," for which cf. Delitzsch, *Sumerisches Glossar*, p. 255.

[28] It seems better to follow the text of C, which reads *me-a-zu* = *me-a-za-e-me-en*, "where art thou?" (Poebel, *Grundzüge der sumerischen Grammatik*, § 242), just as *a-na-zu* means "what of thee?" (Poebel, *ibid.*, § 239).

[29] This is the view of A. Schott, who has given cogent reasons for it. It may be added that Jacobsen's brilliant analysis of the language and style of the great Sumerian king-list (*The Sumerian King List*, 1939, pp. 128 ff.) has made a date for the bulk of it at the very beginning of the Third Dynasty of Ur, perhaps in the reign of Utu-khegal of Erech, very probable, and that this list provides some of the background for increased Babylonian interest in the historical sagas of Sumer.

[30] The existing translations of this line are very unsatisfactory; e. g., Ebeling renders, "Mein Freund ist ein Gott, er wird aufstehen bei meinem Rufe!" which does not fit the context at all. I regard *ibrî-ma* as preterite of *barû* "to see," in the protasis of a hypothetical condition, followed by the enclitic *ma* which often indicates direct discourse. The second half of the verse, *it(t)abbî'am ana rigmiya* I should render literally, "he might keep calling to me at my cry," taking the verb to be a preterite I, 3 form from *nabû*, of the type discovered by A. Poebel, *Studies in Akkadian Grammar* (1939), pp. 1-64. The preterite may even point to a contrary-to-fact condition, removing every shred of optimism from the words of Gilgamesh.

[31] For the text see Meissner, *Mitteilungen der Vorderasiatischen Gesellschaft*, 7 (1902), pp. 1-16; for the translation see Ebeling, *Altorientalische Texte zum Alten Testament*, 1926, p. 194 (the latest translation, that of A. Schott, *Das Gilgamesch-Epos*, Leipzig, 1934 [*Reclamsbibliothek*, Nr. 7235], is not accessible to me).

[32] *Gilgamesh Epic*, XI: 117 ff.

[33] Published in *Cuneiform Texts from Babylonian Tablets in the British Museum*, XV (1902), plate I, and translated by P. Dhorme, *Revue d'Assyriologie*, VII, pp. 11 ff.

[34] The Babylonian "Job," II: 39 ff.; for translation and literature see Ebeling, *op. cit.*

[35] For the translation of these remarkable poems see Alan Gardiner, *The Chester Beatty Papyri*, No. I (1931), pp. 27-38. The papyrus in question, which dates from cir. 1100 B. C., contains an entire book of love-songs, together with some shorter compositions. It is divided into seven long cantos (each called "house"), put alternatively into the mouths of two sweethearts, who address one another as "brother" and "sister," in accordance both with Egyptian custom and with the usage in Canticles. The first, fifth and seventh cantos are attributed to the youth, while the second, third, fourth and sixth are ascribed to the maiden. The literary framework is thus almost identical with that of Canticles. In addition, there are many parallels both in the situations which are described and in the images which are employed. However, direct borrowing from Egypt is quite out of the question. I should assume that the basic Egyptian pattern was transmitted to Israel through Canaanite (Phoenician) channels and that the original Hebrew poems were mainly composed about the ninth century B. C., though they date from about the fourth century in their present form.

[36] For the translation see Ranke in *Altorientalische Texte zum Alten Testament,* p. 28, and for the point of view expressed by the author see my remarks in FSAC 137 f., in which I follow A. Scharff.

[37] This translation has been quoted without change from Paul Haupt, *Biblical Love Ditties,* Chicago, 1902, p. 10. In wording his translation Haupt cooperated with the distinguished Shakesperian scholar, Horace Howard Furness.

[38] See A. D. Nock, *Conversion,* Oxford, 1933.

[39] FSAC 231 f.; *Journal of Bible and Religion,* 1940, pp. 132 f.

[40] E. g., W. A. Irwin in his review of FSAC in the *Christian Century,* March 5, 1941, p. 323 a.

[41] P. Dhorme, *L'emploi métaphorique des noms de parties du corps en Hébreu et en Akkadien* (1923), pp. 112 ff.; cf. also A. L. Oppenheim, JAOS, 1941, pp. 263 ff.

[42] The Massoretic text has *'ehad,* "one," but all the Greek recensions agree in rendering "another heart," presupposing Hebrew *'aher,* which is the same word used in I Sam. 10: 9. It is scarcely necessary to add that this change in reading requires no change in the consonantal text, since *r* and *d* fell together for long periods in Hebrew script. The context and parallels make the Greek reading certain, as recognized by the commentators (e. g., Bertholet, 1936).

[43] C. Spearman, *The Nature of 'Intelligence' and the Principles of Cognition* (1923), pp. 262-276.

[44] On the close parallelism between the laws of evolution in biology and archaeology cf. above, n. 5.

[45] FSAC 129 f.

[46] FSAC 126 ff., with references.

[47] In the first volume of his work *Thought and Things,* p. 16 (cf. also Vol. III, pp. 10 ff.).

[48] K. T. Preuss, *Die geistige Kultur der Naturvölker* (1924).

[49] Franz Boas, *The Mind of Primitive Man* (1922).

[50] R. R. Schmidt, *Dawn of the Human Mind,* translated by R. A. S. Macalister (1936), which must be used with extreme caution because of the adventurous contentions of the author.

[51] Cf. his useful paper. "La structure de la mentalité primitive" in *Revue d'Histoire et de Philosophie Religieuses,* VIII (1928), pp. 1 ff., 149 ff. See also the very good summary of then current views by A. Goldenweiser, *Early Civilization* (1922), pp. 327-398.

[52] The head of this school is Alfred H. Korzybski, who founded an "Institute of General Semantics" at Chicago in 1938; cf. especially his book *Science and Sanity, an Introduction to Non-Aristotelian Systems and General Semantics,* 1933. The non-Aristotelian aspect of his work has been vigorously supported by Oliver Reiser, *The Promise of Scientific Humanism* (1940), but the latter's attempt to prove that Aristotelian logic must be abandoned and replaced by non-Aristotelian logic has succeeded only in exposing the inherent weakness of the whole "semantic" position. E. g., he tries (pp. 100 f.) to prove that the Aristotelian principles of identity, contradiction, and excluded middle are false by a brief symbolic "demonstration" in which he assumes the applicability of the law of identity, excusing himself on the ground that Aristotelian logic is only a special case of non-Aristotelian logic! Another absurdity is pointed out below, n. 55.

[53] See below, Chap. III, § 2.

[54] The problem of the degree of early man's inventiveness has been vigorously debated, but is not easy to solve. On the affirmative side note especially Lord Raglan, *How Came Civilisation?* (1939). It is perhaps safe to say that early Near-Eastern man was considerably more inventive than the average savage of the past century. At the same time, his inventiveness consisted rather in quickness to appreciate the value of an accidental discovery than in any application of the method of trial and error.

[55] This view is seriously stated, e. g., by Oliver Reiser, *The Promise of Scientific Humanism,* pp. 15 f., 43 f., 72 f. It is, however, quite certain that the number of functional relationships that can be expressed by language is strictly limited, and that most languages cover nearly all possible ground with the syntactic and morphological structure at their disposal. Linguistic syntax is something quite different from logical syntax. Philological semantics has been systematically and ably applied to the classification of all known functional relationships which are expressed in language by F. R. Blake, in his forthcoming work, *Semantics, the Science of Meaning.*

[56] The only partial exception is in Babylonian astronomy, which reached its culmination in the fourth century B. C., perhaps already under indirect Greek influence; cf. FSAC 262.

[57] FSAC 135 ff., 253.

[58] FSAC 254.

[59] FSAC 204 f.

[60] FSAC 170 ff.

[61] On the philological disciplines among the Babylonians and Assyrians see B. Meissner, *Babylonien und Assyrien*, II (1925), pp. 324 ff. During the past fifteen years the work of B. Landsberger and his pupils has conclusively established the fact that the "canonical" Babylonian grammatical and lexicographical texts, all arranged in the form of lists, were first composed during the First Dynasty of Babylon (cir. 1900-1600 B. C.).

[62] Cf. provisionally Jastrow, *Die Religion Babyloniens und Assyriens,* II, pp. 803 ff. Moreover, line 3 of Rm 2, 135 is euphemistic rather than favorable, and thus stands in definite contrast to line 2.

[63] Cf. FSAC 130, 161 ff.

[64] It must be emphasized that my phrase "prelogical intuition" is not intended to have any pejorative connotation whatever; that is, I do not mean to place prelogical mentality on a lower plane than logical, except with reference to their relative positions in the scale of human evolution. *Sub specie aeternitatis* there is no difference, so far as we can say, between the two in relative importance in the scheme of things. Nor do I intend to use "intuition" as though it were in itself an inferior form of mental activity. For all my "rational empiricism" (FSAC 318, n. 21) in dealing with nature *and* history, I believe firmly that the world of nature and history which mortals can comprehend is insignificant when compared to the vast realms beyond nature and history. I sympathize strongly with the point of view expressed by Coomaraswamy, *Review of Religion,* 1942, p. 138, paragraph 3. It follows from my theistic standpoint that prelogical intuition may be a much more direct and satisfactory means of divine revelation than any amount of logical ratiocination. God controls evolution just as surely as evolutionary principles control human progress in nature and history (cf. above, n. 5).

NOTES TO CHAPTER II

[1] See the short bibliography in FSAC 313, n. 1. For an appraisal of books dealing with Palestinian archaeology and its history see my sketch in BASOR 52 (1933), pp. 12 ff., and my brief survey of the literature in the field, JPOS XVI (1936), pp. 50 f. We now have an admirable general introduction to the subject in Millar Burrows' book, *What Mean These Stones?* (New Haven, American Schools of Oriental Research, 1941, price $2.50 postpaid), and a valuable systematic treatment in A. G. Barrois's *Manuel d'archéologie biblique,* Vol. I (Paris, 1939).

[2] There is now a very extensive literature on the subject, which is listed and indexed in the excavator's valuable work, *Ugaritica* (Paris, 1939), to which additions have been made by Gordon in his invaluable *Ugaritic Grammar.* For a very good brief account of the material see Zellig S. Harris in the *Smithsonian Report* for 1937, pp. 479-502.

[3] BASOR 52, pp. 4 ff., 53, pp. 18 f. So far no satisfactory reading has been proposed.

[4] See Virolleaud, *Revue Hittite et Asianique,* V (1940), p. 173, for the

synchronism between Niqmed of Ugarit, to whose reign some, at least, of our copies belong, and Suppiluliuma of Khatti. For the date, cir. 1365 B.C., at which the cuneiform tablets of the temple library passed through earthquake and conflagration, see Schaeffer, *Syria*, XVIII, pp. 137 ff., and *The Cuneiform Tablets of Ras Shamra-Ugarit* (London, 1939), pp. 22 f., 35; Albright, *Journal of Egyptian Archaeology*, 1937, pp. 195, 203.

⁵ Cf. FSAC 175. For illustrations of the relatively early date of these texts note that the horse and chariot scarcely ever appear in them, and that there is considerable divergence between the mythical *dramatis personae* of the epics and the deities actually worshipped at Ugarit according to the sacrificial rituals.

⁶ See the standard edition by Knudtzon, in two large volumes, Leipzig, 1907-15. For a brief account of subsequent finds of cuneiform tablets at Amarna and for a discussion of the possibilities of further interpretation see my paper, *Journal of Egyptian Archaeology*, 1937, pp. 190-203. The English edition of the Amarna Letters in two volumes by S. A. B. Mercer (Toronto, 1939) can be used only with great caution; see my review, JBL 1940, pp. 313 ff.

⁷ See especially R. du Mesnil du Buisson, *Le site archéologique de Mishrifé-Qaṭna* (Paris, 1935), and the preliminary reports in *Syria*, VII-XI. The cuneiform tablets were published by Virolleaud, *Syria*, IX, pp. 90 ff., and XI (1930), pp. 311-342; cf. now my remarks, BASOR 78, pp. 23 f.

⁸ For the tablets see provisionally Sidney Smith, *Antiquaries Journal*, 1939, pp. 38-48; *Alalakh and Chronology* (London, 1940).

⁹ See especially Hrozny in Sellin's *Tell Ta'annek* (Vienna, 1904), and *Eine Nachlese auf dem Tell Ta'annek* (Vienna, 1906); A. Gustavs, *Zeitschrift des Deutschen Palästina-Vereins*, 1927, pp. 1-18, and 1928, pp. 169-218. *Inter alios* see also B. Maisler, *Klausner Volume* (1936), pp. 44-66, and A. Sachs, *Archiv für Orientforschung*, XII (1939), pp, 371 ff. I have been intending for years to publish my own study of the tablets.

¹⁰ See Böhl, *Zeitschrift des Deutschen Palästina-Vereins*, 1926, pp. 321 ff. I expect to publish a revised translation of the letter in the near future.

¹¹ For the preliminary reports of Parrot see *Syria*, XVI-XX. Dossin's provisional reports on the tablets will be found mainly in *Syria*, XIX, pp. 105-126, XX, pp. 97-113, as well as in numerous shorter articles in various publications. For general orientation cf. my articles, BASOR 67, pp. 26 ff.; 77, pp. 20 ff.; 78, pp. 23 ff.

¹² On these documents see the publications of J. Lewy, especially his paper in *Revue de l'Histoire des Religions*, CX (1934), pp. 29-65.

¹³ Cf. JPOS, 1936, pp. 18 f., where the earlier literature is cited, and below, Chap. III.

¹⁴ See my preliminary discussion of the material published by G. Posener in 1940, BASOR 81, pp. 16 ff., 83, pp. 30 ff., where references to the older literature will be found.

¹⁵ For these inscriptions and the literature on them see especially J. W. Flight, *Haverford Symposium on Archaeology and the Bible* (1938), pp. 114 ff.

[16] E. g., my tentative decipherment of the Proto-Sinaitic inscriptions, JPOS, 1935, pp. 334 ff., still remains problematic, since no confirmatory material has since turned up.

[17] See Flight, op. cit. I expect to deal with several of these inscriptions at an early opportunity.

[18] On this date see my discussion in the Leland Volume.

[19] For the ninth-century date of the earliest inscriptions from Sardinia see BASOR 83, pp. 14 ff.

[20] See especially R. Dussaud, Les origines cananéennes du sacrifice Israélite (1921).

[21] See R. du Mesnil du Buisson, Mélanges syriens offerts à M. R. Dussaud, I (1939), pp. 421-434, and my detailed treatment, BASOR 76, pp. 5-11. My knowledge of the second tablet I owe to the kindness of Dr. Harald Ingholt, who sent me photographs. For utilization of this latter text, which is not quite so important as the first, we must await du Mesnil's publication.

[22] These documents have been studied particularly by Sachau and Lidzbarski; for earlier bibliography see G. A. Cooke, A Textbook of North-Semitic Inscriptions (1903), pp. 159 ff. A renewed treatment, especially of the inscriptions of Panammu I and II, is badly needed. The oldest and most important text, that of Kilamuwa, has been repeatedly studied; for the literature see especially Lidzbarski, Ephemeris, III, pp. 218 ff. and Bauer, Zeitschrift der Deutschen Morgenländischen Gesellschaft, 1913, pp. 684 ff., with subsequent contributions by Bauer, ibid., 1914, pp. 227 f., Albright, JPOS, 1926, pp. 84 f. and most recently by Alt, Zeitschrift für die Aegyptische Sprache, 75 (1939), pp. 16 ff.

[23] Published by Ronzevalle, Mélanges de l'Université St. Joseph, XV (1931), pp. 235-260; see especially Bauer, Archiv für Orientforschung, VIII (1932), pp. 1-16, and G. R. Driver, ibid., VIII, pp. 203 ff. (to be used with great caution). This inscription (now in the Aleppo Museum) needs systematic examination by a competent epigrapher and Aramaic scholar.

[24] Published by H. Pognon in 1908; see especially Lidzbarski, Ephemeris, III, pp. 1 ff. On the place where it was found cf. JPOS, 1926, pp. 85 f., and BASOR 49, p. 31.

[25] The latest independent translation is that of G. A. Cooke, op. cit., pp 186 ff. The interpretation of the Agbar text, in particular, requires drastic revision in places.

[26] See now especially A. Cowley, Aramaic Papyri of the Fifth Century B. C. (1923); N. Aimé-Giron, Textes araméens d'Egypte (1931); A. Vincent, La religion des Judéo-Araméens d'Eléphantine (1937). On the still unpublished leather documents belonging to Egypto-Persian archives from the late fifth century cf. Chap. V, n. 22.

[27] The Mesha Stone needs a new treatment by a scholar who is trained in modern linguistic and topographical analysis. The inscription agrees with the documents from Samaria in such linguistic peculiarities as the use of forms like šat(t) for Biblical Hebrew šanah, "year," and the regular contraction of diphthongs, which was a peculiarity of the Northern dialect as opposed to the

Southern dialect of Jerusalem, which we call Biblical Hebrew. It differs from them in having a masculine plural ending in *n* instead of *m*, in the survival of the archaic *ifte'al* form in the verb, etc.

[28] See Chap. V, notes 41 and 110.

[29] See H. Torczyner, *The Lachish Letters* (1938), *Te'ûdôt Lakhîsh* (1940). The most convenient orientation, as well as the latest translations, with full citation of the pertinent literature, will be found in my articles in BASOR 61, pp. 10 ff.; 70, pp. 11 ff.; 73, pp. 16 ff.; 82, pp. 18 ff.

[30] For this material see especially Diringer, *Le iscrizioni antico-ebraiche palestinesi* (1934), and his articles in PEQ, 1941, pp. 38 ff., 89 ff., on stamped impressions from Lachish. On stamped impressions of seals from Beth-shemesh see Grant and Wright, *Ain Shems Excavations* V (1939), pp. 78 ff. A fair number of additional seals and graffiti from other sites have been published since the appearance of Diringer's book; most of them will be found in recent numbers of PEQ and BASOR.

[31] C. F. A. Schaeffer, *Syria*, XVI, p. 155; see Schaeffer, *The Cuneiform Texts of Ras Shamra-Ugarit* (1939), p. 8, on the excavator's general view of their chronology and on the third temple, about which little is yet known. These temples are said to date back to the Middle Bronze, though they continued in use in Late Bronze.

[32] C. W. McEwan, AJA, 1937, pp. 8 ff.; G. E. Wright, *The Biblical Archaeologist*, IV, pp. 20 f.

[33] R. du Mesnil du Buisson, *Syria*, IX, pp. 6 ff.; *Le site archéologique de Mishrifé-Qatna* (1935), pp. 71 ff. Great caution is necessary in appraising the results of du Mesnil's excavation of the cultic installations connected with the temple of the goddess Beltekalli.

[34] See M. Dunand, *Fouilles de Byblos*, I (1939), pp. 79 ff., 288 ff., for the architectural remains and the objects found in the area. The chronology has been approximately established by R. J. Braidwood, AJSL, 1941, pp. 254 ff. The oldest of the three temples belongs to the First Intermediate Age of Egyptian history and cannot be older than the late Sixth Dynasty (minimum chronology cir. 2300-2120); the latest is contemporary with the foundation jars of the Middle Empire, which probably date from the first half of the 18th century B. C. (see AASOR, XIII, pp. 70 f., 74).

[35] See now Alan Rowe, *The Four Canaanite Temples of Beth-shan* (1940), and for the two earlier temples of the fourteenth century (so, cf. Wright, AJA, 1941, p. 485) see Rowe, *The Topography and History of Beth-shan* (1930), pp. 10 ff., where references to his earlier publications will be found.

[36] See Mme. Marquet-Krause, *Syria*, XVI, pp. 329 ff.

[37] Tufnell, Inge and Harding, *Lachish II: the Fosse Temple* (1940), and on the chronology see the review by G. E. Wright, AJA, 1941, pp. 634 f. On the temple see also L. H. Vincent, *Revue Biblique*, 1939, pp. 269 ff.

[38] An archaic rectangular shrine has been found in Stratum XIX; three small temples were found in XV, near the great altar (n. 44) from about 2000 B. C.; a temple of the Ugaritic Dagan type, with three phases, turned up in VIII-VIIA (cir. 1400-1150 B. C.); a shrine was excavated in V. Details must await the appearance of *Megiddo* II; cf. May, JBL, 1942, p. 287.

[39] See provisionally BASOR 14, p. 10, and 53, pp. 13 f. This temple, which appears to resemble the Megiddo temple of the same general age in its plan, dates from not later than about 2000 B. C.

[40] The problem of the "temple" of Balâṭah has been curiously complicated by the lack of harmony among members of the staff of the expedition: one group, headed by E. Sellin, who directed nearly all the work there, insists on the sacred origin of the structure, while G. Welter and his followers deny it with equal vigor. On this controversy see especially H. Thiersch, ZAW, 1932, pp. 76 ff., J. Hempel, ZAW, 1933, pp. 156-169, and K. Galling, *Biblisches Reallexikon,* col. 511. Welter excavated a building on the lower slopes of Gerizim above Balâṭah, which he considered as a temple (*Jahrbuch des Deutschen Archäologischen Instituts, Archäologischer Anzeiger,* 1932, col. 313 f.), but in view of its characteristic Canaanite house-form, with a central court and rooms on all four sides, I have no hesitation in regarding it as a patrician villa of the sixteenth century B. C. At Nuzi in eastern Mesopotamia patrician villas of the fifteenth century were found at some distance from the mound on which the town proper stood.

[41] See the references in note 39, and also Glueck, AASOR, XIV, pp. 45 ff.

[42] See provisionally BASOR 14, p. 6; AASOR VI, p. 59.

[43] See Glueck, *loc. cit.* On the *maṣṣebôth* of Khirbet Iskander see Glueck, AASOR XVIII-XIX, pp. 128 f. Note that all these groups of menhirs in Transjordan may be tentatively dated by pottery to the late third millennium B. C.

[44] Cf. provisionally Engberg in *The Biblical Archaeologist,* III, p. 47.

[45] AASOR XVII, pp. 64-68.

[46] Cf. Chap. V, n. 58.

[47] See *Ausgrabungen in Sendschirli,* I, pl. VI, and IV, pp. 362 ff.; *Carchemish,* II, plate B 25. For a convenient summary with cuts see Galling, *Biblisches Reallexikon,* cols. 205 ff.

[48] Note especially the well executed stela representing Baal (*Syria,* 1933, plate XVI, and Schaeffer, *The Cuneiform Texts of Ras Shamra-Ugarit,* plate XXXII), which must date from about the fifteenth century; the stela of the tree-god (*Syria,* XII, plate VIII, 2, and for the character of the deity see BASOR 50, p. 20), probably from the period 1350-1250; the stela of a goddess with Egyptianizing garb from about the same time (*Syria,* XII, plate VIII, 1); the crudely made stela with a seated god (*Syria,* XVIII, plate XVII, and Schaeffer, *ibid.,* plate XXXI), which I should date stylistically to the latest period of the city's history, about 1200 B. C.

[49] Cf. Gressmann, *Altorientalische Bilder zum Alten Testament,* plate CXXV, No. 307, and the accompanying text on pp. 88 f. To judge from the style and treatment of the relief, I should date this stela early in the first millennium. Unfortunately, no facsimile of the nearly effaced text has been published, so far as I know.

[50] See Alan Rowe, *The Topography and History of Beth-shan,* plates 33 (Makal) 48 and 50 (both belonging to Anath). All three Egyptianize so strongly that there remains some doubt as to whether they would be accepted by the Canaanites as normal cult-objects.

[51] AASOR XVII, pp. 42 f., 117 f. The discovery of the Shechem plaque, also from the sixteenth century (Böhl, *Zeitschrift des Deutschen Palästina-Vereins*, 1938, pp. 1 ff. and plate I), as well as Schaeffer's discovery of two copper statuettes of the seventeenth century with the same garments (*Ugaritica*, pp. 128 ff.), has caused a number of scholars (e. g., Galling, *Biblisches Reallexikon*, col. 459) to explain the serpent as the thick fringe of her robe. In the same picture belongs a copper statuette of a male deity from Qatna (*Syria*, VII, plate LXX), dating probably from about the same time. There can be no doubt that the thick fringe of the robes of the Syrian deities does resemble the "serpent" so closely that the latter might be a kind of boa (though much too slender to have any appreciable value as protection against the cold). After a close study of the Qatna figurine, I am convinced that the supposed fringe is partly, perhaps entirely, detached from the garment, and that it therefore may represent a stylized serpent. The photographs of the statuettes from Ugarit point in the same direction. On the other hand, there can be no doubt whatever, in my mind, that the stela from Tell Beit Mirsim actually represents a large python coiled around the legs of a goddess, just as seen by Père Vincent (at first, before the surface had been thoroughly cleared of lime dust, we had considered it as a tree around which was wound a serpent.) There has evidently been a good deal of reciprocal artistic and iconographic influence between thick fringe and winding serpent.

[52] See Dussaud, *Monuments palestiniens et judaïques* (1912), pp. 1-4. I formerly proposed (BASOR 14, p. 9) a date about the Hyksos period for this remarkable monument, which may possibly represent the god Ḥaurôn, to judge from the headdress (which identifies the figure as a Canaanite deity), and from the Horus-falcon behind it (BASOR 84, p. 9). Glueck's explorations have, however, shown that Moab was no longer occupied by a sedentary population in this period. Moreover, the loin-cloth belongs to an Egyptian type which was worn extensively in the Fourth and Fifth Dynasties both by kings and by commoners (e. g., by Snefru on his Sinai tablet, Petrie, *Researches in Sinai*, fig. 50), so I should now date it between 2500 and 2200 B. C. (allowing for a certain lag, especially in the garb of deities. It may be a little older than the original Balû'ah stela.

[53] See Horsfield and Vincent, *Revue Biblique*, 1932, pp. 417 ff.; E. Drioton, *ibid.*, 1933, pp. 353 ff.; Alt, *Palästinajahrbuch*, 1940, pp. 34 ff. Drioton has proved that the Egyptianizing representation must date from the twelfth (or the eleventh) century B. C. I maintain that the stela has been reused and that it was originally erected (with or without a figured relief) in the late third millennium (JAOS, 1936, p. 129, n. 8). To my arguments (the first three of which have been accepted by Alt, *loc. cit.*), I can now add the fact (suggested in my fifth point) that there is a striking similarity between the weathered characters of this inscription and the characters on the two published inscriptions in the early Byblian syllabic script from the same period. Weill's idea that the script of the Balû'ah stela is Minoan is unacceptable for many reasons, despite Alt's cautious endorsement (*loc. cit.*).

[53a] A very interesting stela with a relief of the god Melcarth has just been

190 ARCHAEOLOGY AND THE RELIGION OF ISRAEL

published by M. Dunand (*Bulletin du Musée de Beyrouth*, III, pp. 65-76). It dates from the reign of Ben-hadad of Syria, in the ninth century B. C.

⁵⁴ See *Year Book of the American Philosophical Society*, 1940 (Philadelphia, 1941), pp. 287 f., and a forthcoming article by S. N. Kramer in the *Proceedings of the American Philosophical Society*, 1942, entitled "Sumerian Literature: a Preliminary Survey of the Oldest Literature in the World."

⁵⁵ See W. von Soden, *Zeitschrift für Assyriologie*, XL, pp. 164 ff. It must be said, however, that A. Poebel does not believe in the separate existence of this dialect but regards it as an artificial literary language, made up of elements from different sources (*Studies in Akkadian Grammar*, 1939, pp. 71 ff.). Since both Landsberger and Poebel accept the fact that these poetic texts are written in a special linguistic form of their own, it seems to me that the difference of opinion is terminological.

⁵⁶ Cf. FSAC 173, with the references there given.

⁵⁷ Cf. W. von Soden, *Zeitschrift der Deutschen Morgenländischen Gesellschaft*, 1935, pp. 164 ff. (following Landsberger).

⁵⁸ On the general development of temple plans see especially W. Andrae, *Das Gotteshaus und die Urformen des Bauens im alten Orient* (1930) and V. Müller, JAOS, 1940, pp. 151-180.

⁵⁹ Babylonian temple plans continued to exercise strong influence on Aramaean religious architecture down at least into the third century A. D., as we know from the excavations at Dura.

⁶⁰ See now especially the fine volume of H. Frankfort, *Cylinder Seals*, London, 1939.

⁶¹ For general orientation see FSAC 133 f. These important documents have happily now received scholarly treatment commensurate with their significance. Kurt Sethe, the foremost Egyptian philologist of the past generation, published an exceedingly painstaking critical edition of the text in his monumental work, *Die altägyptischen Pyramidentexte*, I-IV, 1908-1922. Since his death in 1934 at least four volumes of his translation and commentary, covering spells 213-506, three-fourths of what he had left behind him in completed form, have been published by J. J. Augustin, Glueckstadt and Hamburg (no date). There is no good translation of these documents available in compact form, though the late J. H. Breasted utilized them to great advantage in his works, *The Development of Religion and Thought in Ancient Egypt* (1912), *The Dawn of Conscience* (1933).

⁶² Spells 273-4. The latest and best interpretation of this text is Sethe's (cf. note 61); a good translation may be found in Erman, *Die Literatur der Aegypter* (1923), pp. 30 ff. (translated by A. M. Blackman into English, *The Literature of the Ancient Egyptians*, London, 1927).

⁶³ Erman, *Die Religion der Aegypter* (1934), p. 209.

⁶⁴ A scientific edition of these texts, based on exhaustive collation of hundreds of sarcophagi from the Middle Empire, has been undertaken by the Oriental Institute of Chicago, under the direction of A. de Buck and Alan Gardiner. Two volumes (1935-1938) have so far appeared.

⁶⁵ There are a number of sumptuous publications of outstanding papyrus

manuscripts of the Book of the Dead, as well as several complete translations, all quite antiquated in detail. A good beginning along more scientific lines is H. Grapow's critical edition and commentary of selected chapters of the collection: *Urkunden des Aegyptischen Altertums*, V, *Religiöse Urkunden*, I-III (1915-1917), with accompanying translation of these chapters into German.

⁶⁶ The religious poems and litanies of the Bremner-Rhind Papyrus (fourth century B. C.) have now been competently translated, on the basis of the latest knowledge, by R. O. Faulkner, in *Journal of Egyptian Archaeology*, 1936-38, where the Songs of Isis and Nephthys, the Ritual of Bringing in Sokar, the Book of Overthrowing Apophis, etc., are all studied, with references to other comparable literature.

⁶⁷ Sethe, *Dramatische Texte zur altägyptischen Mysterienspielen*, 1928. The Ramesseum papyrus dates from about the 18th century B. C., but the Shabako stone, written about 700 B. C., is a copy of an older document from the Pyramid Age.

⁶⁸ The festal calendar from Medînet Habu has been recorded with exemplary precision by the expedition of the Oriental Institute, under the direction of H. H. Nelson, and has been published as Vol. III of the Medînet Habu publication (1934). No detailed translation or study of this text, the longest hieroglyphic inscription from ancient Egypt, or of its congeners, has yet been made. The Papyrus Harris, which is the longest extant papyrus roll, has now been conveniently and accurately transcribed from hieratic into hieroglyphics by W. Erichsen, *Bibliotheca Aegyptiaca*, V (Brussels, 1933), and this has been followed by a more intensive study of the priceless document of the twelfth century, e. g., by H. D. Schaedel, *Die Listen des grossen Papyrus Harris* (1936).

⁶⁹ These texts will all be found translated in Erman, *Die Literatur der Aegypter* (1923), with English translation by Blackman (1927). They have been admirably discussed by Breasted, *Dawn of Conscience, passim*; cf. also FSAC 135 ff.

⁷⁰ The Proverbs of Amenemope were not published until 1923; the most recent independent translation is that of H. Ranke, in Gressmann's *Altorientalische Texte zum Alten Testament* (1926), pp. 38-46. This work bears so striking a resemblance to chapters of Proverbs that literary dependence of the latter is certain. The Proverbs of Ani survive only in a very corrupt manuscript of about the ninth century, but they may go back several centuries in their original form; the latest translation of the entire text, as far as it is intelligible, is given by Erman (*op. cit.*, pp. 294 ff.) and Blackman.

⁷¹ On the latest interpretations of this text cf. FSAC 137 f.

⁷² For the Thinite and Memphite periods, which cover most of the third millennium, we now have admirable treatments by G. A. Reisner, *The Development of the Egyptian Tomb down to the Accession of Cheops* (1936) and *A History of the Giza Necropolis*, Vol. I. The literature on the following periods is too vast to be summarized briefly.

⁷³ G. Lefebvre, *Le tombeau de Petosiris*, 1923-24.

⁷⁴ See now the admirable survey of the present state of our knowledge by J. Friedrich, *Entzifferungsgeschichte der hethitischen Hieroglyphenschrift*, Stuttgart, 1939.

[75] On their religious contents see provisionally the excellent synopsis by A. Goetze in his book *Kleinasien* (1933) in the *Kulturgeschichte des Alten Orients* (*Handbuch der Altertumswissenschaft*, III, 1, 3), and for a much more detailed, though less competent, treatment see G. Furlani, *La religione degli Hittiti* (1936).

[76] See H. L. Ginsberg, *Orientalia*, 1939, pp. 317 ff.; A. Goetze, JBL, 1941, pp. 353 ff.

[77] On the Hurrians in Western Asia see especially A. Goetze, *Hethiter, Churriter und Assyrer* (Oslo, 1936), pp. 79 ff.; for a brief statement of the situation as I then saw it, see my sketch in *From the Pyramids to Paul* (*G. L. Robinson Anniversary Volume*, New York, 1935), pp. 9-26.

[78] All the older interpretations by Ramsay and Sayce, etc., possess only historical interest at present. The only excavated site which can be called "cultic" without reservation is at Yazilikaya near Boghazköy, where excavations have been undertaken by K. Bittel. Naturally the excavations at such sites as Carchemish and Alalakh in Syria throw light on Hittite religion as well as on Syrian. The cultural background of the remarkable open-air sanctuary on the summit of Jebelet el-Beida in northern Mesopotamia, which dates from the early third millennium, is still uncertain; cf. Max von Oppenheim, *Der Tell Halaf* (1931), pp. 199-220. On current progress in the interpretation of the hieroglyphic monuments see above, n. 74.

[79] This will be clearer after Maria Höfner, a pupil of the foremost South-Arabian philologist of our day, N. Rhodokanakis, has published her studies on the verbal system of the different dialects, on which she read a paper at the International Congress of Orientalists at Brussels in 1938.

[80] See especially BASOR 73, pp. 3-9.

[81] Winnett, *A Study of the Lihyanite and Thamudic Inscriptions* (Toronto, 1937), and his remarks in *The Moslem World*, April, 1940, p. 4, n. 8. For my own views see BASOR 66, pp. 30 f.; they are intermediate between Winnett's first position and that of W. W. Tarn.

[82] For the best and latest collection of the divine names in the South-Arabian inscriptions see G. Ryckmans, *Les noms propres sud-sémitiques*, I (1934), pp. 1-35. This repertory also includes all divine names so far identified in the early North-Arabian inscriptions, though great caution must be exercised in utilizing the latter. The reconstructions of South-Arabian religion by Hommel and Nielsen require drastic critical revision before they can be safely employed by historians of religion.

[83] For the still unintelligible (and nearly all extremely brief) inscriptions and graffiti in an early form of this script from the Late Bronze see especially J. F. Daniel, AJA, 1941, pp. 249-282.

[84] See especially Martin P. Nilsson, *The Minoan-Mycenaean Religion and its Survival in Greek Religion* (1927), *Homer and Mycenae* (1933). Hurrian and Hittite religion formed in turn a bridge between the Semitic world and the Aegean, reflecting as many points of contact with the latter as with the former, though it must be said that the parallels with Aegean religion seem more fundamental.

[85] See provisionally C. W. Blegen, AJA, 1939, pp. 564 ff.

[86] On behalf of the Negebite hypothesis see especially Virolleaud, *La légende de Keret* (1936), pp. 15-33; Dussaud, *Les découvertes de Ras Shamra* (1937), pp. 55 ff., 96 ff. Both are surpassed by R. Weill, whose long papers reach the most fantastic conclusions, with scarcely a shred of serious criticism: *Journal Asiatique*, 1937 (published in 1939), pp. 1-56; *Revue des Etudes sémitiques*, 1937, pp. 145-206. Among the most ardent followers of this school was T. H. Gaster, but he has now disavowed its hypotheses.

[87] Cf. JPOS, 1934, pp. 37 ff.; BASOR 63, pp. 27 ff., 32; BASOR 71, pp. 35 ff.

[88] Among others, see R. de Vaux, *Revue Biblique*, 1937, especially pp. 535 ff.; A. Bea, *Biblica*, 1938, pp. 437 ff.; J. Pedersen, *Berytus*, VI (1941), pp. 63, 105, *passim*.

[89] E. g., Dussaud, *Revue de l'Histoire des Religions*, CV (1932), pp. 285 ff., and now T. H. Gaster, *Mélanges Dussaud*, II (1939), pp. 577 ff.

[90] Cf. BASOR 83, pp. 30-36; J. J. Clère, *Mélanges Dussaud*, II, pp. 829 ff.

[91] Cf. especially my discussion, JBL, 1918, pp. 120 ff. Subsequent research (mostly still unpublished) has further extended the list of comparative mythological parallels from other sources.

[92] Cf. JPOS I, pp. 51 ff., APB 149 ff., FSAC 35 ff.

[93] First shown by B. Landsberger; cf. JBL, 1924, p. 370.

[94] Bliss and Macalister, *Excavations in Palestine*, pp. 31 ff.; the best treatment from the cultic point of view has been given by L. H. Vincent, *Canaan*, pp. 103 ff. However, the building in question closely resembles contemporary private houses at Tell Beit Mirsim—or rather it represents two adjacent houses with the partition wall removed. The peculiar relation of the side walls to one another makes it obvious that there were originally two houses, not one. The average size of each house was then comparable to the average size of a Tell Beit Mirsim house in stratum A (ninth-sixth century B. C.). Moreover, the stone pillars at Tell eṣ-Ṣâfi are almost identical in measurements and disposition with similar ones at Tell Beit Mirsim (see AASOR XXI/II, pp. 50-55, for details; my hesitation on p. 54 about the comparison with Tell eṣ-Ṣâfi probably overshot the mark, since the treatment of the pottery evidence by the two excavators [p. 35] is confused, and the floor-level of the high place was only 16 or 17 feet from the surface of the ground).

[95] On behalf of this theory see Thiersch, ZAW, 1932, pp. 73 ff.

[96] See Watzinger, *Denkmäler*, I, pp. 101 f.; Grant and Wright, *Ain Shems* V, pp. 68 f.; AASOR XXI/II, pp. 54 f.; McCown, BASOR 98, pp. 2-15.

[97] *The Foundations of Bible History* (1931), p. 383.

[98] R. D. Barnett, *Iraq*, II (1935), pp. 198 ff. With Barnett's archaeological and historical treatment of this material I am in full accord, but with regard to his mythological comparisons I am very skeptical.

[99] For the development of this art and for its repertoire see especially Poulsen, *Der Orient und die frühgriechische Kunst* (1912), which is antiquated in detail but still fundamental; Watzinger in Walter Otto, *Handbuch der Archäologie* (1938), pp. 805-812, a very valuable sketch; Gordon Loud, *The Megiddo*

Ivories (1939); Crowfoot and Sukenik, *Early Ivories from Samaria* (1938); also my discussion of the Phoenician ivories in the *Leland Volume*, pp. 46 ff.

[100] On this subject from a different point of view cf. Beatrice L. Goff, JBL, 1939, pp. 157 ff.

NOTES TO CHAPTER III

[1] On this subject see the detailed treatment in my paper " The Role of the Canaanites in the History of Civilization" in *Studies in the History of Culture* (*Waldo Gifford Leland Volume*, Menasha, 1942), pp. 11-50.

[2] This fact is established by the existence of numerous specifically Northwest-Semitic place-names attached to some of the earliest settlements in Palestine (e. g., Jericho, Beth-yerah, Megiddo), by the names of Palestinian towns in the Fifth Dynasty (JPOS, 1935, p. 215) and by the Palestinian words borrowed by the Egyptians before the Pyramid Age (JPOS, 1935, pp. 212 f.).

[3] This fact has remained unrecognized and the political situation has, accordingly, been completely misunderstood by all historians; for detailed discussion see my paper quoted above, n. 1.

[4] BASOR 83, pp. 14 ff.; cf. my fuller discussion in the *Leland Volume*, pp. 33 ff.

[5] FSAC 243, 334; JBL, 1941, pp. 209 f.

[6] R. de Vaux, *Revue Biblique*, 1939, p. 597; cf. JBL, 1940, p. 106.

[7] The precise meaning is not, after all, as I have given it since 1932 (see most recently JBL, 1940, p. 106), but as proposed by J. A. Montgomery as early as 1933 (JAOS, LIII, 111). We may vocalize approximately:

'ima 'El mabbikê naharêma   qirba 'ap(i)qê tihâm(a)têma

That *mabbiku*, " source," is plural in this verse seems to be required by the metre. The expression in the first hemistich cannot be separated from Sumerian *id-ka-min-na*, Accadian *pî nârâti*, " the source of the two rivers," with which I have dealt at length AJSL, XXXV, 1919, pp. 161-195. A good deal of confirmatory material has since been discovered; on the Babylonian symbolism see especially Mrs. E. D. Van Buren, *The Flowing Vase and the God with Streams* (1933); my interpretation of the Sumerian *ka* and *kun* of canals (p. 169, n. 2) has, e. g., been confirmed from entirely different evidence by A. Poebel, *Zeitschrift für Assyriologie*, XXXIX, pp. 160 f. The word *mabbiku* has been tentatively combined with the Semitic name of Bambyce-Hierapolis in Syria by J. A. Montgomery (*loc. cit.*). On this name see Honigmann in Pauly-Wissowa, *Suppl.-Band* IV (1924), cols. 733 f., and on its etymology see Nöldeke, *Nachr. Gött. Ges. Wiss.*, 1876, pp. 5-8; it was originally *Mabbigu*, " Fountain," from Syriac *nbg*, " to gush forth," a partial assimilation of Heb.-Can. *nbk* with the same meaning. With change of the short *i* to short *u* or *o* after the labial, this became later Aramaic *Manbug* or *Mabbog*, Greek *Manbog-* or *Bambukê*, Arab. *Mambij*. The Assyrian *Nappigi* or *Nampigi* represents a genuine Accadian form of the name, dissimilated according to Barth's law from an original *Mappigu* or *Mabbigu*. It is safe to suppose that the local myth (told by Lucian in *De dea Syria*, § 13), according to which a fissure under the temple of

Atargatis represented the crevice through which the water of the Great Flood was drained off, is somehow based on an aetiological interpretation of the name of the town, perhaps first told after the fountain had run dry, leaving only a gaping fissure in the earth. In any case, the annual ceremony in which water was brought from the sea and poured into this fissure, shows that some connection was thought to exist between the latter and the subterranean source of fertility-bringing fresh water in the Great Deep.

[8] Cf. especially my discussion, AJSL XXXIX, pp. 15 ff.

[9] Whether Ba'al-shamêm is intended by "Uranus" is not yet clear; on this deity see especially Eissfeldt, ZAW, 1939, pp. 1 ff.

[10] In view of Heb. *šáhar*, "dawn," which occurs frequently in the Bible, and Aram. *šahrâ*, Arab. *sáhar*, Accad. *šêru*, as well as of the Canaanite mythological figure Helel ben Shahar in Isa. 14: 12, there can be no reasonable doubt about the original meaning of the first name, which corresponds then roughly to Greek *Eos* and Latin *Aurora*. In this case the second name can scarcely be separated from Accadian *šalam šamši*, "sunset."

[11] There can be no reasonable doubt that *Al'iyân(u)* is an abbreviation of the full formula, *'al'iyu qurâdima qâriyêya ba'arși malhámati*, "I prevail over the heroes who meet me in the land of battle," found several times in the Baal Epic; see especially my remarks, BASOR 70, p. 19, on V AB, C, lines 10-12 (Virolleaud, *La déesse 'Anat*, p. 31), also FSAC 198 and 325, n. 41. It must be remembered that the longer formula regularly appears in strict parallelism with the shorter name, and that *ânu* or *anu* (with short *a*) was one of the commonest endings of abbreviated names (hypocoristica) in Ugaritic, as I showed in a paper presented before the Society of Biblical Literature, Dec. 31, 1941.

[12] On Canaanite *Zabûlu ba'lu 'arși* and Baal-zebul see especially my remarks, JPOS, 1932, pp. 191 f., 1936, pp. 17 f.

[13] See AJSL XLI, pp. 73 ff., 283 ff., XLIII, pp. 233 ff.

[14] Since my proposed explanation of the name *'Anat* as meaning originally "destiny, providence" (AJSL XLI, 1925, pp. 94 ff.), I have seen that the Accadian word *ettu*, "sign, omen," cannot be separated from it (cf. FSAC 339 f., n. 51). Heb. *'et*, Aram. *'enet* (in *ke'enet* = Heb. *ka-'et*), "sign (of the heavens), time, destiny" (Psalms 31: 16 [15], "My destiny [*'ittôt*] is in Thy hands") is either originally identical with *'anatu-ettu* or is a parallel word from the same stem. Cf. also below, Chap. V. The name *'Anat* then probably meant originally "sign, indication of purpose, active will," and was originally applied to the personified or hypostatized will of Baal (BASOR 84, p. 15). It is thus parallel to the Canaanite and Israelite conception of the *panîm* of Baal or Yahweh as the active presence or power of the deity (FSAC 228). It is still uncertain whether there was a male counterpart 'An, though recently published personal names from Mari support the existence of the latter.

[15] *Qâniyatu 'elîma* (cf. H. Bauer, ZAW, 1933, pp. 89 f.).

[16] See my remarks as quoted by Burrows, BASOR 77, pp. 6 f. (*bâmatu* has a long vowel in the first syllable, for which cf. Chap. IV, n. 24, and may thus be derived from a lost stem *bwm* related to *wbm*).

[17] For this explanation of the name *Qdš* see AASOR XVII, p. 69, n. 18; *Mélanges Dussaud*, I, p. 118, n. 2 (with which cf. BASOR 78, pp. 26 f., n. 21, where further parallels are adduced). However, I overlooked the convincing evidence for this thesis which is found in Keret, lines 197 f., where we read *laqudši 'Atir(a)ti Ṣurrîma*, literally, "to the holiness of Asherah of the Tyrians" (BASOR 94, p. 30, n. 4). *Qdš* often equals Asherah in Dan'el and Keret.

[18] *Mélanges Dussaud*, I, pp. 114 ff.

[19] Virolleaud, *Le déesse 'Anat*, pp. 13 ff., with a revised translation by J. Aistleitner, ZAW, 1939, pp. 206 ff.

[20] Not "in the valley" with Virolleaud and Aistleitner, but "mightily," as pointed out by Gordon (*Ugaritic Grammar*, p. 105, s. v. *'mq*) and Gaster.

[21] For the meaning of these lines see FSAC 325, n. 45.

[22] See FSAC 198 f., and above, n. 11.

[23] Cf. above, n. 17.

[24] On this deity and his name see especially my discussion in *Oriental Studies* (*Paul Haupt Anniversary Volume*, 1926), pp. 146 ff., and BASOR 84, pp. 11 f.

[25] See *Archiv für Orientforschung*, VII, pp. 164 ff. Though attempts to find a reference to Eshmûn in the tablets of Ugarit have been made, they are quite unsatisfactory and my explanation of the name as a comparatively late corruption of earlier Phoenician **Ša(l)mûn* (for Can. *Šulmân*) remains highly probable. From the divine name *'šmn* are derived Heb. *'ešmannîm*, "good health," and Graeco-Phoen. (**asir-*)*ismunim*, "(herb of) good health" (Dioscorides).

[26] Eshmûn was also identified with Melcarth as the composite deity Eshmûn-Melcarth (cf. Baudissin, *Adonis und Esmun*, pp. 275 ff.). Melcarth was also, primarily, lord of the underworld; see n. 29 and BASOR 87, pp. 28 f.

[27] On the god Mukal and his congeners see now BASOR 90, pp. 33 f. Here it is necessary to warn students against taking such ancient equations too seriously and following them to their logical conclusion, since it would be easy to make out a specious case for the identification of every deity with every other by following such a chain of identifications. A drastic example of the absurdities to which application of Aristotelian logic to prelogical data will inevitably lead, is Hugo Radau's book, *Bel, the Christ of Ancient Times* (Chicago, 1903).

[28] On this god see AJSL LIII (1936), pp. 1-2; BASOR 84, pp. 7-12.

[29] Cf. AJSL LIII, 11. My contention that the appellation "king of the city" has nothing primarily to do with Tyre, but refers to the underworld in general, is now confirmed by Dunand's publication of an Aramaic stela of Ben-hadad king of Damascus, dating from the middle of the eighth century, dedicated to Melcarth (see Chap. II, n. 53a). While the stela was found in a Roman site north of Aleppo, there can be little doubt that it was brought there from a site further south. It is scarcely credible that an Aramaean king of Syria in the ninth century would set up a votive stela to the city-god of Tyre in a region so far away from Tyre and would inscribe it in Aramaic.

[30] On this god and his name see especially G. Hoffmann, *Zeitschrift für Assyriologie*, II (1896); H. L. Ginsberg, BASOR 72, p. 13, and *Orientalia*, IX (1940), pp. 39 ff.; Albright, JAOS, 1940, pp. 296 f. Hoffmann's combinations, which seemed rather adventurous at the time, have been confirmed

almost throughout. For other references see R. Dussaud, *Les découvertes de Ras Shamra et l'Ancien Testament* (1937), pp. 72 ff.

[31] See a forthcoming article on "The Creation of the Composite Bow in Canaanite Mythology" by Albright and Mendenhall in JNES, 1942. The materials from which a composite bow is made (hard wood, horn, sinew) are listed in the hitherto unintelligible passage II D, 6, lines 20-25.

[32] See Hoffmann, *loc. cit.*, Albright, *loc. cit.*, on Kôshar.

[33] See J. A. Wilson in Gordon Loud, *The Megiddo Ivories* (1939), pp. 12 f., where the hieroglyphic text is exceedingly well treated. I expect to deal with it elsewhere; cf. provisionally below, Chap. IV, n. 97.

[34] See BASOR 70, p. 22; Dussaud, *Revue de l'Histoire des Religions*, CXVIII (1938), pp. 155 f.; Ginsberg, *Orientalia*, 1940, pp. 42 ff.

[35] On the Hurrian elements see especially Ginsberg, *Orientalia*, 1939, pp. 317-327; Goetze, JBL, 1941, pp. 353-374. It may be particularly emphasized that the parallelism of members which is so characteristic of Semitic poetry, especially in Ugaritic, appears rarely in the hymn to Nikkal.

[36] On his popularity in very early times see already AASOR VI, p. 74. Many Northwest-Semitic personal names formed with *Yaraḥ* (whence *Eraḥ*) are mentioned in cuneiform tablets of the early second millennium; cf. the list given by Theo Bauer, *Die Ostkanaanäer* (1926), p. 76. I know of no certain occurrences of the name in composition after the middle of the second millennium, though some fossilized examples, no longer understood by their bearers, are likely to have persisted for several centuries.

[37] See JPOS, 1932, p. 195, n. 28, for a possible etymology.

[38] Published by Virolleaud as IV AB in *Syria* XVII (1936), pp. 150-175. The best revised translation is that of H. L. Ginsberg, *Orientalia*, 1938, pp. 1-11.

[39] A drastic account of the rape of Anath by Baal is preserved in an Egyptian magical text from about the thirteenth century B. C., recently published by Alan Gardiner, *Hieratic Papyri in the British Museum, Third Series*, Vol. I (1935), pp. 61 ff. The Semitic origin of the myth is illustrated by the fact that the few lines of it which are preserved are full of Semitic words, a fact not noted by Gardiner. Anath bathes on the shore of the sea (written syllabically *ḥa-pú*, according to my system of transcription, that is, Ugaritic *ḥâpu*, later Hebrew *ḥôf*), at an unknown place named Hamkat. Then we read that Seth (i. e., Baal) ". . . her arse, leaping her as the sacred ram of Amun leaps, forcing her ('*mq*, on the meaning of which see above, n. 20) as a . . . forces . . ." That rape and not voluntary submission is involved, is clear from a later passage in the same text which states that Seth "copulated (with Anath) in fire, and deflowered her with a chisel." There may be a direct connection between the two myths, since the scene of Anath's meeting with Baal in the Ugaritic myth is "on the bank ('*aḥ* = Accad. *aḥu*, "river-bank, sea-shore," according to Virolleaud) of *Šmk*," or "in the alluvial plain ('*aḥ* = Heb. *'aḥū*, with Ginsberg) of *Šmk*." The similarity between the names *Hmkt* and *Šmk* is at all events quite remarkable and may point to a corruption in the Canaanite transmission of the story. It must be remembered that we

have now several cases where we find a myth or part of a Canaanite myth transmitted through Egyptian as well as through Ugaritic channels; cf. JPOS, pp.
18 f.

⁴⁰ See Virolleaud, *Syria* XVI, pp. 247-266. For revised translations see
especially Ginsberg, JPOS, 1936, pp. 138 ff.; Montgomery, JAOS, 1936, pp.
226 ff.; Gaster, *Acta Orientalia,* XVI, pp. 41 ff.

⁴¹ Published by Virolleaud as I AB, *Syria,* XII, pp. 193-224, and XV, pp.
226-243. I AB has been translated subsequently in whole or in part by a number of scholars, including the reviewer; the best treatment is by Ginsberg,
Orientalia, 1936, pp. 193 ff.

⁴² Cf. FSAC 176 f., with my note. The changes made here are insignificant,
affecting only minor points.

⁴³ The best commentary on this passage is Sir James Frazer's *Adonis, Attis
and Osiris* (third edition, 1914). On details see especially Dussaud, *Revue de
l'Histoire des Religions,* CIV (1931), pp. 388 ff.

⁴⁴ Published by Virolleaud as II AB, *Syria,* XIII, pp. 113-163. For a revised
translation see my preliminary essay, JPOS, 1934, pp. 101-132, and Ginsberg,
Kitvê Ugarit (1936), pp. 47 ff.; Cassuto, *Orientalia,* 1938, pp. 265-290, offers
further improvements in the first part of the text.

⁴⁵ A reason for Baal's refusal to have windows in his abode has been most
ingeniously suggested by Cassuto, *ibid.,* pp. 285 f. Cassuto quotes Jer: 9: 20
(21), " Death (*Mawet* = Ugar. *Môt*) hath come up through our windows, hath
entered into our palaces," to show that windows were considered as suitable
entrances for Death. This curious idea was doubtless originally based on occa-
sional observation that the night air can be dangerous in pulmonary diseases,
but it could easily be transferred to dislike of architectural innovations, as windows were undoubtedly at one time.

⁴⁶ It must be confessed that we cannot be sure about the reading *yômu,*
" day," first proposed by Montgomery, and that Virolleaud's *yênu,* " wine," is
also possible, though in my opinion very unlikely.

⁴⁷ On the meaning of this appellation see BASOR 83, p. 41, n. 19, and 85,
p. 14, n. 2. To H. L. Ginsberg Gapnu and Ugaru were two gods (BASOR 95)

⁴⁸ The passage is difficult, as will be seen by consulting previous treatments
of II AB, viii: 1 ff. New is my suggestion that these two mountains with non-
Semitic names stand on the boundary between the upper and the nether worlds
and that the enigmatic word *ǧsr* is connected with Arab. *ǧdr,* which I should
tentatively equate with Heb. *'ṣr* and Accadian *eṣêru,* whence *uṣurtu,* " outline,
limit," etc. Line 4 may then be rendered provisionally, " to the two mounds at
the edge of the underworld."

⁴⁹ Almost exactly the same expression is used in the same way in Psalm
88: 5 (4), " I was counted with those who go down to the Pit," employing the
same verb *yarad.* This passage contains a number of equally striking Canaanite
reminiscences, including Canaanite *bêtu ḫuptati 'arṣi,* " guest-house (?) of the
underworld," corresponding to the corrupt *bmtym ḥpšy* of the Massoretic
Hebrew text of the following verse.

⁵⁰ See my discussion, BASOR 83, pp. 39 ff., with Ginsberg's remarks, BASOR

84, pp. 12 ff., and my rejoinder, pp. 14 ff. Cassuto has happily compared Hab. 2: 5, where the throat of Sheol is in parallelism with Death (*Mawet*).

[51] For the most recent treatment, with references, see my article, BASOR 84, pp. 16 f. For completeness it may be noted that Dussaud (*Revue de l'Histoire des Religions*, CXVIII, pp. 143 f., and Aistleitner, ZAW, 1939, p. 198, have also recently translated this passage. In general our renderings are in agreement.

[52] For the text see Virolleaud, *Syria*, XVI, pp. 29-45. The best translation is that of Ginsberg, JPOS, 1935, pp. 327-333; cf. also my observations, JPOS, 1936, pp. 17-20, which are concerned mainly with comparative material from other sources.

[53] For these texts see Virolleaud, *La légende phénicienne de Danel, La légende de Keret* (both 1936). The Keret tablet has been most recently treated, with full synopsis of its contents, by J. Pedersen, *Berytus*, VI (1941), pp. 63-104, and especially by H. L. Ginsberg, *The Legend of King Keret* (BASOR, *Suppl. Stud.*, 2/3, 1946), where all three tablets are included. For the latest synopsis of the Dan'el or Aqhat Epic, as far as preserved, see Gordon, *The Living Past* (1941), pp. 149 ff. For these texts see also BASOR 63, pp. 23 ff.; 71, pp. 35 ff.; 72, pp. 13 ff.; 94, pp. 30 ff.; 97, pp. 3 ff.; 98, pp. 15 ff.

[54] On this see S. Gsell, *L'histoire ancienne de l'Afrique du Nord*, III, pp. 405-10; L. Poinssot and R. Lantier, *Revue de l'Histoire des Religions*, 1923, pp. 32-68.

[55] Cf. Eissfeldt, *Ras Schamra und Sanchunjaton* (1939), pp. 69 f.

[56] Cf. provisionally my remarks, AASOR XVII (1938), p. 68.

NOTES TO CHAPTER IV

[1] FSAC 193 ff., 210 ff. For more detailed discussion of the course of the Conquest see my articles, BASOR 58 (1935), pp. 10-18; 74 (1939), pp. 11-23. For criticism of some of my positions, with penetrating analysis of the ecological and territorial problems involved see Alt, *Palästinajahrbuch*, 1939, pp. 8-63.

[2] Against my views see the detailed criticism to be published by T. J. Meek in JBL under the title, "Monotheism and the Religion of Israel." Meek has generously placed a copy of this forthcoming article at my disposal, a courtesy for which I am greatly indebted to him. He has tried to be fair and has provided an excellent background for clarification of my published views, which have not always been clearly understood by my readers. However, I do not regard any of his criticisms as valid, except in a few non-essential points.

[3] FSAC 203 ff.

[4] For the Sleib see especially Werner Pieper, *Le Monde Orientale*, 1923, pp. 1-75, and the numerous references in the indices of Musil's *Arabia Deserta*, p. 624 b, and *The Manners and Customs of the Rwala Bedouins*, p. 708 a. There is an excellent parallel in India, where the Doma of Hunza "are, in a casteless Mohammedan territory, a caste of iron-workers and musicians of low social status," as noted by Emeneau, *Language*, 1940, p. 356.

[5] Of course, the Kenites may have been much more prosperous in comparison than the Sleib, who are notoriously poor and are despised by their Arab neighbors. The gypsies are sharply distinguished from the Arabs by their physical type and especially by their language, which is a Hindu dialect.

[6] On Gen. 4: 19-22 see especially S. Mowinckel, *Avhandlinger utgitt av Det Norske Videnskaps-Akademi i Oslo, Hist.-Filos. Klasse,* 1937, No. 2, pp. 46 f., 81 f., together with my observations JBL, 1939, p. 96. There is, however, no justification for the theory of Eduard Meyer, accepted by Mowinckel, that the three sons of Lamech reflect " the three ' classes ' of the desert tribes."

[7] For the scene see Newberry, *Beni-Hasan,* I, pl. 31 and Gressmann, *Altorientalische Bilder zum Alten Testament* (1927), pl. XXI. The two objects which I identify as portable bellows have remained enigmatic until now, so a few indications may be given; a full discussion will be published elsewhere. For Egyptian representations of bellows from the New Empire (fifteenth century B. C. onward) see Wreszinski, *Atlas zur altägyptischen Kulturgeschichte,* I, plates 82, 153, 316. On the bellows in antiquity see also Daremberg et Saglio, IV, 1227, s. v. *follis;* Ebert, *Lexikon der Vorgeschichte,* II, p. 26 a, s. v. *Blasebalg.* For the bellows among the Canaanites about the middle of the second millennium note especially the fact that the god Hîyân is mentioned as using *mpḫm,* "bellows," in the Baal Epic of Ugarit. The Beni-Ḥasan objects are clearly made of skin (presumably goat-skin as in a fifth-century example from Greece), with two rigid pieces and an aperture for air (only one is shown, since only one side of the bellows is visible).—It must be emphasized that the Egyptians of the nineteenth century were very familiar with Asiatics, as we may infer from the certain fact that Palestine, Phoenicia and southern Syria formed part of the Egyptian Empire during the entire Twelfth Dynasty (see now BASOR 81, pp. 16-21, 83, pp. 30-36, and J. A. Wilson, AJSL, 1941, pp. 225-236). Nor may we forget the known fact that the Semites overran northern Egypt in the First Intermediate Period (about the 21st century B. C.). Unless the group portrayed at Beni-Hasan was very unusual in character there was, accordingly, no conceivable reason for devoting such particular attention to it.

[8] The problem of the Apiru is still very obscure; cf. FSAC 182 f.; A. Alt, *Palästinajahrbuch,* 1939, pp. 56-63; J. Lewy, *Hebrew Union College Annual,* XIV (1939), pp. 587-623; XV, pp. 46-58. However, it must be said that *'Ibrî,* " Hebrew," must still probably be derived from *'Apiru;* for linguistic parallels cf. APB 206 f., BASOR 77, pp. 32 f., and below, n. 43. If the equation is correct, it follows that the ancestral Hebrews were equally anomalous in socio-economic status: they were intruders in every land where they are attested by documentary evidence; they were neither sedentary nor nomadic; they were sometimes condottieri and were often employed as forced laborers, e. g., in Egypt (on the Apiru there cf. the admirable paper of J. A. Wilson, AJSL XLIX, 1935, pp. 275-280). To treat the term as applying primarily to travelling tinkers, etc., would be quite unwarranted on the basis of our present evidence.

[9] In one passage they are called '*rbrb*, in the other '*spsp* (disregarding the somewhat questionable transmitted vocalization in each case). Both terms are reduplicated collectives of the type discussed by Gesenius-Kautzsch, *Hebräische Grammatik* [28th ed.], pp. 244 f.), derived from verbs meaning, respectively, " to change, mix," and " to gather."

[10] Our knowledge of this situation is due entirely to the researches of Nelson Glueck, on which cf. briefly FSAC 30-32 and Glueck, *The Other Side of the Jordan*, 1940, pp. 114-157, with the references there given. For an extension of his investigation to the region between the Jabbok and the Yarmuk see BASOR 86, pp. 14 ff. and his forthcoming detailed report in AASOR.

[11] On the Ghawârneh and the Budûl see my observations BASOR 14, p. 4, and 57, p. 19, n. 3, together with the references there given. The Ghawârneh are mainly of negro ancestry and the Budûl appear to be of gypsy origin—or at least to represent an older group of the same general character.

[12] This exaltation of the nomad is essentially different from the exaltation of the nomadic ideal which we find in Israel during the eighth and seventh centuries, on which cf. especially J. W. Flight, JBL XLII, pp. 158-226 and my brief sketch in Lovejoy and Boas, *A Documentary History of Primitivism*, I (1935), pp. 429-31. The former is based principally on family pride and is associated with the continued vogue of classical literature exalting the nomad's *muruwwah*, " manly valor," and parallel qualities, while the latter is essentially a method of escape from the evils of sedentary society.

[13] On this subject see especially M. Noth, *Das System der Zwölf Stämme Israels* (1930), pp. 3-28, though I cannot agree with him in many details; e. g., his impression that the list of the twelve spies in Nüm. 13: 4-16 is " very late " (sehr jung, p. 19) is contradicted by the consistent archaism of the names, where they are fully preserved. Even the hypocoristica (abbreviated names) show archaic forms, as in the numerous names ending in *y*, which are often paralleled among the Ugaritic personal names of the fourteenth century B. C. which are now known to us. I regard the list in question as very ancient and important, though I should not care to insist that it referred originally to the spies.

[14] See Noth, *op. cit.*, pp. 39-60.

[15] Cf. APB 159 ff., FSAC 215.

[16] See especially H. Kjaer, JPOS, 1930, pp. 87-174, and *I det Hellige Land* (Copenhagen, 1931), together with my remarks, APB 57 f.

[17] BASOR 68, p. 25, especially n. 11. This ware and its chronological significance will be fully dealt with in my forthcoming publication of the excavations at Bethel.

[18] The genealogy of Abiathar, as indicated in II Sam. 8: 17, etc. (see the commentators and *Encyclopaedia Biblica*, I, col. 13 on the passage), I Sam. 14: 3; 4: 11, 19 ff., etc., gives the following scheme; the average length of a royal or noble generation in the ancient Near East is known to have been about 25 years and about 20 years when primogeniture was the rule (with maximal variation cir. 15-28 years):

Eli (short for a name like *Yeḥaw'elî* of Samaria)   c. 1100(+)-1050
|
Phinehas II   c. 1080-1050
|
Ahitub (born before fall of Shiloh)   c. 1060
|
Ahiah (short for Ahimelech, as he is usually called)   c. 1040-1010
|
Abiathar (a youth under David and still alive under Solomon) c. 1020-950

[19] Cf. J. Morgenstern, JAOS, 1916, pp. 324 ff.

[20] Cf. G. Dossin, *Mélanges syriens offerts a M. R. Dussaud*, II (1939), p. 986, and *Revue d'Assyriologie*, XXXVI, p. 52.

[21] See my remarks, JPOS, 1935, p. 227, n. 107, and further observations in my paper in the *Leland Volume*, p. 22.

[22] See above, Chapter III.

[23] See JPOS, 1934, p. 120, n. 86, and Gordon, *Ugaritic Grammar*, p. 95 b. For the same meaning in Biblical Hebrew see JBL, 1938, p. 227.

[24] After long opposition and recent hesitation I have finally become inclined to accept the often suggested Phoenician derivation of Greek *bōmós*, " raised platform, statue-base, pedestal, altar " (see most recently in the fanciful book of Z. Mayani, *L'arbre sacré et le rite de l'alliance chez les anciens Sémites*, Paris, 1935, p. 30). This combination has also been considered sympathetically by J. A. Montgomery, in a recent letter. In favor of it is not only the almost identical cultic meanings of the two words, but also their etymological form. Gr. *bōmós* has no satisfactory etymology (as may be seen by reading what Leo Meyer and Boisacq have to say about the word) and the lost Phoenician form of Heb. *bāmāh* (from a stem *bwm*, with originally long *a* in the first syllable, as pointed out by J. Barth, *Nominalbildung*, p. 9) must have been something like *bōmóh* from *bômatu*. The Greek ending has obviously been assimilated to a class of nouns ending in accented *mos* (cf. Meyer, *Griechische Etymologie*, III, p. 110). In other words we appear to have perfect phonetic, as well as semantic parallelism. We are becoming increasingly familiar with the significance of raised platforms within the temple: cf. the raised platforms in the back of the sanctuaries of the late second millennium B. C. at Beth-shan, described by A. Rowe, *The Four Canaanite Temples of Beth-shan*, passim, on the temples of " Amenophis III," of " Seti I," and the two temples of " Rameses III " (on the chronology of these temples see now Wright, AJA, 1941, pp. 484 f.).

[25] *Geschichte des Altertums*, I, 2 (3rd. ed.), pp. 423 f. Graham and May, *Culture and Conscience* (1936), pp. 45 ff., associate the standing stones of Gezer with early cult of the dead in the third millennium, but the treatment of the subject is too fluid to be clear. Eduard Meyer's explanation has been accepted by C. Watzinger, *Denkmäler Palästinas*, I (1933), p. 63, and by K. Galling, *Biblisches Reallexikon*, col. 371, though somewhat hesitantly.

[26] W. Andrae, *Die Stelenreihen von Assur* (1913).

[27] *Gezer*, II, p. 398 below. On p. 404 Macalister states that the evidence of scarabs and pottery showed that the "high place" had been founded in the

second half of the third millennium. While he does not give a concrete demonstration of this early date, it must be confessed that parallels from Ader, Bâb edh-Dhrâ' and Lejjûn in southern Transjordan all point to the same period (see Chap. II, n. 43). On the other hand, since standing pillars of such size had to be set in fairly deep holes in order to be firm, it is unlikely that Macalister's evidence was really decisive. That the stones were in position in the Late Bronze Age is archaeologically certain, and this age may accordingly be taken as the *terminus ad quem* for their erection.

[28] Ugaritic *skn* I derive from Accad. *šiknu,* "form, image" (alternating with *ṣalmu,* "image, likeness"), hence "stela with image," and finally "stela." For the phonetic change cf. the identical case of Accadian *šipru,* "message," from which Canaanite *sipru,* Heb. *sefer,* "letter, book," is derived (both loans probably go back to the third millennium). For the context in which *skn* occurs see n. 30.

[29] Like *nefeš,* "breath, soul, life," which means "mortuary stela" in Aramaic inscriptions, *peger* had earlier developed the same sense; see n. 30 and Lev. 26: 30 (*pigrê gillûlêkem* is "stelae of your idols").

[30] These stelae were published by Dussaud in *Syria,* XVI (1935), pp. 177-180, and have been elaborately treated by J. Obermann, JAOS, 1941, pp. 31-45. The latter has for some reason omitted the clear *h* at the end of line 2 of the second inscription (B), which brings with it a false translation, but he has corrected the final *t* of Dussaud in the third line of the same text to a more probable *m.* My translation diverges slightly from both:

A. [1]*skn . d-š'lyt* [2]*A(?)ryl . l-Dgn . pgr* [3]*[š]w-'alp l-'akl*
"Stela which Aryal(?) has offered to Dagon: a mortuary offering of a sheep and an ox for food."
B. [1]*pgr . d-š'ly* [2]*zn . l-Dgn . b'lh*[3]*š w-'al]p . b-mḥrm*(!)
"Mortuary offering which 'Uzzênu offered to Dagon his lord; a sheep and an ox as an inviolable offering."

These stelae cannot well be explained except as connected somehow with the prospective funerals of the persons whose names they bear.

[31] The interpretation of the word *'el'eb* as equivalent to Latin *manes* (plural of an unused noun), "(divine) shades of the dead," occurred independently to Goetze (see JAOS, 1938, p. 278, n. 80, where it is hesitantly rendered "divine ancestors") and me. For several years I have been connecting the word with Heb. *'ôb,* "ghost, shade which returns to earth," which has long been connected with Arab. *'âba,* "to return." Ugaritic *'eb* (*'ibu*) would then reflect a more original vocalization than Hebrew *'ôb* (for *'ubu*), which has been affected by the labial consonant. On the word cf. also A. Bergman, JBL, 1936, pp. 224 ff. and H. G. May, AJSL, 1939, p. 53.

[32] For my preliminary report see BASOR 57, pp. 18-26.

[33] For the most detailed account of these high places see G. L. Robinson, *The Sarcophagus of an Ancient Civilization,* New York, 1930, where references to previous literature will be found.

[34] Cf. most recently T. Canaan, *Mohammedan Saints and Sanctuaries in Palestine* (1927), pp. 3 ff.

[35] Cf. G. F. Moore in *Encyclopaedia Biblica*, II, col. 2065 ff.

[36] The best concise treatment of the history of the Old-Testament priesthood from the orthodox Wellhausenist point of view remains the article "Priest" by W. Robertson Smith and Alfred Bertholet in *Encyclopaedia Biblica*, III, cols. 3837-3847.

[37] We may observe that such uncompromising rigidity of unilinear evolution is without good historical parallel and that historical evolutionary processes are more given to oscillation than to advance in a straight line; cf. FSAC 79 ff. While interpolation is often quite justified where the line of historical evolution is fixed by earlier and later data, extrapolation, where only data of later date are known, is perilous to the highest degree and ought to be abandoned by historians.

[38] On the organization of this state see especially E. Meyer, *Sitzungsber. Preuss. Akad. Wiss., Phil-Hist. Klasse*, 1928, pp. 495 ff., and H. Kees, "Herihor und die Aufrichtung des thebanischen Gottesstaates" (*Nachr. v. d. Ges. d. Wiss.*, Göttingen, 1936).

[39] *Revue Biblique*, 1939, pp. 394-405.

[40] ZAW 17 (1940-41), pp. 1-29.

[41] In this connection it may be pointed out that the word *ḫrṣn* on the copper ceremonial adzes which formed the starting point of the decipherment of Ugaritic, does not mean "adze" at all, in spite of the ingenious parallels which have been adduced, but is the name of the chief priest, *Ḫaruṣennu* (as the name is written in Accadian transcriptions). In other words, the correct decipherment of Ugaritic began as the result of a mistake! Analogies are more frequent in scientific research than commonly supposed.

[42] The word *lawiyu* can be proved to have existed with this approximate meaning, as should be clear from the following considerations. The Minaean inscriptions of Dedan (el-'Ulā) in North Arabia, dating, as shown by F. V. Winnett (BASOR 73, pp. 3-9), from the Persian period or a very little later, mention a class of male and female temple personnel called *lawi'u, lawi'atu*. From the texts themselves and from parallel documents it has been shown independently by N. Rhodokanakis (who is the foremost living authority on South-Arabian inscriptions) and H. Grimme that *lawi'u* meant something like "person pledged for a debt or vow"; cf. Gressmann, *Altorientalische Texte zum Alten Testament*, p. 464, note 1, and *Le Muséon*, XXXVII (1924), pp. 169-199. Grimme has correctly compared Hebrew *lawah*, "to borrow," *hilwah*, "to lend," from the common Semitic stem *lwy*. However, he was unaware that in Neo-Babylonian the word *lawûtânu* (*lamutanu*) exists in the sense "apprentice, clerk," i. e. pledged or articled clerk; cf. M. San Nicolò, *Neubabylonische Rechts- und Verwaltungsurkunden*, I, p. 719, and A. Ungnad, *Beiheft*, p. 82. In 1919 I connected this word with the Levites (*Revue d'Assyriologie*, XVI, p. 184), but with unsatisfactory philological derivation. We can now treat the word as a characteristic Neo-Babylonian loanword from Aramaic, like *yârîtûtu*, "inheritance," from *yâretûtâ* (preserved in Jewish Aramaic) and especially *raśûtânu*, "creditor," from Aramaic *reśûtâ*, "loan" (still found in Jewish Aramaic), itself from the verb *reśâ, 'arśî*, "to lend." The North-Minaean spelling shows that the word had been borrowed from Aramaic, where inter-

vocalic *y* changed to   t a very early date. In the Persian period, of course, North Arabic was saturated with Aramaic commercial influence. For possible Canaanite occurrence of the word *law(i)yu* see my remarks, *Vocalization of the Egyptian Syllabic Orthography* (1934), p. 8, n. 16, where the word should be rendered "person pledged to (El)," instead of "client of (El)." The phonetic development of the word is simple: *lawiyu* > **liwyu* (cf. Late-Canaanite *milk*, "king," from *maliku*) > **lēw* (like Heb. *gēw*, "back," from **giwyu*). For the derived *Lēwî* see the next note.

⁴³ On the etymology of "Kenite" see most recently JBL, 1939, pp. 95 f., and FSAC 195 f. For the derivation of *ḥofšî* from *ḥupšu* cf. especially JPOS, 1934, p. 131, n. 162, and Mendelsohn, BASOR 83, pp. 36 ff. Strictly parallel in formation is Heb. *nokhrî*, "foreigner," from an old word *nukru*, on which see my remarks, BASOR 77, p. 31, n. 48. On the word "Hebrew" see above, n. 8.

⁴⁴ It is generally recognized that Samuel cannot have been a Levite by genealogy, since there is not a hint of it in I Sam. 1: 1, and his early career is against it. On the other hand, it is not necessary to suppose that the Chronicler invented the Levitic genealogy found in I Chron. 6: 22 ff., since an erroneous identification of the Kohathite Elkanah (Ex. 6: 24) with Samuel's father (exactly like the false identification of Ezrah, the putative ancestor of the musicians Ethan and Heman [cf. I Kings 4: 31, etc.], with Zerah son of Judah in I Chron. 2: 6) would have been quite sufficient. On the Levitic genealogies, their origin, composition and date, see especially the valuable study of K. Möhlenbrink, ZAW, 1934, pp. 184-231.

⁴⁵ For the date see n. 42; Grimme's extreme date about the tenth century B. C. (*op. cit.,* p. 193) cannot be taken seriously.

⁴⁶ Contrast the learned but highly subjective discussion of the subject by H. H. Rowley, "Zadok and Nehushtan," JBL, 1939, pp. 113-141. Rowley thinks that Zadok was the Jebusite priest of the sanctuary of Nehushtan in the latest pre-Davidic Jerusalem.

⁴⁷ Jud. 18: 30, on which cf. the commentators and the B recension of the LXX.

⁴⁸ See provisionally FSAC 229; I hope to publish my detailed treatment in the near future.

⁴⁹ The name Kushan occurs as that of two districts or possibly tribes in the second millennium. There was a region or tribe of this name in southern Transjordan, as we know from the archaic passage in Hab. 3: 7; this may be tentatively identified with the district of Kushu in this same general region in the 19th century B. C. (BASOR 83, p. 34, n. 8). There was also a district of Qusana-ruma, i. e., Kûšân-rôm, "Kushan is high," or "high Kushan," in northern Syria in the thirteenth and twelfth centuries B. C., as we know from the list of Ramesses III. Since the Egyptians could not distinguish clearly between *k* and *q* before *u*, as we know from many transcriptions, and since one of the sibilants which became *shin* in Hebrew always appears as *s* in Egyptian, reflecting older Canaanite pronunciation, there is no phonetic difficulty. The Syrian Kushan was in the region called Naharaim (Nahrêna) by the Egyptians.

[50] There are numerous names of towns in northern Mesopotamia in the great list of Asiatic cities conquered by Ramesses III, as I hope to demonstrate conclusively at an early opportunity.

[51] See Alan Rowe, *The Topography and History of Beth-shan* (1930), p. 38, and G. M. FitzGerald, *Palestine Exploration Fund Quarterly Statement,* 1932, pp. 138 f. On the chronology and the attribution of Stratum VI to Ramesses III see AASOR XVII, p. 77, and G. E. Wright, AJA, 1941, p. 485.

[52] On the chronological and historical sequence of the inscriptions of Ramesses III see W. F. Edgerton and J. A. Wilson, *Historical Records of Ramses III* (1936).

[53] E. g., Amarna (Knudtzon ed.), No. 84, lines 36 ff.

[54] JPOS I, p. 55, n. 1; cf. Alt, *Die Staatenbildung der Israeliten in Palästina* (1930), pp. 12 f., n. 25.

[55] Cf. especially Burney, *Judges* (1920), pp. 78 ff.; Morgenstern, *Jewish Quarterly Review,* IX (1919), pp. 359-69; Albright, JPOS I (1921), pp. 55 ff.; BASOR 62, pp. 26 ff., 78, pp. 8 f.

[56] FSAC 211.

[57] For the meaning cf. the parallel name *Yarob'am* (Jeroboam), the first element of which must be derived from the verb *rbb*, "increase," in view of numerous analogies (cf. AJSL XXXVIII, 140 f.).

[58] The date may be roughly fixed by the following considerations. As Eduard Meyer (*Die Israeliten und ihre Nachbarstämme,* p. 381) showed, we must almost certainly combine the war with Midian in the days of Hadad king of Edom (Gen. 36: 35) with the movement which led to Gideon's victory over the Midianites. Our new recognition of the significance of the story of Gideon as a monument of the earliest great camel-raid (FSAC 120 f.) lends double force to this important synchronism between Israelite and Edomite history. Since the Edomites seem to have transmitted the throne through the distaff side, to judge from the fact that, while no king is son of his predecessor, the name of the last king's wife, as well as of her mother and grandmother, is recorded in Gen. 36: 39, we may reckon the average reign at about twenty years, just as in the case of a normal patrilineal dynasty. Even if the Edomite throne was "elective" as supposed by some scholars, this length of reign would be a good average, to judge from ancient Near-Eastern parallels. If the last king in the list was an earlier contemporary of David, Hadad's reign may be placed not far from cir. 1080-1060 B. C., which would be roughly the date of Gideon's career. Abimelech, who was the son of Gideon by a Shechemite woman, was born and grew to maturity after Gideon came into prominence, so we can scarcely date his reign before cir. 1050 B. C. In other words it must be placed after the fall of Shiloh (not later than cir. 1050; cf. note 18, above), in the period covered by Samuel's career in southern Israel. That this date is not too late is shown by other facts; e. g., the Song of Deborah can scarcely be dated before the last quarter of the twelfth century (BASOR 62, pp. 28 f.), and the career of Gideon certainly followed it. A date for Abimelech in the third quarter of the eleventh century would explain how we find such a circumstantial prose narrative of the events in question; Israel had now settled down completely and had become historically minded.

[59] By "Amorite" I mean Northwest-Semite, especially as applied by the Accadians of Mesopotamia to the nomads from the edges of the Syrian Desert and by the Egyptians to the inhabitants of eastern Syria and Palestine. As is well known, the E document, originating in the north, shows a tendency to prefer "Amorite" to "Canaanite," whereas J, which took shape in the south, preferred the latter. Cf. FSAC 109 ff., 119 ff., with the references there given.

[60] See Dossin, Syria, 1938, p. 108.

[61] AJSL LIII (1936), pp. 1-12; BASOR 84, pp. 7-12.

[62] The usual translation, "Man of Baal," is linguistically difficult, and must, in my opinion, be replaced by the rendering given in the text. Note that in the Baal Epic of Ugarit the resurrection of Baal is greeted with the triumphant words, " And I know that triumphant Baal lives (ḥy), that the Prince, lord of the earth, exists ('it, which would be 'iš in later Canaanite)." Moreover, there are several passages in the Bible where 'iš or 'eš is employed instead of classical yeš.

[63] It is very hard to separate the expression used here, kᵉbîr ha-'izzîm, from the parallel śᵉfîr ha-'izzîm, used in several passages in the clear sense of "he-goat." The first word is derived from the verb kbr, which means "to be large, old" in Aramaic and Arabic, and "to be fat" in Accadian. If it meant "old he-goat," it would be easy to see how effective the latter's half-concealed head, with black beard and burning eyes, would be as a substitute for a sick man. As for "teraphim" in this passage, I suggest the possible rendering "old rags"; in Canaanite trp is now known to have meant "to wear out," or the like (BASOR 83, p. 40; and 84, p. 15, on the parallel verb which appears as škḥ in Hebrew). For other parallels to kᵉbîr ha-'izzîm note śᵉ'îr 'izzîm, "he-goat"; śeh 'izzîm; gᵉdî 'izzîm.

[64] See provisionally my discussion in Mélanges Dussaud, I, pp. 118 f., with references. A fuller description will appear in AASOR XXI.

[65] Mélanges Dussaud, I, p. 119, notes 3-4.

[66] FSAC 85 and passim.

[67] FSAC 196 ff., 227 f., etc.

[68] Cf. FSAC 253. These lines come from the so-called "Babylonian Job," which was certainly composed between cir. 1200 and 800 B. C., and probably toward the end of the second millennium.

[69] Cf. APB 167 (where I should now write "with concomitant tendency toward territorial henotheism," instead of "with concomitant henotheism)." On the tendency toward institutional differentiation in the Early Iron Age see Alt, Staatenbildung (1930), pp. 1 ff., 34 ff. For particularism in types of pottery (which may be observed in spite of basic similarities) see Glueck, The Other Side of the Jordan (1940), p. 145.

[70] See JBL, 1935, p. 204; BASOR 62, p. 30; 63, p. 10, n. 7 on Grimme's priority.

[71] On Qaus cf. Glueck, BASOR 72, pp. 11 f., and Albright, JAOS, 1940, p. 295, n. 39.

[72] Southern Gilead and northern Moab passed from Moabite to Ammonite suzerainty after cir. 750 B. C., as we must infer from such passages as Amos

1: 13; II Chron. 26: 8; 27: 5; Jer. 49: 1, etc., cf. also E. Forrer, *Provinz-einteilung des assyrichen Reiches*, p. 64, on·the vicissitudes of this region in the late eighth and the seventh centuries, though his suggestions must be taken with serious reservations.

[73] Cf. W. Eichrodt, *Theologie des Alten Testaments*, I (1933), p. 45 and n. 4.

[74] Cf. FSAC 236.

[75] On this site cf. E. E. Voigt, JPOS, 1923, pp. 79-87, with modifications by the writer, *Jewish Quarterly Review*, XXII (1932), p. 413. The alternative localization for the priestly settlement has, however, been subsequently given up for lack of adequate evidence. Since the alternative site was *ed-Djib*, three miles from Gibeah in the opposite direction, the principle of contiguity to the royal residence is not affected at all.

[76] FSAC 230 ff.

[77] Max Löhr, *Asylwesen im Alten Testament* (1930).

[78] S. Klein, " Cities of the Priests and Levites and Cities of Refuge " (in Hebrew) in *Mehqarim Ereṣ-Yisraeliyim* (continuation of *Palästina-Studien*), Vol. III, 4. See now my study, *Louis Ginzberg Jubilee Volume*, pp. 49-73.

[79] Contrast Noth, *Das Buch Josua* (1938), pp. 100 f., who insists on the post-Deuteronomic date of the list of Levitic cities in Jos. 21.

[80] Unfortunately the publication of Margolis's invaluable posthumous work, *The Book of Joshua in Greek*, has only reached chapter 19, but 21 is covered by my notes, taken in the autumn of 1924 (cf. ZAW, 1926, pp. 225 ff.). It is interesting to note that an independent reëxamination of this chapter made recently, yielded results which proved to be virtually identical with those of Margolis. For instance, the Hebrew omits verses 36-37 (so numbered in Kittel's Bible), which the Greek preserves. In v. 16, where Joshua has " Ain " and the Chronicler " Ashan," the latter is proved to be correct by the Vaticanus recension of Joshua. In v. 25, where the Hebrew of Joshua erroneously repeats the " Gath-rimmon " of the preceding verse, where it is correct, the Vaticanus recension offers a reading which is only a slight corruption of the " Bileam " of the Chronicler, which was originally written in the longer form " Ibleam " in Joshua. For Margolis's method see H. M. Orlinsky, JAOS, 1941, pp. 81 ff.

[81] For example, the strange " Aner " of I Chron. 6: 70 (A. V.), though supported by Vaticanus, is transparent haplography for the Hebrew of Joshua: *'t-T'nk*. In v. 28 of Joshua we have " Kishion " where the Chronicler has " Kedesh." However, the Vaticanus family offers " Kishion " instead of " Kishion," and the Egyptian transcriptions of the name from the fifteenth century B. C. prove that the Greek text is right. The difference in early square character between the correct *Q-y-š-w·n* and *Q-d-š-w-* is so slight that a scribal error of the Chronicler or his copyist becomes certain. In verse 29 of Joshua we have " En-gannim " where the Chronicler offers " Anem." The Greek has " Fountain of Books " (!), which probably goes back, through an inner Greek scribal error (see *Louis Ginzberg Jubilee Volume*, pp. 70 f., for details), to En-anem, or the like (*'Ên-'ônám* = Arab. *'Ên-'ôlam*), which is the original form which I reconstructed in 1926, on the basis of the other Greek and Hebrew variants (*ibid.*, pp. 231 f.). The list of the Levitic towns of Zebulun is

curiously corrupt. The Hebrew of Jos. 21: 34 f. has four names, while the Greek has three; in Chronicles both Hebrew and Greek have preserved only two names. On inspection, it appears that "Kartah" is accidental repetition of "Kartan" two verses above, while the "Kadesh" of the Vaticanus family is a similar repetition of the "Kadesh" mentioned two verses above. Then the "Tabor" of the Chronicler is not a traditional variant of the "Nahalal" of Joshua, but both are correct; the original list included the Zebulunite towns of Jokneam, Rimmon, Nahalol and Tabor, all well-known places. It must be emphasized that the foregoing illustrations are merely samples, and that not a single probable ancient variation between the prototypic lists is left after the same or similar methods have been applied systematically throughout the lists.

[82] See my discussion of the equation Eltekeh = Khirbet Muqenna' (BASOR 15, p. 8; 17, pp. 5 f.).; the equation has been accepted by Alt and his disciples. For the identification of Tell el-Melât with Gibbethon, accepted by Alt and the writer, see von Rad, Palästinajahrbuch, 1933, pp. 37 ff.

[83] On the sites and their history see especially AASOR IV, pp. 156 f., and BASOR 62, pp. 18-26 (on the soundings of E. P. Blair and A. Bergman), especially p. 26.

[84] This we know from the fact that the frontier between Israel and Damascus in the ninth century ran south of Aphek, mediaeval Afîq and modern Fîq in southern Jôlân, and from the fact that Karnaim (Qarnên), modern Sheikh Sa'd, was a province of Damascus and later of Assyria in the eighth century (Forrer, Provinzeinteilung, p. 62). There is ample corroboratory evidence.

[85] Cf. JPOS, 1925, pp. 28 ff., 38 ff.; 1931, pp. 249 ff.

[86] Cf. A. Bergman, JPOS, 1936, pp. 243 f.

[87] Op. cit., pp. 17 f. I disagree with his view that the two lists are divergent and that one of them (he left the relative priority open) is somewhat posterior to the other.

[88] JPOS, 1925, pp. 20 ff.; A. T. Olmstead, History of Palestine and Syria, p. 330.

[89] ZAW, 1926, p. 236; JBL, 1938, p. 226.

[90] Cf. A. Alt, Sellin Festschrift, pp. 13-24; M. Noth, Josua, pp. ix ff.

[91] Cf. n. 77 f., as well as Morgenstern, Heb. Un. Col. Ann., VII, 57; VIII, 79.

[92] Cf. now the excellent popular article by O. R. Sellers, The Biblical Archaeologist, September, 1941, passim.

[93] Cf. especially JAOS, 1940, pp. 296, f. and n. 45.

[93a] I expect to show elsewhere that šarîm, "singers," formed a class of temple personnel at Ugarit, cir. 1400 B. C.

[94] I disagree vigorously with the attribution of any part of the Balaam poems to the period after the Disruption of the Monarchy. The most elaborate recent treatment of the Balaam cycle, by Mowinckel (ZAW, 1930, pp. 233-271), agrees with most earlier discussions in attributing the "Yahwistic" poems in Numbers 24 to the United Monarchy, but he is much too radical in assigning the "Elohistic" poems in chapter 23 to the time of Josiah. So far from dating the verses Num. 24: 20-24, to a "very late" date, perhaps even to the early

Greek period, with Mowinckel and most recently R. H. Pfeiffer (*Introduction to the Old Testament,* 1941, pp. 277 f.), I should like to call attention to the extreme archaism of the language and to the fact that the text obviously became more and more unintelligible with the passage of time. I believe that the enigmatic references to "Kittim" and "Asshur" are misinterpretations of ordinary words, and that the passage refers only to Amalek, the Kenites, and Eber. There is, in fact, no serious reason to doubt that these verses go back to the age of Balaam (thirteenth century B. C.); see my paper, "The Oracles of Balaam" (JBL, 1944, pp. 207-233) for details. In any case, most scholars refer the poems in Num. 24: 3-19 to the tenth century B. C.

⁹⁵ There can be no reasonable doubt that the word *'ezraḥ* meant originally "aborigine," just as it is regularly rendered in the Greek Bible (*autóchthōn*). Just as the Canaanite meaning of such words as *ḥofshî* and *'Ibrî* still appears in a few passages, so this sense of *'ezraḥ* is absolutely clear in passages like Num. 9: 14, to which Mr. Arthur Hertzberg has drawn my attention. Both Hebrew and Greek agree on the translation, "There shall be one statute for you and for the *ger* and for the native (*'ezraḥ*) of the land." Here and in several other verses in the Pentateuch three classes are distinguished. In course of time the distinction between Israelite and Canaanite or Hebrew aborigine faded out, but even in most of these passages the *ger* is assigned the judicial standing of an *'ezraḥ*, not of a true Israelite. On the erroneous identification with Zerah see above, n. 44.

⁹⁶ Heb. *maḥōl* (from *ḥwl*, "to circle") has a meaning very much like that of Greek *orchēstra*, from *orchéomai*, "to dance," hence "semi-circular place for dancing," whence the English word "orchestra."

⁹⁷ For an excellent treatment of the inscriptions see J. A. Wilson in Gordon Loud, *The Megiddo Ivories* (1939), pp. 12 f. The dissimilation by which *Kulkul* became *Kalkol* offers no difficulties at all; cf. JAOS, 1940, p. 298 for parallel phenomena in Hebrew and Phoenician.

⁹⁸ Ptaḥ was identified with the Canaanite god Chusor, older Kôshar; see above, Chap. III, n. 30.

⁹⁹ I expect to discuss this question in detail elsewhere; I may refer provisionally to the lists of names in JPOS, 1934, pp. 227-229.

¹⁰⁰ A few provisional indications must suffice for the present. With *Kalkol* cf. Assyrian or Aramaic *Kulkulânu* (also written *Kukkulânu, Kakkulânu, Akkulânu,* etc., all forms applying to the same man; see Tallqvist, *Assyrian Personal Names,* pp. 110 f.), evidently derived from the plant-name *kakkulu* for **kulkulu*. With *Darda'* cf. Heb. *dardar* and note that Heb. *qarqa'* is *qaqqaru* (for **qarqaru*) in Accadian. Cf. also the name of the prophet-musician Habakkuk (Hab. 3: 1), which cannot be separated from the Accadian plant-name *ḥambaqûqu*. Note also the name of a Babylonian female musician of about the thirteenth century, *Qaqqadânîtu*, which can scarcely be separated from the plant-name *qaqqadânu* (literally, "having a head").

¹⁰¹ For the Ugaritic parallels in the poetical books of the O. T. see my forthcoming paper, "The Psalm of Habakkuk," in the T. H. Robinson anniversary volume to be issued by the British Society for O. T. Study.

[102] Cf. *Jour. of Bible and Religion*, VIII (1940), pp. 134 f. There are an increasing number of cases where the vocabulary of the eighth-century prophets is elucidated from Ugaritic literature, but real stylistic parallels seem to be lacking.

[108] On this psalm see now U. Cassuto, *Tarbiz*, XII (1941), pp. 1-27. The number of parallels may be still farther extended by materials which I have in preparation. The sanest pre-Ugaritic study of this psalm is that of M. Buttenwieser, *The Psalms* (1938), pp. 29-47, who insists on the close relationship between parts of the psalm and the Song of Deborah, though it is scarcely necessary to go back quite that far for its composition. Ugaritic parallels show that his sharp cleavage between 68 A and 68 B is not warranted, though we may grant that there has been a reworking of older materials, not necessarily after the tenth century B. C.

NOTES TO CHAPTER V

[1] The date of Shishak's accession is dependent on Israelite chronology, for which see note 4.

[2] The Assyrian dates are based on the Khorsabad List, which was discovered by the expedition of the Oriental Institute of the University of Chicago in 1933, and which has become partly known, thanks to published photographs and statements.

[8] The latest and best account of the fluctuations of Assyrian power in northwestern Mesopotamia has been given by Emil Forrer in his article " Assyrien" (*Reallexikon der Assyriologie*, I, especially pp. 286-297) which appeared in 1930.

[4] For my chronological system see now BASOR 100, pp. 16-22. Though influenced strongly by the work of Kugler (*Von Moses bis Paulus*, 1922), Lewy (*Die Chronologie der Könige von Israel und Juda*, 1929), Begrich (same title, 1929), Mowinckel (*Acta Orientalia*, 1932, pp. 161-277) and E. R. Thiele (JNES, 1944, pp. 137-186), it strikes out several new paths, particularly in emphasizing the importance of datings of events (sometimes preserved only by the Chronicler) according to the regnal years of kings of Judah.

[5] For Winckler's drastic reduction of the extent of David's conquests and Solomon's empire see especially the third edition of Schrader's *Keilinschriften und das Alte Testament* (1902), pp. 230 ff. Guthe's views are compactly presented in the maps of his *Bibelatlas* (2nd ed., 1926), especially No. 3.

[6] On the Assyrian references to Zobah see E. Forrer, *Die Provinzeinteilung des assyrischen Reiches* (1921), pp. 62, 69. Since there has been much confusion on this point, it should be emphasized that the writings *Subutu, Subite* exhibit the normal vocalic assimilation of the Assyrian dialect and reflect an original *Subātu*; cf. BASOR 67, p. 27, n. 6, for parallels.

[7] Forrer's arguments appear decisive in this question, especially when supplemented by Harper, *Letters*, No. 414, which proves that Subatu was a rendezvous of the Arabs in the seventh century B. C. and hence must have been situated on the edge of the desert.

[8] For these names cf. Albright, *The Vocalization of the Egyptian Syllabic Orthography*, p. 40, No. 19, and p. 60, C. 7. According to the Papyrus Anastasi I Ṭubikhu was near Kadesh on the Orontes, and the Amarna Tablets suggest a location south of the latter (to judge from the character of the political and geographical references as well as from the fact that the scribe was a Canaanite, not a Hurriaǹ like the scribes of Kadesh and Qatna). I have long thought of Baalbek as perhaps on the site of ancient Ṭubikhu.

[9] See Chapter III, n. 4.

[10] See my article in the *Leland Volume* (Menasha, 1942), pp. 43 f., n. 101.

[11] See BASOR 83, pp. 17 ff.

[12] Cf. JPOS II, p. 285. However, it is not impossible that the verb *gûr* in Jud. 5: 17 is denominative from the Canaanite word which is preserved in the Egyptian loan-word *kur(a)*, "ship." Our deduction is not changed.

[13] Cf. FSAC 120 ff.

[14] On Ophir cf. J. A. Montgomery, *Arabia and the Bible* (1934), pp. 38 f., 176 ff., with references. The most recent treatment of the problem, by the late J. J. Hess in a paper presented at the International Congress of Orientalists at Oxford in 1928 on "Die Lage von *Pwn-t*," was never published, so far as I know; he maintained that both Punt and Ophir were in Yemen, though with possible extension to the opposite, African, coast of the Red Sea.

[15] See provisionally BASOR 83, p. 21 and n. 31.

[16] In the Story of the Shipwrecked Sailor (from the period 2000-1800 B. C.), line 165, the serpent-king of Punt is represented as giving the sailor all kinds of precious things, including such African products as ivory, and at the end of the list, just as in the Bible, *gf* and *ky* monkeys. The first word, pronounced approximately *qôfe* at the time of Solomon, was borrowed in Hebrew as *qôf*, as in I Kings 10: 22; the second word is clearly the same as biblical *t-k-y* (Massoretic *tukkîyîm* in plural) in the same passage. As a matter of fact we find the feminine *kyt* instead of the masculine *ky* in later Egyptian (though the two probably coexisted) and the initial *t* is obviously the Egyptian feminine article, which is often found attached to loanwords from Egyptian in other languages. That the feminine Egyptian word became masculine in Hebrew is not at all unusual; cf. Arabic *timsâh* "crocodile" (for Eg. *t-emsâh*), where exactly the same thing has taken place. Though this explanation is practically certain and was first given in 1921 (Albright, AJSL XXXVII, 144), it has been consistently overlooked and the antiquated rendering "peacock" keeps recurring. It may be added that two kinds of monkeys also appear among articles brought from Punt in the early fifteenth century (Breasted, *Ancient Records*, II, § 265, where *gf* and *'n'n* monkeys are mentioned). The Egyptian names (which may include the name *Ophir* itself) certainly point to Africa.

[17] As is well known, a reign of three years in earlier Hebrew antedating practice may mean only one full year and parts of two others. Three days may also imply one full day and parts of two others.

[18] Cf. JAOS 45 (1925), pp. 238 ff. and the fuller treatments referred to in n. 120. Peake has since succeeded in demonstrating the equation Magan = 'Omân in southeastern Arabia; see *Antiquity*, 1928, pp. 452 ff., and my favor-

able comment JAOS 56 (1936), p. 142. This proves that Melukhkha lay beyond 'Omân and does not exclude a possible extension as far as Punt.

[19] See provisionally my account of this chapter in the forthcoming Lutheran commentary on the Old Testament, in which I list some of the arguments for this date. Cf. also FSAC 327, n. 74.

[20] Cf. Burrows, *What Mean These Stones?* (1941), p. 39. This was first pointed out by Hugo Winckler.

[21] For details see my forthcoming treatment in BASOR.

[22] The leather letters of Arsames, written cir. 410, my acquaintance with which I owe to the courtesy of E. Mittwoch, who will publish them. On these documents see Franz Rosenthal, *Die aramaistische Forschung* (1939), pp. 37 f.

[23] See H. Schäfer, *Sitz. Preuss. Akad. Wiss., Phil.-Hist. Kl.*, 1931, pp. 730-738.

[24] It stands to reason that the royal traders bought their wares as cheaply as possible. The objections raised by Lamon and Shipton to this ratio (*Megiddo I*, 1939, p. 44) do not reckon with the fact that the manufacture of a chariot was then a slow and difficult process, requiring special technical skill and expensive imported materials. A horse simply grew; there is not the slightest evidence in the Hittite literature on horse-breeding and training that such things as pedigrees were yet known, and the only two elements to be considered by buyers were probably the district from which a horse came and the animal's own appearance and qualities.

[25] Cf. *Megiddo I*, pp. 43 f. Lamon and Shipton are, however, overlooking the fact that cavalry was not introduced into Syria or Palestine, to judge from our present evidence, until the ninth century. At the battle of Qarqar, in 853 B. C., the North Syrians had some cavalry, but Israel had none. Cavalry had already become the most important part of an Assyrian army. Once introduced into the Near East by the Indo-Europeans (Medes, Cimmerians, etc.) about the twelfth century B. C. cavalry spread rapidly. In the late twelfth century the Babylonian king Nebuchadnezzar already employed cavalry, and by the tenth century we find armed riders represented at Gozan (Tell Halâf) in northern Mesopotamia. On this question see the comprehensive treatment of Joseph Wiesner, *Der Alte Orient*, 38 (1939), 2-4, pp. 69 ff.

[26] See Glueck, *The Other Side of the Jordan* (1940), pp. 93 ff., supplemented by BASOR 79, pp. 3 ff. See also BASOR 90, pp. 13 f.

[26a] On state (crown) slavery in Palestine see now I. Mendelsohn in BASOR 85.

[27] BASOR 83, pp. 21 f.

[28] See Glueck, *op. cit.*, pp. 50-88.

[29] This is often denied, but I see no reason whatever for rejecting the explicit statements of II Sam. 8: 1, 12; I Kings 5: 4 (English, 4: 24), etc. I Kings 5: 1 (English, 4: 21) and II Chron. 9: 26 are ambiguous, since the territory under Solomon's control is explicitly said to extend from the River (Euphrates) to the border of Egypt and since the earlier passage is defective and may have included originally a brief list of the principal subject countries. The argument derived from the reference to the Egyptian storming of Gezer, northeast of

15

214 ARCHAEOLOGY AND THE RELIGION OF ISRAEL

Philistia (I Kings 9: 16), cannot be called serious; the text seems to be corrupt (there are now two successive statements that Solomon built Gezer), since Macalister found no trace of destruction by fire in this period, and since it is geographically and historically improbable (for my substitute theory that " Gezer " is here a corruption of " Gerar " see my discussions JPOS, 1924, pp. 142-4, and AASOR XII, § 98).

[30] *Amos Studies* (1941), pp. 183-205.

[31] See his valuable study, *Die Staatenbildung der Israeliten in Palästina* (1930), *passim.*

[32] See Alt, "Jerusalems Aufstieg," in *Zeits. Deutsch. Morg. Ges.*, 1925, 1-19.

[33] Alt, *op. cit.*, p. 48; cf. Albright, JBL LI (1932), p. 80.

[34] See Albright, *loc. cit.*

[35] Möhlenbrink, *Der Tempel Salomos* (1932); cf. FSAC 225.

[36] Scott, JBL LVIII (1939), pp. 143 ff.

[37] See especially Alt, *Alttestamentliche Studien zu R. Kittels 60. Geburtstag* (1913), pp. 1 ff.; Albright, JPOS, 1925, pp. 25 ff.

[38] I adhere as strongly as ever to my former view on this point, in spite of Alt, *Staatenbildung*, p. 54, n. 30.

[39] See his study, "Samarie aux temps d'Achab," in *Syria*, 1925-1926.

[40] JPOS, 1925, pp. 38 ff.; 1931, pp. 248 ff. For the latest bibliographic survey of the material see Diringer, *Le iscrizioni antico-ebraiche palestinesi* (1934), pp. 50-57. I am more than ever convinced that none of the places mentioned in these ostraca is located outside Western Manasseh.

[41] See BASOR 73, 21, n. 38. Increasingly numerous epigraphic finds make it certain, in my judgment, that the ostraca published by Reisner in 1924 date from the reign of Jeroboam II. Since the ostraca extend from the ninth to the seventeenth year of some king (see below, n. 110), Jeroboam's predecessor, who is credited with only sixteen years, drops out. Epigraphically these ostraca cannot go back into the ninth century.

[42] See Forrer, *Provinzeinteilung des assyrischen Reiches* (1921), pp. 60 f., 69; Albright, JPOS, 1925, pp. 43 f.; Alt, *Zeits. Deutsch. Paläst.-Ver.*, 1929, pp. 220-242, where Alt has brilliantly refuted Jirku's attempts to weaken Forrer's system.

[43] See K. Möhlenbrink, *Der Tempel Salomos* (1932), which is by far the most thorough recent treatment, but is archaeologically rather weak; C. Watzinger, *Denkmäler Palästinas*, I (1933), pp. 88-95, admirable from the comparative archaeological side; G. E. Wright, *The Biblical Archaeologist*, IV, 2 (May, 1941), brief but excellent, utilizing material of first importance which has only now become available.

[44] A drastic illustration is the work of Gabriel Leroux, *Les origines de l'édifice hypostyle* (1913), pp. 159-162. Because Leroux rejected the idea that there could be Phoenician influence on early Greek architecture he was forced to deny the validity of the striking parallel to the earliest classical Greek temple-plans which is provided by the Temple of Solomon. The discovery of the Tainât temple has effectually spiked this point of view, since it has practically

the same ground plan as some of the archaic Doric temples, e. g., at Syracuse and Selinus, but is over two centuries older than they are. Temples C and D at Selinus, which resemble the Tainât plan very closely, are generally dated cir. 570-560 B. C. (cf. e. g., D. S. Robertson, *Handbook of Greek and Roman Architecture*, 1929, pp. 71 ff., and chronological tables).

⁴⁵ *American Journal of Archaeology*, 1937, p. 9, fig. 4; Wright, *Biblical Archaeologist*, May, 1941, p. 21 and fig. 3. On the comparative architectural associations of this type cf. V. Müller, JAOS 60 (1940), p. 162.

⁴⁶ Cf. the observations of G. E. Wright, *loc. cit.* There is crying need for an up-to-date critical study of all this accumulated material, for which see especially the recent survey by C. Watzinger, *Handbuch der Archäologie* (1938), pp. 805-816. To this must now be added the remarkable collection of ivories from the thirteenth century and the first half of the twelfth, discovered in 1937 at Megiddo (Gordon Loud, *The Megiddo Ivories*, 1939), as well as an important painted pilaster capital of the proto-Aeolic type, found in Stratum V (cir. 1050-950 B. C.) of Megiddo in 1935.

⁴⁷ Cf. Scott's list, JBL, 1939, pp. 143 f.

⁴⁸ Cf. Scott, *ibid.*, pp. 144 f.

⁴⁹ *Lectures on the Religion of the Semites*, new edition (1894), pp. 487-490.

⁵⁰ See BASOR 85, pp. 18-27.

⁵¹ See Th. Reinach and Hamdy Bey, *Une nécropole royale à Sidon* (1892), pp. 89 f. and fig. 35.

⁵² The coins are later, but reflect traditional practice.

⁵³ Karl Wigand, *Thymiateria* (*Bonner Jahrbücher*, No. 122, 1912).

⁵⁴ For the soundest and one of the most recent iconographic analyses of the early Egyptian *djed* pillar see H. Schäfer in *Studies Presented to F. Ll. Griffith* (1932), pp. 424 ff.

⁵⁵ See Montet, *Byblos*, Plate LIV: 241-5.

⁵⁶ *Harvard Excavations at Samaria*, II, Plate 64 m.

⁵⁷ In Old Coptic we find the pronunciation *tat* preserved; since Coptic short *a* reflects New Egyptian short *i* in accented closed syllables, we may safely reconstruct the original as *djid*. The Egyptian sound conventionally transcribed *dj* virtually always appears in Semitic transcriptions of Egyptian words as *ṣade*, and inversely Semitic *ṣ* is transliterated *dj* in Egyptian in all historical periods.

⁵⁸ For *ḥammân*, "incense-stand," see H. Ingholt, in *Mélanges Dussaud*, Vol. II (1940), and K. Elliger, ZAW, 1939, pp. 256-65, who conclusively disposes of Lindblom's objections (cf. FSAC 333, n. 45). The original sense of the word *ḥammân* must have been "stand for heating, brazier," from the common Semitic verb *hmm*, "be hot," causative "to heat." The word then applied primarily to a large class of terra-cotta braziers and objects of similar form and function, including incense-stands; for previous treatment cf. especially Watzinger, *Tell el-Mutesellim*, II (1929), pp. 38 f., May, *Material Remains of the Megiddo Cult* (1935), pp. 20-23, Alan Rowe, *The Four Canaanite Temples of Beth-shan* (1940), pp. 52 ff. I am not suggesting that all these objects were braziers or incense-stands; some were undoubtedly pot-stands, others were stands for offerings, still others were sacred "flower-pots." The largest and

most instructive collection remains that from the archaic temples of Ishtar at Assur, where we can distinguish sharply between high narrow stands (which continue in the West down to about the twelfth century B. C.), squat stands of brazier type, and "house"-stands, the original purpose of which is obscure. For the conclusive demonstration that the tall slender terra-cotta stands of the second millennium B. C. were suitable for use as braziers see Ingholt's experimental proof, *Kgl. Danske Videnskabernes Selskab, Archaeol.-kunsthist. Meddelelser*, III, 1 (Copenhagen, 1940), pp. 52 f. and plate XVI, 1. From at least as early as the tenth century B. C. until the Roman period we have slender limestone altars of incense with four horns, clearly identified as *hammânim* by the evidence cited by Ingholt and Elliger. It would seem that the stone altars replaced pottery stands at the beginning of the Iron Age.

[59] The problem of this deity, who was worshipped at Sham'al in northern Syria in the ninth century and who later became the chief god of the Tyrian colonists at Carthage, is still unsolved. The recent theory of Hurrian origin is possible, but very questionable. Cf. most recently Eissfeldt, *Ras Schamra und Sanchunjaton*, pp. 36-42.

[60] Cf. AASOR XVII (1938), § 5 and n. 3.

[61] For these inscriptions see above, n. 36.

[62] For the cosmic pillars cf. Job 26: 11. On this motif, and on the supposed exact orientation of the Temple to permit the rays of the rising sun to shine directly into the Holy of Holies at the autumnal equinox, see especially Morgenstern, *Hebrew Union College Annual*, VI (1929), pp. 1-38; Hollis, *Myth and Ritual* (edited by S. H. Hooke), pp. 87 ff.; H. G. May, JBL LVI (1937), pp. 309 ff. While Morgenstern's argument is impressive I am still a little skeptical. Hollis's far-reaching suggestions cannot be taken seriously; cf. my review, JPOS, 1934, pp. 154 f.

[63] Their name, *kîyôr*, is also Mesopotamian, as shown by the fact that the word appears as *kiuru* in the Assyrian inscriptions of Sargon II, with the same meaning, and that it has a Sumerian etymology (see below in the text, on the portable platform with the same name). The writer called attention to this equation in 1916 (JAOS 36, p. 232; cf. JAOS 40, p. 317, n. 18), and the combination of *kîyôr* with *kiuru* was again made much later by J. Friedrich, quite independently (see *Archiv Orientální*, 1932, pp. 66-70). Friedrich's view that the word is of Urartian origin is improbable; it is far more likely that Ur. *kiri* was derived from *kiuri*. It may be observed that he cites (as having parallel formation in Hebrew) the word *kishôr*, "spindle" (synonymous with *pelek*, derived from Accadian *pilakku*), which has been happily derived from a Sumerian *ki-sur*, literally, "place of spinning." Note the identity of vocalization. [On Sum. *kiur* see now Falkenstein, *Zeits. f. Assyr.*, 34, 23 f.]

[64] Cf. Wright, *The Biblical Archaeologist*, May, 1941, pp. 28 ff.

[65] On the cherubim see Dhorme and Vincent, *Revue Biblique*, 1926, pp. 328 ff., 481 ff.; Graham and May, *Culture and Conscience* (1936), pp. 195 f., 249 ff.; Albright, *The Biblical Archaeologist*, I, 1 (1938). There is now a great deal more material which is available for the corroboration of the thesis that the cherub was conceived as a winged sphinx (human-headed lion).

⁶⁶ E. g., Benzinger, *Hebräische Archäologie*, 3rd ed. (1927), p. 329. For older discussions cf. Benzinger in the *Encyclopaedia Biblica*, col. 4341.

⁶⁷ Cf. A. Jeremias, *Das Alte Testament im Lichte des alten Orients*, 3rd ed. (1916), p. 488 and n. 1. His reference to the *apsû* is correct (cf. Albright, AJSL XXXV [1919], p. 185, etc.), but it is very unlikely that the *tâmtu* which was set up by the Cossaean king Agum II (cir. 1500 B. C.) in the temple of Shamash, in connection with his celebration of the return of the images of Marduk and Ṣarpânît, had anything to do with a basin of water, even if the reading is correct, which is uncertain.

⁶⁸ Even the Deluge, *abûbu*, was portrayed in art as a winged dragon; cf. Amarna, No. 22 (Knudtzon edition), iii: 5, 25; ii: 51; iv: 4; Thureau-Dangin, *Huitieme campagne de Sargon* (1912), lines 373, 379.

⁶⁹ See JPOS, 1936, 18.

⁷⁰ E. g., Gen. 49: 25; Deut. 33: 13; Psalms 42: 8 (7); 148: 7.

⁷¹ E. g., Isa. 51: 10; Job 3: 8 (JBL LVII, 227); 7: 12; 9: 8; 26: 12; Psalms 74: 13.

⁷² E. g., Psalms 74: 15; Hab. 3: 8-9 (cf. Cassuto, *Annuario di Studi Ebraichi* 1935-1937, Rome, 1938, pp. 17 ff.).

⁷³ For untenable speculations on this subject see L. Venetianer, *Ezechiels Vision und die salomonischen Wasserbecken* (Budapest, 1906). He explains the *ôfannim* as "water-channels" instead of as "wheels," comparing Accadian *epinnu*, but the latter is now known to mean "plough," as first shown by M. Witzel.

⁷⁴ Cf. Weidner, *Archiv für Orientforschung*, VII (1931), pp. 170-178, especially pp. 174 f.

⁷⁵ Animals became most popular as supports of furniture precisely in the Early Iron Age. In the second millennium we frequently find animals decorating the sides of basins (e. g., AASOR XVII, § 76).

⁷⁶ Cf. JAOS 40, 316 f.

⁷⁷ See Dalman, *Arbeit und Sitte in Palästina*, I, pp. 45-48.

⁷⁸ The stem appears as *nqp*, whence also Ugaritic *nqpt*, used in parallelism with *šnt*, "year." Heb. *teqûfah*, "season," is derived from the secondary *qwp*, "encircle," which is closely related to South Arabic *qyf* with the same meaning (cf. Rhodokanakis, *Wiener Zeitschrift für die Kunde des Morgenlandes*, 1936, pp. 216 ff.).

⁷⁹ Albright, JBL XXXIX (1920), pp. 137-142.

⁸⁰ J. de Groot, *Die Altäre des salomonischen Tempelhofes* (1924), which is original in its ideas, but must be used with caution; K. Galling, *Biblisches Reallexikon*, p. 22; Galling in A. Bertholet, *Hesekiel* (1936), pp. 153 ff.

⁸¹ I see no reason to doubt that this passage refers to the original altar of burnt offering as built by Solomon, presumably described from memory (see n. 84, below) and very possibly altered somewhat in detail during the intervening centuries.

⁸² The Targum renders this peculiar expression as *tashwîthâ*, "pavement."

⁸³ There is no reason to suppose that the omission of this description by the editor of Kings was due to anything but accident; the religious reasons sometimes adduced are arbitrary.

[84] Cf. Galling in Bertholet, *Hesekiel*, pp. xix-xxi.

[85] See my remarks JBL, 1920, p. 139. The false assumption that the first element in the word *ạri'el*, etc., means etymologically " hearth " seems ineradicable. That the *har'el* served as an " altar-hearth " is true, but there is nothing in the name to require this interpretation.

[86] A few indications must suffice; the subject will be taken up elsewhere in detail. The word first occurs as a Canaanite loan in Egyptian (thirteenth century), used synonymously with *'udir* (Heb. *'ōzer*), " helper," and *dubi'* (Heb. *ṣōbe'*), " warrior(s) " in Pap. Anastasi I, 23: 9, in the sense of " warrior, hero," or the like; it is written *'i-ir-'i-ra*, i. e., *'er'el*, since there was no *l* in Egyptian (for the vocalization cf. Albright, *Vocalization of the Egyptian Syllabic Orthography*, 1934, p. 35, III. C). Next it occurs in the same sense II Sam. 23: 20. In the Moabite Stone, lines 12-13, we must probably render, " And I brought back from there Ôrî'el (Uriel) its chief (*dawîd*, used as in the Mari documents) and I dragged him before Chemosh at Qerîyôt." This passage thus drops out of the picture. In Isa. 29: 1 ff.; we have some remarkably interesting plays on words, using the word first in the sense of " hero," second in that of " shade." Since it is a dirge, closely imitating Canaanite models and employing many Canaanite words, the following lines are significant:

And thou shalt become like an *'er'el* (so for *'ari'el* of the text) . . .
And lower than the ground shalt thou speak,
    and thy utterance shall sink below the dust;
And thy voice shall be like a ghost from the underworld,
    and from the dust shalt thou chirp thy utterance.

For a possible occurrence in a ninth-century Phoenician inscription from Cyprus see BASOR 83, p. 16 and n. 12. The shift in meaning from " hero " to " shade " or inversely was common in the ancient Near East; cf. Heb. and Can. *rfa'îm*, " Rephaim," and Greek *hērōs*. Other data of equally striking character will be dealt with elsewhere.

[87] Cf. my discussion JBL, 1920, p. 137.

[88] This mountain, which bore the Accadian name *Khurshân* (without ending, and hence to be treated as a proper name, "*The* Mountain") has been discussed by H. Zimmern, *Zum babylonischen Neujahrsfest, zweiter Beitrag* (Leipzig, 1918), pp. 3 f., n. 2.

[89] That this word was borrowed directly from Sumerian, not through Accadian as usual, has been happily suggested by A. Poebel, *Zeitschrift für Assyriologie*, XXXIX (1929), p. 145; cf. JAOS 57 (1937), 71, n. 95.

[90] On the Tower of Babel see H. Gressmann, *The Tower of Babel* (New York, 1928), pp. 1-19. For the latest and most reliable reconstruction of the *ziqquratu* E-temen-an-ki at Babylon, see W. Andrae, *Mitteilungen der Deutschen Orient-Gesellschaft*, No. 71 (1932), pp. 1 ff.

[91] Cf., e. g., the Rassam Cylinder of Sardanapalus, vi: 29, and the *ṣit shamshi* of *Shilkhak-in-Shushinak*, king of Elam in the twelfth century B. C. (Vincent, *Canaan*, p. 144), which exhibits two stage-altars or temple-towers (?), each with four broken-off " horns " at the four corners of the top stage.

[92] *Zeitschrift für Aegyptische Sprache*, 73, pp. 54 ff.

[93] See Schaeffer, *Syria*, XIV, pp. 122 f. and plate XVI.

[94] *Egyptological Researches*, I (1906), p. 30 and plate 40.

[95] The shape suggests a possible connection with the sacred box which was the palladium of Israel for so many centuries.

[96] See above, n. 63.

[97] Delitzsch, *Sumerisches Glossar*, p. 49.

[98] For possible associations cf. JAOS 40, p. 317, n. 18.

[99] FSAC 228-30 and references. I hope to publish my treatment of this material at length soon.

[100] I cannot agree at all with Morgenstern's ingenious and plausible discussion of I Kings 13 in his *Amos Studies*, I (1941), pp. 161 ff. His treatment of the date of Jeroboam's annual pilgrimage feast at Bethel (*ibid.*, pp. 146-160) is useful because it directs attention to neglected features of the problem, but I cannot accept his conclusion. To me it is far more likely that Jeroboam revived an obsolete—or nearly extinct—alternative date for the festival, which was already celebrated in Jerusalem at the same time of the year as we find to be the case later. Jeroboam undoubtedly posed as a reformer, not as an innovator, and his changes were clearly intended to restore older practices (cf. Ex. 32) which had been abandoned by normative Yahwism, or which had been supplanted by the latter.

[101] "Das Gottesurteil auf dem Karmel" in *Festschrift Georg Beer* (1935), pp. 1-18.

[102] In his valuable study, "Ba'alšamēm und Jahwe," ZAW, 1939, pp. 1-31, especially pp. 19 ff.; see also *Der Alte Orient*, 40 (1941), pp. 18 f.

[102a] It is now certain that Melcarth was a deity of cosmic origin as well as cosmic function; see Chap. III, n. 29.

[103] Cf. JAOS 60 (1940), p. 298, and Baethgen, *Beiträge zur semitischen Religionsgeschichte*, p. 150.

[104] This may follow from the name of Abel-beth-maachah (modern Tell Âbil), literally, "Stream(so!) of Beth-maachah," since early Canaanite place-names of this type almost invariably contain a divine element (cf. AJSL, 1936, pp. 6 f.). Note the feminine ending and the fact that the name is nearly always under suspicion of being either gentilic or non-Israelite where it appears in the Bible (e. g., the mention in Gen. 22: 24 refers to the district by this name; the patronymics in I Kings 2: 39; I Chron. 11: 43; 27: 16 may all be derived from Beth-maachah, just as "Shamgar ben Anath" means "Shamgar of Beth-anath," and Hadad-ezer ben Rehob" is equivalent to "Hadad-ezer of Beth-rehob"; the names of wives or concubines of founders of tribes like Caleb and Machir often reflect mixture with non-Israelite elements; the wife of the father of Gibeon, I Chron. 8: 29; 9: 35, was presumably non-Israelite like the original population of that town).

[105] It must be remembered that a queen-mother was often an exceedingly important person in the ancient Near East. Illustrations are numerous; we may select as particularly instructive the cases of Jezebel and Athaliah, of Nehushta, mother of Joiachin (early sixth century; cf. JBL, 1932, p. 91), of Sammuramat (Semiramis), mother of Adad-nirari III (late ninth century), and of Naqi'a, mother of Esarhaddon (early seventh century).

[106] *Syria,* XVIII, p. 164.

[107] On the meaning of *mkrm* see my forthcoming discussion in BASOR.

[108] Lucian, *De dea Syria,* § 22 (*kárta hirón* is the expression used); for the most recent translation see Clemen, *Der Alte Orient,* 37, p. 16.

[109] I should read the first two words *zinḫî 'eglaikh,* with no change in the consonantal text (it must be remembered that there could be no difference between "thy calf, thy two calves, thy calves," in the orthography of the Northern Kingdom as we know it from the eighth-century ostraca). For the meaning of the word written *sh-b-b* (perhaps *ś-b-b*) see BASOR 84, p. 17, n. 26.

[110] On the general date see above, n. 41. For the seventeenth year see the discussion in Diringer, *Le iscrizioni ántico-ebraiche palestinesi* (1934), pp. 57 f., and note that Reisner's facsimile copy is obviously a somewhat stiff rendition of the Hebrew scribe's ligature of the numerical signs for X and V. Previous skepticism was therefore quite unwarranted, since the following unit strokes are both very clear.

[111] This is not infrequently asserted, but without proof, by scholars. Curiously enough this position has been taken more emphatically by such " conservative " scholars as Eerdmans and Harold Wiener than by any of their " critical " colleagues.

[112] For the time at which the decline of Phoenician maritime power must be placed cf. above, Chap. III, § 1. For archaeological verification of the approximate correctness of the traditional date of the foundation of Carthage see the impressive evidence given by D. B. Harden from the sacred precinct of Tanit at Carthage (*Iraq,* IV, 1937, pp. 85 ff.).

[113] See Eissfeldt, *Molk als Opferbegriff im Punischen und Hebräischen und das Ende des Gottes Moloch* (1935) and cf. my review, JPOS, 1935, p. 344, as well as de Vaux, *Revue Biblique,* 1936, pp. 278-282.

[114] See N. Schneider, *Biblica,* 1937, pp. 337-343; A. Bea, *Biblica,* 1939, p. 415, and G. Dossin, *Revue d'Assyriologie,* XXXV, p. 178, n. 1. For much later survivals cf. P. Jensen, *Zeitschrift für Assyriologie,* 1934, pp. 235 ff.

[115] In Hebrew cf. *dagan,* "grain," from the name of the god Dagan; *ashterôt haṣ-ṣôn,* "sheep-breeding," from the name of the goddess Astarte; perhaps *tîrôsh,* "wine," from the name of a Mesopotamian deity (cf. Poebel, *Zeitschrift für Assyriologie,* 39, p. 157); in Accadian cf. *Shakkan, Sumuqan, Nisaba, Gira,* etc., as words for " cattle, grain, fire," etc., respectively. The same development of meanings is familiar from Greek and Latin.

[116] This city is certainly the same as Assyrian Shabarain (pronounced *Sabarain,* with the Aramaic dual ending, since the Assyrians reversed the Babylonian sibilants, as proved to satiety by transcriptions, on which see most recently BASOR 82, pp. 16-17), which was attacked by Shalmaneser V in his accession year (727 B. C.) and was probably destroyed, since the destruction of Sepharvaim is presupposed in four other passages in the Bible, from the year 701 B. C. The exact consonantal equivalent of the Aramaic form which is found in Assyrian, is Hebrew *Sibraim* (Ezek. 47: 16), name of a town situated between the lands of Hamath and Damascus, somewhere in the region of Ḥumṣ.

[116a] See A. Pohl, *Biblica*, 1941, pp. 35-37.

[116b] In Northern Mesopotamia we find references to the sacrificial cremation of sons to the god Adad in documents extending from the tenth to the seventh century; cf. Kohler-Ungnad, *Assyrische Rechtsurkunden*, pp. 455 f. and Meissner, *Festschrift Max Freiherrn von Oppenheim gewidmet* (1933), p. 74. Cf. also Blome, *Opfermaterie* (1934), pp. 407 ff.

[117] See Eissfeldt, *op. cit.*, pp. 48 ff., and against him nearly all his reviewers.

[118] See his book, *Ras Schamra und Sanchunjaton* (1939), pp. 69 ff., and cf. above, Chap. III, § 4.

[119] JBL LX (1941), pp. 289-310.

[120] Vincent, *La religion des Judéo-Araméens d'Eléphantine* (Paris, 1937), on which cf. my brief review, *Jewish Social Studies*, I, p. 128.

[121] The word *semel* (which appears later in Phoenician as *sml, smlt*, apparently with the same meaning) is clearly connected with Accadian *sim(m)iltu*, "step(s), stairway," on which see especially Meissner, *Beiträge zum assyrischen Wörterbuch*, II (1932), pp. 53-55, and Landsberger, *Zeits. f. Assyr.*, 41, pp. 230 f.; 42, 166, whence Heb. *sullam*, "stairs" (in Jacob's dream at Bethel) and Aramaic *sibbiltâ* (for *simmiltâ*), with the same meaning. The original sense of *sim(m)iltu* was something like "slab," to judge from the fact that its synonym *askuppu* or *askuppatu* meant just that. Like *askuppatu*, which came to mean both "wall-slab, orthostate" and "door-slab, threshold," *simmiltu* seems to have meant both "slab" and "step"; steps were usually made of single slabs of stone in northern Mesopotamia and Syria. The sense "slab," i. e., "stela with hewn faces," perfectly fits all passages where *semel* occurs.

[122] Like the original Accadian *uknû*, properly *uqnû*, both "lapis-lazuli" and "purple," on which see Thureau-Dangin, *Syria*, XV (1934), pp. 140 f.

[123] Gaster's treatment (*op. cit.*, p. 291) gives an entirely false impression of the text, since *'ilm*, "gods" is a wholly unwarranted addition of his, for which the original offers no place. The text actually reads *'iqn'u . šmt[--]n . šrm*, with one or two letters missing in the middle; since the paragraph includes only these two short lines, any translation must be hazardous until a good parallel has been pointed out in another text.

[124] At best Babylonian *ḫarû*, which generally means "to dig," is only very remotely connected with *ḫurru*, "cave." which is etymologically identical with Heb. *ḥor*. The meaning of the expression *Nabû ša ḫarê* is wholly unknown, though it may well mean "Nabu of digging," in which case the sacred building called the *bit ḫarê* has a corresponding sense. Canal digging was one of the most important functions in Babylonian society.

[125] Heb. *ḥor* means here simply "hole (in the wall)," and is clearly a device by which to give the prophet unobserved access to the closed chamber.

[126] The cognate Accadian *erêbu* "to enter, set" (also in Hebrew as *'arab*) is used of the heliacal setting of the planets as well as of the setting of the sun and stars; cf. Kugler, *Sternkunde und Sterndienst in Babel*, I (1907), p. 278 a. It is scarcely necessary to call attention to the fact that Ishtar was goddess of the planet Venus, called *Dilbat* after a common appellation of the goddess.

[127] So also a number of previous scholars, e. g., A. Bertholet, *Hesekiel* (1936), *ad loc.*

[128] We can scarcely regard learned scribal reference to the Sumerian Damu in one of the Byblus Letters of Amarna as evidence of actual cult; on the passage see O. Schroeder, *Orientalistische Literaturzeitung*, 1915, cols. 291 ff. This ideographic writing proves nothing about the name of the Adonis of Byblus, which cannot have been Sumerian in any case.

[129] Cf. above, n. 62.

[130] See Struve, "*Zur Geschichte der jüdischen Kolonie von Elephantine*," in *Bulletin de l'Académie des Sciences de l'URSS*, VI. Serie, Tome XX, pp. 445-454.

[131] Vincent's contention (pp. 364 f.) that the Greek and Phoenician graffiti of Ipsambul belong to the time of Psammetichus I instead of to that of Psammetichus II (593-588) does not suit the epigraphy of either script, since both Phoenician and Greek are more closely related to the script of the late sixth century than to the script of the seventh.

[132] Cf. Cowley, *Aramaic Papyri of the Fifth Century B. C.* (1923), pp. 65-76, and Albert Vincent, pp. 542-560. [See continuation at bottom of page.]

[133] JBL, 1937, 387-394; JAOS, 1939, pp. 82 ff.

[134] See Langdon, *Revue d'Assyriologie*, 26 (1929), pp. 189 ff.; Weidner, *Archiv für Orientforschung*, VIII (1933), pp. 29 ff.

[135] The Hadad inscription of Panammû, lines 16, 21.

[136] *Une communauté judéo-araméenne à Eléphantine* (1915), pp. 82 ff.

[137] *Op. cit.*, pp. 360 f., 566, n. 3.

[138] For the preliminary report on the excavations at Bethel see BASOR 56, pp. 2-15, especially p. 14. Intensive work on the pottery since the publication of this report leads clearly to the deduction stated in the text. I hope to publish the Bethel volume within the coming two years.

[139] Two Assyrian governors of Samaria in the seventh century are now known: Nabû-mukîn-akhi, who was eponym in 690, and Nabû-shar-akhkhêshu, who was eponym after 648 B. C. For long continuance of ruling provincial families cf. the history of the house of Sanballat in the fifth and fourth centuries, as well as that of the Tobiad house, which can be followed from the fifth to the second century.

[140] See FSAC 286 f. and the references there given.

[141] *Op. cit.*, pp. 579 ff.

[142] Cf. above, Chap. III, n. 14.

[143] On this form of the name see especially my observations, JBL XLVI (1927), pp. 175 ff.

[144] FSAC 196-207, 219 ff., 228, 236, 251 ff. My insistence that the central principles of Yahwism remained essentially the same in more spiritual circles from the Mosaic age to the time of Ezra has been misunderstood by some reviewers as implying that I reject the principle of evolution!

[132] (con.) Cassuto (*Kedem*, I, 1942, pp. 47-52) has shown that these payments were in light shekels (1/20 of a *kursh*), and that the 246 shekels paid Yahu came from the 123 Jews whose names are listed; he concludes that Jewish cult was not syncretistic. Against his extreme position see my observations, BASOR 90, p. 40, and especially a forthcoming paper by Dupont-Sommer on a Jewish oath by both Yahu and Khnûm, the ram-god of Elephantine. My views are not affected.

ADDENDA AND CORRIGENDA TO THE THIRD EDITION

(Each new note is prefixed by an asterisk, to simplify cross-references)

*1 Page 8, lines 9 f.—With the steady accumulation of radiocarbon counts since 1948, it has become certain that Late Paleolithic dates must be reduced substantially. It is now probable that all our Aurignacian, Solutrean, and Magdalenian examples of cave art should be dated between about 15,000 and about 8,000 B. C.

*2 P. 26, lines 17 ff.—Since about 1950 I have replaced the term "prelogical" by the much more satisfactory "protological." The former suggests that no logic is involved, whereas it is actually an early stage of thinking on higher levels. Lévy-Bruhl's differentiation between prelogical and logical stages of human thinking was severely criticized by anthropologists during his lifetime, on the ground that savages are quite able to reason logically—even though implicitly—in matters which have to do with their daily life and nourishment. As a result of these criticisms and his own further reflection, Lévy-Bruhl himself abandoned his former position in his private notebooks, written in 1938 and published in 1947 (*Revue Philosophique*, CXXXVII, pp. 257-281), giving up the notion of *prélogique* in principle. As I have pointed out in the French edition of *From the Stone Age to Christianity* (*De l'Age de la Pierre à la Chrétienté*, Paris, 1951, pp. 86-88, 122 f.), all Lévy-Bruhl's reported difficulties with his own earlier theory would have been eliminated by recognizing an additional stage, that of empirical logic, in accordance with the description in the first two editions of this book, pp. 28 ff., as well as in the French edition of FSAC. It may be added that an eminent European authority on the history of mathematics, who is very much interested in the origins of Greek logic, spent much of the year 1947-48 reading translations of the Hebrew Bible and ancient Oriental literature for the express purpose of disproving my sharp distinction between empirical and formal logic. At the end he admitted failure. The closest approach to formal logic appeared in the Assyrian astrological reports of the seventh century B. C., where implicit syllogisms are found. It was reserved for the Greeks to work out the basic principles of formal logic, codified by Aristotle. When we eliminate all implicitly logical thinking, we still have a large body of material which does not follow any of the formal principles developed by the Greeks from the early sixth century B. C. on. This material is restricted to those domains of higher culture where mistakes in reasoning cannot easily be corrected by experience. Yet the term "prelogical" is not quite satisfactory, because this early thinking does have its own principles of analogy, etc., and was undoubtedly influenced marginally by empirical logic. The term "protological" is thus preferable, and I expect to employ it henceforth.

*3 P. 31, line 19.—Read "Northwest-Semitic" for "Canaanite." In my opinion we cannot admit any extensive Canaanite influence on early Israelite law. The admirable study of Henri Cazelles, *Études sur le Code de l'Alliance* (Paris, 1946), has established the probability of Mosaic origin of the Book of the Covenant, utilizing earlier Hebrew customary law and modified somewhat by later court decisions and commentary. In distinguishing Hebrew law more sharply from Canaanite law I have also been influenced by the investigations of my pupils, particularly of Drs. George E. Mendenhall and Sidney O. Hills.

*4 P. 33, line 11.—I do not, of course, mean that Aristotelian logic is the last word in formal logic, any more than that Israel's empirical logic is the last word of experience. But within its formal categories no mathematical logician has been able to disprove any essential principle of Aristotle—any more than a relativist can demonstrate the inadequacy of Newtonian mechanics for the civil and mechanical engineer or the geodesist. Reichenbach's three-valued logic does not contradict Aristotle's two-valued system; it merely supplements the latter by allowing for situations where we necessarily have to reckon with what is true, false, and uncertain or indeterminate.

*5 P. 37, line 7 from below.—Since 1948 the excavation of Ugarit has been resumed by Schaeffer, with extraordinarily important finds, particularly of art objects and economic and administrative documents in alphabetic North Canaanite and Accadian cuneiform.

*6 P. 38, line 4.—In 1945 a second alphabetic inscription in this same sinistro-grade variety of the Ugaritic alphabet was published by S. Yeivin as coming from near Mount Tabor in northern Palestine; see my remarks in BASOR, No. 99, p. 21.

*7 P. 38, line 12.—This is now replaced by the same author's *Ugaritic Handbook* (Rome, 1947), containing a revised and expanded grammar, complete transliteration of all then available Ugaritic texts, and a comprehensive glossary.

*8 P. 38, line 5 from below and *passim.*—For additional references to publication of tablets from Qatna and Alalakh, etc., see notes *52 ff. below.

*9 P. 40.—The dates for early Northwest-Semitic inscriptions are in need of correction on the basis of the writer's subsequent work: e. g., the earliest inscriptions come well down into the fifteenth century at Serābîṭ el-Khâdim; see below, n. *58. The inscriptions from the following period (Lachish, Beth-shemesh, Megiddo, Byblos, etc.) extend from about the fourteenth to the twelfth centuries; see n. *59 below. The Ahiram Sarcophagus and all other so far published Byblian alphabetic inscriptions except the " enigmatic " one belong to the tenth century and perhaps the beginning of the ninth; see n. *60 below.

*10 P. 41, line 11.—For the Gezer Calendar see especially my paper, BASOR, No. 92 (1943), pp. 16-26, and now A. M. Honeyman, *Journal of the Royal Asiatic Society*, 1953, pp. 53-58. For a survey of other recent studies see S. Moscati, *L'epigrafia ebraica antica* (Rome, 1951), pp. 8-26. On the significance of the Gezer Calendar and other early epigraphic material from the first millennium B. C. for our understanding of the evolution of Hebrew biblical orthography and language, see the monograph by Drs. Frank M. Cross, Jr., and D. N. Freedman, *Early Hebrew Orthography: A Study of the Epigraphic Evidence* (New Haven, 1952).

*11 P. 46.—Some of the dates on this page must be corrected in accord with discoveries since 1946. My date for the First Dynasty of Babylon is 1830-1530; the date 1700-1530 extends from Hammurabi's conquest of Larsa to the end of the Dynasty. We now know that Gudea actually flourished toward the end of the Third Dynasty of Ur, thanks to S. Kramer's announcement of the discovery of the prologue to the Laws of Ur-Nammu (Zur-Nammu), mentioning his defeat of Namkhani (Nammakhni), *ensi* of Lagash before Gudea. The great Gudea is thus the same as the *ensi* of Lagash in the reign of Shû-Sîn, in the early twentieth century B. C. (Falkenstein chronology).

*12 P. 48, line 5.—We must now add the results of the Iraq Government's excavations at Eridu since 1946, which have carried our knowledge of the earliest precursors of the temple tower far back into the ' Obeid period, in the middle centuries of the fourth millennium.

*13 P. 54, line 18.—This situation is rapidly changing, thanks to Helmuth Th. Bossert's discovery of the Phoenician and hieroglyphic Hittite bilingual inscriptions of Karatepe since 1947. For the rapidly growing literature see the bibliography published in *Die Ausgrabungen auf dem Karatepe* by H. Th. Bossert, U. B. Alkım, H. Çambel, N. Ongunsu, and İ. Süzen (Ankara, 1950), pp. 76 ff., and recent issues of the *Jahrbuch fur kleinasiatische Forschungen*, founded by Bossert in 1950. It is still dangerous to employ Hittite hieroglyphic inscriptions for the study of religious questions.

*14 P. 57, line 4.—The first four campaigns of the American Foundation for the Study of Man in South Arabia (1950-1953), organized and headed by Wendell Phillips, with the author as chief archaeologist in the first two campaigns (1950-1951) and Dr. F. P. Albright (not related) as chief archaeologist in the third and fourth campaigns (1952-1953), are in process of revolutionizing our knowledge of South Arabian cultural history and chronology. Under my editorship we hope to publish a series of quarto volumes on the results of these and subsequent campaigns in Qatabân, Saba', and Zafâr ('Omân). The results hitherto obtained demonstrate the political and cultural primacy of Saba' (Sheba) in the early centuries of the first millennium B. C. Among the rock inscriptions of Qatabân discovered by the expedition epigrapher, A. Jamme, are texts going back to the beginning of the first millennium, if not even earlier. One of the mounds of Qatabân (Hajar Bin Humeid) was founded not later than cir. 1000 B. C., and other towns had probably been founded during the immediately preceding centuries. No monumental inscriptions antedating the eighth century have yet been discovered. The priest-kings of Saba' now known, are to be dated between about 800 and 450 B. C.; they were followed by kings, whose power passed into the hands of the Minaean kings in the fourth century B. C. In the last century B. C. Ma'în and its southern rival, Qatabân, were destroyed, and the whole of South Arabia passed under the control of the Sabaeans and people of Hadramaut, who established a powerful empire about the turn of the Christian era. The kingdom of Saba' and Dhû Raydân was founded about A. D. 60, and by the fourth century A. D. South-Arabian civilization was rapidly declining. It finally collapsed in the course of the sixth century A. D. Among papers relating to the chronological and historical results of our work note W. F. Albright, BASOR, No. 119 (1950), pp. 5-15; BASOR, No. 128 (1952), pp. 39-45 (on the Chaldaean inscriptions from the eighth-seventh centuries B. C. in South-Arabian script); BASOR, No. 129, pp. 20-24 (on Minaean chronology); an article "Dedan" in the Albrecht Alt *Festschrift* (dealing with Northwest-Arabian history and chronology); G. W. Van Beek, "Recovering the Ancient Civilization of Arabia," *Biblical Archaeologist*, XV (1952), pp. 2-18.

*15 P. 57, line 20.—Since the death in 1945 of the great authority on South-Arabian philology, N. Rhodokanakis of Graz, his pupil, Dr. Maria Höfner, has led in this field. J. Ryckmans of Louvain is the recognized chief among South-Arabian scholars. Dr. Höfner has published an excellent grammar (*Altsüdarabische Grammatik*, 1943), and is at work on a lexicon. Systematic collaboration on an elaborate plan of systematizing our knowledge of South-Arabian paleography has also begun.

*16 P. 57, line 3 from below.—We now have one large fragment of a Late-Bronze Cypriote tablet, discovered by Dikaios in a context which probably points to the thirteenth century B. C. This must be the harbinger of many such finds.

[17] P. 58, line 18.—On points of contact between the customs and phraseology of the Homeric Epics and the Ugaritic epics see C. H. Gordon, *Introduction to Old Testament Times* (Ventnor, N. J., 1953), pp. 89-99.

[18] P. 58, line 23.—The tablets from Cnossus have now been completely published by Sir John Myres in *Scripta Minoa*, II (1952), and the 1939 lot of 600 from Messenian Pylos was published by E. L. Bennett: *The Pylos Tablets* (Princeton, 1951). In the summer of 1952 some 400 more were excavated by C. W. Blegen at Pylos and some forty were found by A. J. B. Wace at Mycenae itself. Successful beginnings of decipherment are already reported from competent sources.

[19] P. 59, line 4.—In my detailed study, AJA 54 (1950), pp. 162-176, I propose a date about the first half of the tenth century for the oral composition of both Homeric Epics in approximately their present form.

[20] P. 63, line 9.—See now my study of the Wen-amûn Report in *Studies Presented to David Moore Robinson*, Vol. I (St. Louis, 1951), pp. 223-231; further studies by myself and G. Glanzman are in preparation. J. Černý has conclusively demonstrated that the papyrus containing our only copy of the Report, was written as an administrative document, not as a literary work (*Revue Egyptologique*, VI, p. 41, n. 8, and elsewhere). We can accept its statements in detail without necessarily endorsing its author's opinion of himself and his own ability.

[21] P. 70, line 16.—O. Eissfeldt, in his *Sanchunjaton von Berut und Ilumilku von Ugarit* (Halle, 1952), has tried to show that Sanchuniathon lived in the second half of the second millennium B. C., between 500 and 1000 years before my preferred date. However, the proper names associated with his tradition all point toward the period between 700 and 500 B. C., and other considerations seem to me to support this general date.

[22] P. 72, line 2.—It is increasingly clear that the home of these Canaanite epics was in Phoenicia Proper and its Syrian hinterland, as illustrated particularly by place-names such as Lebanon, Shirion (Antilibanus), Tyre, Sidon, Smk (Lake Ḥûleh), Harnem (Hermil in the northern Biqâ'; see BASOR, No. 130 [1953], pp. 26 f.). All national epic literature tends to come from some one region in any ethnic nexus; e. g., the *Iliad* and *Odyssey* arose in Ionia (whatever their ultimate roots may have been).

[23] P. 73, line 20.—On the god El see now the detailed treatment by O. Eissfeldt, *El im ugaritischen Pantheon* (*Berichte . . . der Sächsischen Akademie der Wissenschaften, Phil.-hist. Klasse*, 98:4, 1951).

[24] P. 74, line 5.—See now A. S. Kapelrud, *Baal in the Ras Shamra Texts* (Copenhagen, 1952).

[25] P. 79, line 9.—There is no attested form " Rashpon "; the supposed place-name Rašpuna from which it was restored by E. O. Forrer (who idenfied it with Apollonia) must be read Kašpuna (Donald Wiseman, *Iraq*, XIII (1951), p. 23, and Pl. XI, line 8), pronounced Kaspuna (Kaspôn) by the Assyrians.

[26] P. 80, line 21.—On Ḥaurôn see John Gray, *Journal of Near Eastern Studies*, VIII (1949), pp. 27-34, with some additional references; his main thesis that Ḥaurôn was closely related to Eshmûn and Asklepios, chthonic gods of healing, is probably correct, though he rather over-emphasizes it. See n. *27, on the chthonic character of the related Melcarth.

[27] P. 81, line 16.—Any subsisting doubt as to the chthonic character of the Tyrian Melcarth should be dispelled by H. Seyrig's demonstration (*Syria*,

XXIV, pp. 62-80) that the Herakles-Melcarth of Tyre was still identified with Nergal, the Accadian lord of the City of the Underworld, as late as Roman times.

*28 P. 84, line 12.—Only a little more of the Baal Epic has been published since Virolleaud's *La déesse 'Anat* (Paris, 1938), and it appears that only some badly worn or extremely small fragments remain to be published. On the other hand, it is probable that some otherwise attributed fragments belong to the Baal Epic. For the most recent and complete interpretation of this epic see T. H. Gaster, *Thespis* (New York, 1949), pp. 115-224; see also the translations by H. L. Ginsberg, *Ancient Near Eastern Texts Relating to the Old Testament* (edited by J. B. Pritchard, Princeton, 1950), pp. 129-142, and C. H. Gordon, *Ugaritic Literature* (Rome, 1949), pp. 9-56. The writer has given specimen translations of various parts of the Baal Epic in *The Interpreter's Bible*, I (New York, 1952), pp. 259 ff.

*29 P. 90, line 7 from below.—For the Keret and Aqhat (Dan'el) Epics see also Ginsberg, *op. cit.*, pp. 142-155, Gordon, *op. cit.*, pp. 66-103, and for the Aqhat Epic see Gaster, *op. cit.*, pp. 257-313, where a detailed interpretation of the text will be found.

*30 P. 91, lines 8-4 from below.—While these observations remain true, we now know much more about Hurrian cosmogony, thanks especially to H. G. Güterbock, whose *Kumarbi* (Zürich, 1946) has uncovered close parallels between Hurrian myths of beginnings and Sumero-Accadian, on the one hand, and with Phoenician and Hesiodic, on the other.

*31 P. 96, lines 8 ff. from below.—On the question of the date of the effective domestication of the camel see now the admirable monograph by Reinhard Walz, *Zeitschrift der Deutschen Morgenländischen Gesellschaft*, 101 (1951), pp. 29-51. In a subsequent MS study, which Dr. Walz has kindly sent me, he adheres to his position, that the Arabian camel was effectively domesticated in central Arabia between the 16th/15th and 13th/12th centuries B. C. (p. 49). With this I fully agree.

*32 P. 104, line 8.—On archaeological grounds I should now date the fall of Shiloh a little later, in the quarter-century beginning about 1050 B. C.; cf. *The Old Testament and Modern Study* (ed. H. H. Rowley, Oxford, 1951), p. 12.

*33 P. 110, line 12 from below.—I now date the accession of Ramesses III between 1180 and 1175 B. C.; cf. BASOR, No. 130, p. 8, n. 19, with references.

*34 P. 111, line 17.—This date must be fixed about 1060 B. C.; cf. the data cited in notes *20 and *33.

*35 P. 117, line 16.—The Song of Deborah should be dated in the late twelfth century, not far from 1125 B. C.; cf. my Pelican *Archaeology of Palestine* (1949), pp. 117 f.

*36 P. 127, line 9 from below.—The name "Ethan" actually does appear in the lists of personal names from fourteenth-century Ugarit as *'Aty(a)n* (whence *'Aytan* > Ethan); for the characteristic transposition of the *yodh* cf. such cases as Ugar. *Ṣdyn* = *Ṣidôn*, *Qišyôn* (Heb.) = *Qišôn* (Heb. and Egyptian transcription).

*37 P. 128, line 7 from below.—After the studies to which I allude in my paper on "The Psalm of Habakkuk" (*Studies in Old Testament Prophecy*, edited by H. H. Rowley, Edinburgh, 1950), pp. 3-9, which have been continued subsequently by myself and my students, I should modify this statement.

I now believe that Psalms with Canaanite structure and organic Canaanite content can safely be dated to the tenth century or earlier; cf. especially my detailed treatment of Psalm 68, which I regard as a tenth-century catalogue of some thirty beginnings (incipits) of older hymns and lyrics of more secular nature (*The Hebrew Union College Annual*, XXIII, Part I, Cincinnati, 1950-1951, pp. 1-39). In archaizing Psalms which belong to the sixth-fourth centuries B. C. we tend to find isolated verses and expressions, which do not belong to the composition in the same organic way. However, we are still feeling our way with regard to the chronology of the Psalter, and great caution is indicated.

[38] P. 130.—The dates on this page are not necessarily exact. That of Shishak should be cir. 935-914 (BASOR, No. 130, p. 10); the Assyrian dates are still uncertain within a range of two or three years; David was replaced by Solomon about 961 B. C.; see BASOR, Nos. 100, pp. 16-22; 119, pp. 20-22; 130, pp. 4-6.

[39] P. 131, line 5 from below.—This is wrong: Tyre is mentioned in the Wen-amûn Report, though only in passing. Only Sidon and Byblus appear as important commercial seaports.

[40] P. 151, line 3 from below. This must also be modified: it is impossible to date effective Phoenician expansion into the central and western Mediterranean before David destroyed Philistine power between cir. 990 and 980 B. C. Before then the Philistines and their kinsmen on the coast of Palestine controlled the sea (as in the time of Wen-amûn) and the hinterland of southern Phoenicia as far north as Galilee; cf. my Pelican *Archaeology of Palestine* (1949), pp. 122 f., and AJA LIV (1950), pp. 174 ff.

[41] P. 132, lines 10-1 from below.—Cf. n. [31], above, on the date of the domestication of the camel, which must have been speedily followed by the development of camel caravans. In I Kings 10:15 the Arabs are mentioned as already trading with Israel in the reign of Solomon, and in 853 the Assyrian records first mention the Arabs (as members of the Aramaean coalition which included Ahab of Israel).

[42] P. 133, line 1.—On the evidence for still earlier formation of a Sabaean trading empire see BASOR, No. 128 (1952), p. 45, and JBL LXXI (1952), p. 248 f.

[43] P. 135, lines 5 ff.—For a philological discussion of this passage see now my review of J. A. Montgomery's commentary on Kings, JBL LXXI, p. 249.

[44] P. 137, line 11. See N. Glueck, BASOR, No. 90, pp 13 f., and AASOR XXV-XXVIII (1951), pp. 345 ff.

[45] P. 144, line 10 from below.—See now my treatment, BASOR, No. 85, pp. 18-27, and that of H. G. May, BASOR, No. 88, pp. 19-27.

[46] P. 152, lines 12 ff.—See H. J. Lenzen, *Die Entwicklung der Zikurrat* (Leipzig, 1941), pp. 56-60, on the close relation existing between the Babylonian temple-tower and stepped altar. Calling attention to such Hellenistic parallels as the Altar of Pergamum, which was also a building, he thinks that the temple-tower was influenced in its staged development by altar prototypes. A similar situation with respect to the monumental altar of Ba'albek in Syria, which was both building and altar, has been independently pointed out by Paul Collart and Pierre Coupel (*L'autel monumental de Baalbek*, Paris, 1951, pp. 136 ff.). Though quite different in plan and construction from the Babylonian temple-towers, the altar of Baalbek stands on a stepped terrace and access to the top is gained by a complex series of stairways. The background

for stepped altars is further complicated by the fact that they were common in Egypt from the Pyramid Age on, and that the type was borrowed by the Greeks; see Herbert Hoffman, AJA 57, 189-195 (I should disagree with his effort to derive the Greek altars directly from the Egyptians and should propose that we look for Phoenician intermediation—a possibility which would better explain the origin of the stepped altar of the Temple of Solomon).

*47 P. 156, lines 16 ff. from below.—The controversy about the exact nature of the ninth-century god of Carmel is now resolved in favor of my identification of this god with the Tyrian Baal (following earlier scholars) by M. Avi-Yonah's discovery at Carmel of a Greek inscription from about the third century A.D., dedicated to the Heliopolitan Zeus of Carmel. The Baal of Baalbek was also known as Ginai, primarily a lion-god of Nergal type and thus closely related to Baal Melcarth of Tyre (see above, n. *27). It would be strange if the patron deity of Carmel had not been assimilated to the god of Tyre, since the promontory of Carmel is the most important landmark for mariners in the vicinity of Tyre. (On the Baal of Carmel see also the valuable study by R. de Vaux in *Bulletin du Musée de Beyrouth*, V, pp. 7-20.)

*48 P. 160.—On the date of the Ostraca of Samaria see now the excellent summation by Eamonn O'Doherty, *Catholic Biblical Quarterly*, XV (1953), pp. 24-29.

*49 P. 162, lines 5 ff.—Very important new data have been brought forward by R. Dussaud (*Comptes Rendus, Académie des Inscriptions*, 1946, pp. 371-387) from late Punic inscriptions; among more recent discussions cf. my remarks, JAOS 71 (1951), pp. 262 f., J. G. Février, *Revue de l'Histoire des Religions*, CXLIII (1953), pp. 8-18, and W. Kornfeld, *Wiener Zeitschrift für die Kunde des Morgenlands*, 51 (1952), pp. 287-313 (unfortunately without any knowledge of the work done since the end of the thirties).

*50 P. 184, n. 1.—Among books which have appeared since 1942 we may mention particularly C. C. McCown, *The Ladder of Progress in Palestine* (New York, 1943); W. F. Albright, Pelican *Archaeology of Palestine* (Penguin Press, 1949); A. G. Barrois, *Manuel d'archéologie biblique*, Vol. II (Paris, 1953).

*51 P. 185, n. 4.—For the correct vocalization of the name, *Niqmaddu*, see BASOR, No. 95 (1944), pp. 30-32. The date for the earthquake should now be reduced to about 1355, as a result of M. B. Rowton's fixing the date of Ramesses II to 1290-1234/3 B.C.; cf. BASOR, No. 130 (1953), pp. 130 f.

*52 P. 185, n. 7.—For a complete publication of the tablets from Qatna see J. Bottéro in *Revue d'Assyriologie*, XLIII (1949), pp. 1-40, 137-215; XLIV, pp. 105-122 (on which cf. my remarks, BASOR, No. 121, pp. 21 f.).

*53 P. 185, n. 8.—These documents have now been published by D. J. Wiseman, *The Alalakh Tablets* (London, 1953).

*54 P. 185, p. 9.—For the Taanach tablets see especially BASOR, No. 94 (1944), pp. 12-27.

*55 P. 185, n. 10.—For the Shechem tablets see BASOR, No. 86 (1942), pp. 28-31.

*56 P. 185, n. 11.—See also A. Parrot, *Mari, une ville perdue* (Paris, 1936) and the volumes of copies, transcriptions, and translations issued by G. Dossin and others since 1946 (Paris, Geuthner). Five volumes of each series are available as these lines are written.

*57 P. 185, n. 13.—See now the detailed treatment by T. H. Gaster, *Bibliotheca Orientalis*, IX (1952), pp. 82-85; he forgets, however, to mention my long prior treatment of the same material.

[58] P. 185, n. 15.—See now the preliminary account of my decipherment of the proto-Sinaitic inscriptions in BASOR, No. 110 (1948), pp. 6-22.

[59] P. 186, n. 17.—See now my observations, *Actes du XXIe Congrès International des Orientalistes* (Paris, 1949), pp. 100 ff. The most recent studies will be found in BASOR, Nos. 116 (1949), pp. 12-14, and 129 (1953), pp. 8-11 (by A. Goetze).

[60] P. 186, n. 18.—See my detailed treatment in JAOS 67 (1947), pp. 153-160.

[61] P. 187, n. 38.—This material has now been published in *Megiddo* II (Chicago, 1948), pp. 61 ff., 73 ff., 102 ff., 44 ff., respectively.

[62] P. 190, n. 54.—See now S. N. Kramer, *Sumerian Mythology* (Philadelphia, 1944) and a series of important monographs and papers by him which have appeared since.

[63] P. 195, n. 13.—See the summation of the previous discussion, with new material, by S. Ronzevalle, *Mélanges de l'Université de St. Joseph*, XXIII (1940), pp. 28-55.

[64] P. 196, n. 25.—The Dead Sea Isaiah Scroll, 59:10, spells the word *'ašmônîm* or *'ešmûnîm*, thus confirming this obvious derivation.

[65] P. 199, n. 1.—For my most recent account of the Conquest see *The Jews* (ed. L. Finkelstein, New York, 1949), pp. 13-17, and the Pelican *Archaeology of Palestine* (1949), pp. 108 f., 112 f.

[66] P. 199, n. 2.—My own views on the origin of monotheism in Israel have not changed since 1940, though I am greatly expanding their presentation in forthcoming studies.

[67] P. 200, n. 7.—In Nina M. Davies, *Ancient Egyptian Painting* (Chicago, 1936), Pl. XI, we have an accurate reproduction of the bellows.

[68] P. 200, n. 8.—Our material on the 'Apiru has been increasing steadily; see my latest discussion, BASOR, No. 125 (1952), pp. 29 ff., where I adopt the equation Hebrew = 'Apiru after years of hesitation. Since then very valuable new material has been published by D. J. Wiseman (see n. [53]).

[69] P. 202, n. 24.—See also L. H. Vincent, *Revue Biblique*, 1948, pp. 245-278.

[70] P. 210, n. 96.—Heb. *māḥôl*, *meḥōlôt* is Accad. *mēlultu*, " dancing, singing," from the stem *ḥll*.

[71] P. 213, n. 22.—The Arsames correspondence has now been published by G. R. Driver, *Aramaic Documents of the 5th Century B. C.* (Oxford, 1953).

[72] P. 220, n. 113.—See further references in n. [49].

[73] P. 220, n. 115.—Add Heb. *'ašmônîm* (or the like), " good health," from the name of the god; see n. [64].

[74] P. 222, last line of 1946 edition.—For further light on the mixed religion of the Jewish colony at Elephantine see A. Dupont-Sommer, *Revue de l'Histoire des Religions*, CXXVIII (1944), pp. 28-39; *ibid.*, CXXX (1945), pp. 17-28; *Comptes Rendus, Académie des Inscriptions*, 1947, pp. 175-191; *Sabbat et Parascève à Éléphantine* (Paris, 1950). Very important new light comes from the still unpublished Brooklyn papyri (cf. provisionally E. G. Kraeling, *Biblical Archaeologist*, XV (1952), pp. 66 f.

LIST OF ABBREVIATIONS

AASOR = *Annual of the American Schools of Oriental Research* (New Haven, American Schools of Oriental Research, 409 Prospect Street).

AJA = *American Journal of Archaeology* (Archaeological Institute of America).

AJSL = *American Journal of Semitic Languages* (Chicago, Oriental Institute of The University of Chicago)—now replaced by the *Journal of Near Eastern Studies*.

APB = Albright, *The Archaeology of Palestine and the Bible* (New York, 1932-35), out of print.

BASOR = *Bulletin of the American Schools of Oriental Research* (see above).

FSAC = Albright, *From the Stone Age to Christianity* (Baltimore, The Johns Hopkins Press, 1940).

JAOS = *Journal of the American Oriental Society.*

JBL = *Journal of Biblical Literature* (Society of Biblical Literature and Exegesis).

JPOS = *Journal of the Palestine Oriental Society.*

PEQ = *Palestine Exploration Quarterly* (London, Palestine Exploration Fund).

ZAW = *Zeitschrift für die Alttestamentliche Wissenschaft.*

INDEX OF BIBLICAL CITATIONS

(following English Bible)

INDEX OF SUBJECTS AND AUTHORS

235